The Ancient Romans

A Captivating Guide to the People of Rome, Roman Games, Pompeii, and the Colosseum

Free Bonus from Captivating History
(Available for a Limited time)

Hi History Lovers!

Now you have a chance to join our exclusive history list so you can get your first history ebook for free as well as discounts and a potential to get more history books for free!

Simply visit the link below to join.

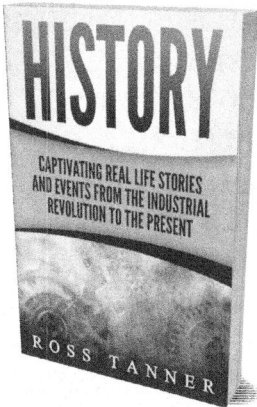

Or, Scan the QR code!

captivatinghistory.com/ebook

Also, make sure to follow us on Facebook, X, and YouTube by searching for Captivating History.

Table of Contents

Part 1: The Romans

A Captivating Guide to the People, Emperors, Soldiers and Gladiators of Ancient Rome, Starting from the Roman Republic through the Roman Empire to the Byzantine Empire

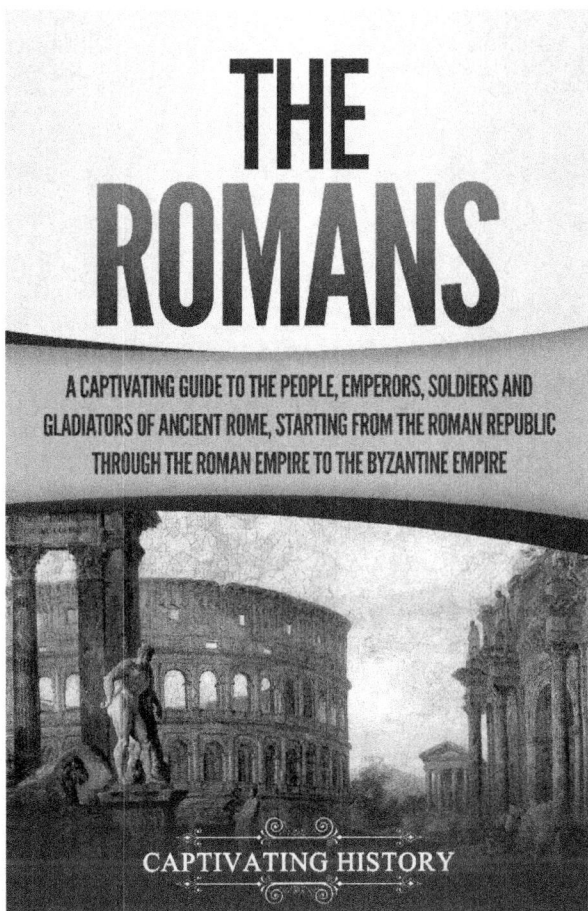

Introduction: The Greatest Show on Earth

Rome always had potential.

People were living there in the Bronze Age when it was just a scattering of huts nestled across small hills near a natural crossing point over the Tiber River. Fragments of their pots and some remains of graves and mud huts tell us these first Romans were farming families.

For centuries, their place was nothing more than that. But it was perhaps due to the boundary of two growing groups of increasingly sophisticated, ambitious people—the Etruscans to the north and the Latins in the south—that a few decades before the year 700 BCE, the scattered settlements formed into one, became organized, were able to use small hills as natural defenses, and developed culturally. In the next 250 years, Rome became powerful at the expense of its two neighbors.

Archaeologists are still trying to uncover the exact reasons for this development. But while they are unsure, the legends are not. Those stories say Rome began when a wolf came across a wooden basket that had floated to a stop at the edge of the Tiber. She sniffed at a bundle inside. It moved! Two human baby twin boys were wrapped together, shivering and frightened. The wolf carefully lifted out the pair and helped them suckle from her full udder. A woodpecker flew down and helped. The foundlings survived, and the wolf and bird continued to care for them until a poor herdsman discovered the boys and took Romulus and Remus into his home as adopted sons. On becoming young men,

Romulus murdered his brother, founded a city at the spot where the wolf had found them, called it Rome, provided wives for his followers in a famous military raid, and the rest is history.

That much is fanciful, but without question, the crossing was a good place to live. It was a natural place to start a city. Travelers preferred to cross the Tiber at Rome because there was an island that made the crossing easier, even though they also might be searched and taxed. The stretch of lagoons and swampy land between there and the coast twenty kilometers (twelve or so miles) away were a buffer from any surprise attacks from the sea and, at the same time, provided convenient access for the ships of foreign eastern Mediterranean merchants who came in peace.

From here, we can follow the sweeping history of Rome's expansion and achievements in three periods, beginning around 750 BCE, without any wolf or woodpecker.

The first families of farmers were united under a series of kings, who laid the city's political and social foundation along that bend in the Tiber. Then, in 507 BCE, the monarchy was replaced by a more public-led republic, which funded and supported Roman armies that disgorged out of the Tiber valley, eventually taking over all of western Europe and the entire Mediterranean Basin. Finally, the democratic-like republic was pushed aside in 27 BCE, and a series of autocrats and dictators ruled as emperors, initially from Rome but also in other cities, until the empire finally disappeared in 1453 CE.

That's a huge span of some two thousand years. Along the way, these Romans developed an astonishing legal system, set up an exceedingly effective military organization, administered vast areas with precision and efficiency, and produced marvels of engineering and literature. At the same time, they took slavery and public debauchery to unbelievable levels.

There's plenty to talk about at each point along the way. Let's start with the kingdom.

Chapter 1 – Kings at the Crossing

No reliable written records survive from the two hundred years or so of the Roman Kingdom. However, it's clear from the archaeological record that something changed at the river crossing starting around the year 700 BCE.

Livy, the well-known Roman historian (59 BCE–17 CE), tries to be helpful. Writing centuries later, he dates the founding to April 21st, 753 BCE, to neatly fit in with the story of Romulus and Remus. Today, historians are skeptical.

We can say that about this time, a town was formed in place of those scattered family clusters. Mud huts were replaced by stone buildings with tiled roofs. Walls went up to protect the town. Slowly, bigger homes added atriums, courtyards, and gardens. Decorated statues and terracotta embellishments appeared with some buildings. There were paved streets. Water was collected and stored in public stone tanks. People now buried their dead in communal cemeteries, and if the family was wealthy, their tombs were above ground.

This much organization could only have occurred if family heads had been unified or replaced (perhaps slowly) by elites and leaders who were able to tax the farming families and organize the growing settlement. These men were buried with armor and weapons. Traditionally, we have called them "kings." There is no hard evidence of how many there were and what authority they had, especially during the first decades of the kingdom. However, we can be fairly certain this leadership and government was some kind of monarchy because there are vestiges of kingship in the early years of Rome's second period, the republic. For example, an ancient inscription dating from the republic years has been found in the Roman Forum containing the word "king," and this suggests there was a king before the republic was established. Remains of a religious building called the Royal House have also been uncovered in the Forum, which could reasonably be said to have replaced a pre-republic king's palace.

Just how a king got to the throne is unclear. But again, there are some clues in the early years of the republic just after those monarchs were replaced. In those initial republic years, leaders were approved by assemblies of Rome's men. It's not a stretch to assume this republican system was a natural carryover from the way Rome had been governed under kings just a few years earlier, as it seems the sovereigns co-ruled with formally organized citizen groups. Traditions and archaeology show the kings were approved by groups of family heads or clans or perhaps even army units. The monarchy was not hereditary.

The king wielded considerable power. For example, he was also the city's chief augur, determining the will of the gods by watching birds and animals and observing thunder and lightning when making decisions and on important state occasions. There were other augurs, but the king was the chief mediator between the people and the gods of Rome. He was called the "bridge-builder," and he must have awed his subjects. Further, he led the religious ceremonies in this highly religious city and appointed priests. Kings also selected public officials, which gave him control and access to information.

Between them and their officials, the Roman kings completed major public works at a time when cities were a relatively new concept in that part of the world. A large public square was built in 650 BCE, and twenty-five years later, impressive community buildings were erected around it. A striking temple was completed nearby in about 550 BCE or even a little earlier.

The Etruscans to the north had been building in stone for some time and no doubt inspired and perhaps advised and built some of these in Rome. But by whatever means, this was pioneering. Rome was being transformed physically and philosophically into a true urban settlement, complete with an ongoing building boom led by dominant kings assisted by assemblies of elite men.

Romulus had originally organized his people in three assemblies, at least according to the traditions. No evidence for that has survived, but formal groups were definitely present during the kingdom. Eventually, people were separated into groups based roughly on where they lived in this new cityscape. If you had enough influence and wealth to set up your household near the king in the most prestigious public areas of the city, you were given more respect and formal rights than your weaker and poorer fellow citizens. What you had became more important than whatever old class or order your family might have belonged to in the past.

By the end of the kingdom period, Rome had swelled to a city of more than 30,000 people spread over some 280 hectares. The people gathered to watch and take part in religious ceremonies, thousands of them cheered at chariot races, and crowds applauded their champions at the annual games held in honor of the god Jupiter. By this time, it seems the first version of the famous Circus Maximus had been built. Here, then, was an urban center enjoying some of the hallmarks of the cities we live in today.

There's a traditional list of seven kings who led this growth, which was compiled centuries later but is complete with dates and a record of their majesties' glorious, long-lasting achievements. Basically, each is said to have founded one or some of the main institutions of the later Roman Republic. This is neat and tidy and has a certain appeal, but it is entirely unsupported by hard evidence.

However, six of these names fit the old Roman naming convention for elite men. From this, we get a hint that perhaps at least the names themselves are authentic since the six individual names are unusual, and their six clans were weak in the early republic years. If a republic writer was inventing the names of those kings, wouldn't he use names and clans that were powerful in the early republic to provide some legitimacy from continuity? Thus, it is thought that the kings' names can be somewhat trusted.

Roman names are interesting, and once you understand how they were given to children, the tangle of names in Rome's long history becomes easier to deal with.

Men from the elite class, the patricians, had a three-part name: a first name followed by the names of their clan and sub-clan. Their first name was randomly chosen by parents from a standard list of twelve names, but the next two names indicating clan and sub-clan were non-negotiable (of course). So, for example, there could be several Julius Caesars at any one time, all from the Julii clan and Caesar sub-clan or family. But the man we remember is instantly distinguished by his first name, his forename, Gaius.

The inferior plebian classes of common people had no clan lineage, so their men carried only a first name and their family designation. So, the pleb Mark Anthony (Antony) of Cleopatra fame had just two names, his first name Marcus and his family name Antonius.

Women were even less distinguished. The daughters of the elite were given the feminine form of their father's clan. The girls in plebian families had to be content with the feminine form of the sub-clan name. So, yes, three daughters in one family would all have exactly the same name. Mark Anthony's two daughters were both called Antonia, for example.

The first name in the list of those ancient Roman kings is Romulus, the wolf-reared founder who murdered his brother and led a famous raid that secured much-needed wives from the neighboring Sabines for the town. His name doesn't fit the Roman naming tradition we've just looked at. Rather, it's just one name, and it apparently comes from the ancient Etruscan word "roma." We haven't yet deciphered the language of ancient Etruria, so we don't know what *roma* means, but we can see it is a feminine noun. The ending of Romulus's name makes it mean "Little Rom." That strongly implies this first king was named after the city rather than the city being named after him.

His is the only name in the list that historians suspect to be fiction. The second is the more reliably named Numa Pompilius, a Sabine who is said to have set up the calendar and Rome's religious center, the Temple of Janus. Numa Tullus Hostilius supposedly came next, who is best known for razing a nearby city. Rome's fourth king, Ancus Marcius, is credited with forming a class of common people (the plebs) from enslaved captives. The next man claimed as king, Lucius Tarquinius Priscus, apparently did better, as he is said to be an Etruscan who completed the city's first major public works program by building a large sewer system. The mysterious Servius Tullius is sixth in the list and is supposed to have written Rome's first constitution, given freedom to the plebs, reorganized the voting assemblies so they were wealth-based, and negotiated a military agreement with other Latin cities.

Lucius Tarquinius Superbus is the seventh on the list. He's closer to the time when written records have survived, and we may be able to discern a few definite things about him from a particular story. It is said that Tarquinius Superbus, also known as Tarquin the Proud, permitted his son to arrange for a woman called Lucretia to be raped. This unfortunate woman was wracked with shame and committed suicide. Then, the story tells us, there was a furious public outcry, the king was tossed aside, and in 507 BCE, the people agreed to set up a republic as an alternative to the monarchy.

Fact or fiction? Well, we can say for a fact that something happened because there was no eighth king, and in place of the monarchy, we suddenly have the republic. Also, we know the names of the first consuls of the republic, and one of them was Lucius Tarquinius Collatinus—the husband of the violated Lucretia. Perhaps some incident involving this woman did actually spark the bonfire that razed the monarchy. On the other hand, this tale was only written down by Livy and others hundreds of years later.

If the end of the kingdom is obscured in time's mists, so is the life of the subjects. But we can learn a little more when we examine the cultural and political influences of their neighbors, the people of Etruria, who initially lived in what we now think of as Tuscany and Umbria. The Etruscan culture and ideas rubbed off on Rome throughout the two hundred years of the kingdom.

We are not yet able to understand the unique Etruscan language, a variant of Indo-European, even though their alphabet was derived from the Greeks, who were setting up city-states in Italy, constantly pushing against Etruria, and complaining of Etruscan pirates on the high seas. But while we currently get no help from their writings, it's reasonable to conjecture they were descendants of very early distinctive migrants from somewhere in central Europe, whose homelands were overwhelmed and totally decimated after they left.

In their new homeland, the Etruscans developed a capable military and a distinct culture different from anything else in Italy. Their cities were small and enjoyed a degree of independence, like Greek city-states. The people seem to have been governed by kings for some time and then by magistrates who were approved for one-year terms by assemblies of landowning men. Although facts and details are scarce, we can see the same general outlines of monarchy and assembly in neighboring Rome.

Early in the 7th century, just as Rome's monarchy was getting established, the Etruscan army pushed across the Tiber, and by around 650 BCE, they had a measure of control over everything as far south as Mt. Vesuvius. Their heavily fortified city of Veii was barely sixteen kilometers (roughly ten miles) north of Rome, and for well over one hundred years, these people were very much a big brother to the Roman monarchy. Rome's politics, military thinking, art, religion, commerce, and even its alphabet couldn't help being affected.

Interaction was everywhere. An inscription from Veii during the Roman Kingdom period includes a Roman name. A temple gift explained in Etruscan writing dating from the monarchy has been found in Rome. Magistrates in Rome used Etruscan symbols. Two Roman kings were Etruscans.

Then, in 524 BCE, the Etruscans overreached themselves. An Etruscan army attacked one of the many Greek city-states in the south, were repulsed, and, within twenty years, had retreated and shrunk to a secondary status. Around 500 BCE, they made a last-gasp attempt to invade Rome. But they failed, as the legends (and later Thomas Babington Macaulay) tell us, when the one-eyed "brave Horatius, the captain of the gate" defended the bridge over the Tiber long enough for Rome to be readied and saved. Rome's army had become a formidable force, with experienced commanders and resources to fund thousands of troops.

In fact, that seventh Roman king, the Etruscan Tarquinius Superbus, possibly owed some of his overthrow in 507 BCE to this abrupt diminution of Etrurian power, as well as the shocking behavior of his son toward the tragic Lucretia.

So, when the last king was tossed out by a revolt of his people, Rome was totally transformed from the late Iron Age cluster of farming families living in wattle and daub huts. It was now decked with impressive buildings, hosted wildly popular entertainments, felt secure behind a high wall, and submitted to powerful religious rituals. The once-dominant Etruscan neighbors across the Tiber River were now weaker than economically sure-footed and culturally confident Rome and its generals.

In a remarkably short two hundred years or so, a truly urban city had been conceived and built by a series of rulers working with assemblies of their subjects. From here, the world would see an eruption of political and military might that's still talked about 2,500 years later.

Chapter 2 – New Citizens and Old Gods

Now that the last king had been thrown out by the crowds in Rome's public squares, what would they put in his place? Perhaps unsurprisingly, they took a safe option and went for more of the same, for a modified version of what they knew. There would be a king-equivalent, and the crowd would still have some control over him.

From now on, the "king" would be several people called magistrates or consuls, and they would only rule for one year unless military duties called them away. These men frequently led the army, and obviously, the city didn't want a change of leadership midway through a distant campaign. So, a one-year term could be extended if needed.

The people's voice would still come from noisy public meetings, but now there were new regulations that filtered the public votes to approve new leaders and pass or reject major pieces of legislation. Those public meetings were organized along class lines, ranked by wealth and landholdings. In this early republic, Rome was still a community of farmers, with the biggest landowners having the most money and political strength.

Tradition also helped. A number of clans that had been given a high status during the kingdom now held on to it. These were the patricians. Just how they came to have this power was not even clear to Roman historians, but they were firmly at the top. Patricians were entitled to wear white linen tunics and red shoes. Certain priesthoods were reserved for them. Everyone else was a commoner or a pleb. They had no prestigious family heritage or traditional connection with power, and they were required to wear dark-colored tunics and plain leather sandals. At the bottom was a relatively small group of slaves. There were few during the early years of the Roman Republic, but their number would swell enormously as the republic's armies took over foreign lands.

So, Romans were not equal, although when you look at the census data of the early republic, the wealthiest class is differentiated from the poorest only by a factor of ten. That eventually changed as Rome's legions brought in wealth from abroad in the later republic, but that all grew from egalitarian roots.

Citizens frequently met as either patricians or plebs to approve or toss out the proposals of the chief magistrates, who had been elected by these same people only a few months earlier. There were other groups, like the Senate, but patrician and plebeian assemblies dominated political life in the republic for hundreds of years.

It's worth looking a little closer at the patrician assembly. Elite men aged 17 to 60 years met in 193 voting groups called centuries. Yes, that's the word we know today as one hundred. It's a hangover from the kingdom when standard army units of 100 men would meet and vote. The name was retained, although in the republic's patrician assembly, the army had no formal voting role and each century had more than 100 members because every free male citizen in the republic had a group where they could debate the issues and vote.

These elite assemblies of patricians discussed important matters. Which laws would come into force? Would specific behavior be judged as criminal? Should war be declared and the army unleashed? Who would be the next chief magistrate?

That last item was particularly important since only those consuls, or chief magistrates, could call an assembly and supervise elections. Further, they drew up the proposals for discussion, and the wording couldn't be modified by members of the centuries.

The men in these patrician centuries would debate and then vote on the consul's proposal. Each century then cast one vote as determined by the majority of the members of their century. So, while thousands of men discussed each issue, there were only 193 ballots to count when the final vote was called.

This system was not as democratic as it might appear. It became weighted in favor of old money by the careful and cunning distribution of votes. Those 193 centuries were arranged so that 18 centuries were filled with men from certain wealthy families and 5 filled with professionals who might have roles in the army. The remaining 170 centuries were occupied by men ranked by wealth, with the richest Romans given more centuries than the less fortunate. Age was also factored in. There were naturally more younger patrician men than older in the city, and this simple demographic was manipulated. At the end of the day, voting could skew to the benefit of well-connected wealthier centuries, where the members' average age was older.

Having said that, though, this was not a system that could always be rigged because, on many occasions, especially in the first one hundred years of the republic, economic hardship brought people out onto the streets and into the assemblies of the common people, where they voted for things like debt relief and financial regulation to support the poor.

There were assemblies for plebs, dating from the earliest days of the republic, and they were set up like the patrician assemblies. From 494 BCE, the plebs voted in their own leaders called tribunes. They had one-year terms, and they formulated proposals that could not be reworded and sent them to the formal groups of common men for debate. The result of those pleb votes determined the single vote of each group.

The plebs were seriously affected by a long economic downturn of those first one hundred years, and their assembly often discussed the issues that are always associated with the poor: hunger, debt, and land reform. But the plebs were also pushing for more political power. Why should wealthy landowners have more voice than the hardworking people who supported them with their labor? There were two major outbreaks of hunger-driven strikes and rioting by the plebs within the first fifty or sixty years of the republic, and it appears this politicized the common people and ensured their assemblies had a definite, even if weak, place in Rome's corridors of power.

Sadly, the early republic's division of people into the haves and have-nots, the traditionally privileged and the poor, which you would hope might give a voice to the economically weak, did not perform like that. Money speaks, and wealthy plebs eventually migrated up into the ruling bodies that were initially only held by patricians, and then together, they ran Rome to the advantage of monied families. Does anything ever change?

This system of chief magistrates, or consuls, working with groups of citizens was a government without a state apparatus as we know it today. There were no ongoing, permanently staffed government institutions. Each new chief magistrate set up his own bureaucracy and disbanded it when his term ended.

There's another group we should mention: the Senate. It is the Roman assembly we perhaps best remember today. Senators had status, and some of it showed. For instance, only senators could wear a distinctive tunic decorated with two wide vertical stripes running from the shoulder. Further, they were personally selected by the consuls at first. Later, this selection passed to lesser magistrates, who chose them from a pool of former magistrates, but both selections ensured senators were spokesmen of the governing classes.

Like the other assemblies, the Senate met at the command of a consul. But to some extent, senators could influence the resolutions that came before them because the consul would open a debate on a matter and, after discussion, produce two resolutions to the situation. Senators would then vote for one of those two. Their decisions were only recommendations, and their power was moral only. But it took a strong consul to ignore a decree of the Senate.

Steering the ship of state also took the help of the Roman gods. When big decisions were being made about the ruling consuls, city politics, or the army, Romans wanted to know what the gods thought. Gods ruled the world, and it would be irreligious and foolhardy to ignore them.

In the early years of the republic, it was widely agreed that only a special patrician could interpret the signs that the gods used to reveal their thinking. He was the diviner, the doorway to the gods. In Rome, dreams were not interpreted, and prophets were ignored.

People with this special ability were called augurs. For thousands of years in Greece and in other parts of the Middle East, augurs had been thought to understand the will of the gods by observing and interpreting natural signs or the actions of animals. These diviners appeared in Rome during the kingdom years and were heeded for well over one thousand years.

There's a certain logic to what augurs did, although they seem strangely out of place to our modern eyes. Romans reasoned that if a god exists, then he must care for his people, and if he cares, he will show them his will. In Rome, an augur would set up in a certain place, point out what part of the sky he was going to watch, then wait for divine direction by listening to claps of thunder or watching how certain birds flew, where they landed, or how they pecked at their food. This revelation didn't spell out exactly what was about to happen. Rather, it answered the question of "Should Rome do this?" with a simple "Yes" or "No."

The republic's first augurs were the chief magistrates. It was accepted that every patrician was eligible to be an augur, but the actual power only came to a man when he was elected chief magistrate. He lost this ability when he left office. Most new magistrates would sit up at midnight on the day of their appointment and watch for what the gods would tell them about their own future.

At the beginning of the republic, the patrician augurs absolutely underpinned the entire political and military structure. When a consul marched his army out of Rome, for example, he would pause to take an oath to the city's chief god, Jupiter Optimus Maximus. Returning victorious, he would throw a massive religious event to celebrate. But it reached into private life also. For example, an augur would be necessary when wedding plans were being made.

The augury system changed over the years of the republic. At one point, a college of augurs was formed. Rules were made increasingly elaborate, and augury became a life-long skill. For several hundred years, an augur could claim another augur's finding was mistaken because the procedures had not been correctly followed. Obviously, this power of veto could be a powerful political tool in the hands of the patricians. That disappeared when plebs were admitted into the augurs' college around 300 BCE.

The early Rome we've been looking at grew more politically than physically. The suburbs, temples, and public buildings remained largely the same. True, it was lively and self-opinionated, but essentially, Rome remained a modest town at a crossing on the Tiber River, influenced and overshadowed to a large extent by the sophisticated Etrurian cities to the north.

For the first years of the republic, it was a city content to build figuratively on the legacy of the kingdom period, to modify the power of rulers, find a balance between its wealthy and its less fortunate citizens, fend off enemies and threats close at hand, work the farms, worship the same ancient gods, and enjoy martial sports like javelin and discus throwing. It also survived a severe decades-long economic downturn in the first one hundred years.

Through all this, Rome managed to save enough public money to find the ransom payment demanded by an army of Gauls, which suddenly appeared outside the young city around 400 BCE. The Gauls breached its limited fortifications and slaughtered enough important people to make future Roman historians cringe and look for ingenious ways to salvage some pride from this shame.

But then things changed. After all, Rome was confident of its political and economic stability. Augurs assured their consuls they should send the army to conquer their home province of Latium and then invade the rest of Italy. By 264 BCE, all of Italy belonged to Rome. Let us now see how this happened.

Chapter 3 – Taking Over the Neighborhood

The takeover of peninsular Italy is one of history's most remarkable military campaigns. It was driven by 250 years of continuous ambition and gluttonous intent and powered by a framework of cunning treaties and unbending administration.

It was a campaign more splendid than any single consul or magistrate, so it ellipses someone like Alexander the Great. It continued longer than any Senate tenure, so its program compares with the Spanish conquest of the New World. Somehow, hubris and arrogance in the heart of Rome, combined with the ancient Roman gods, brought Rome's laws and Latin culture to every Apennine valley and coastal plain in Italy. The cobblers of the republic were always making soldiers' boots.

At first, the fighting was all about survival. The Gauls had taken over Europe by around 500 BCE, the time the republic was founded. One hundred years later, they spilled into northern Italy, looking for new lands. At this time, tribal groups in the south of Italy were pushing toward the Tiber, as were others, through the mountains to the east of Rome. Also, northern Umbrian farmers and their small armies were expanding, creeping ever closer toward the city.

All these groups wanted to take the easy flatlands of Latium, immediately south of Rome, so the Latins had to cooperate militarily. They agreed to assist each other if they were attacked. Rome stayed out of this Latin League because it had once forced an unequal treaty on those cities. They would not attack Rome, and if Rome and the League joined together to attack non-Latins, Rome would take half of any spoils while the League would divide the other half between all their cities. However, Rome assumed it was superior.

This was an uneasy, unbalanced relationship. But actually, it was apparently matched by the facts. In 348 BCE, for example, Carthage, on the distant shore of North Africa, signed a treaty with Rome and not the Latin League. This suggests it thought Rome dominated Latium.

Whatever the exact relationship, Rome and the other Latins often did cooperate, and thousands of their soldiers battled and struggled in what must have seemed like endless small pitched battles and campaigns across their region to beat off tribal invaders. And the League prevailed. A decisive battle against the Umbrians in 431 BCE turned the tide, and by the 390s, they seemed to have been completely and permanently evicted from Latium.

Roman troops were limited and had to be used sparingly. In 435 BCE, they took the Etruscan city of Fidena, a short march north of the Tiber ford. Then they were sent to that southern encounter in 431 BCE and stayed in Latium. Twenty-five years later, their siege machines and war engines were trundled up to the walls of the next Etruscan city, Veii, just a little farther away. It took almost a decade, but Veii eventually fell in 396 BCE, increasing the land Rome controlled by 30 percent to 1,600 square kilometers (about 620 square miles).

This happened just in time. Five years later, Gauls swept across the Tiber ford and stormed into Rome, as mentioned above. The city almost sank in this northern European tidal wave. There are no accurate surviving records of the fighting, although the later patrician histories manage to put a spin on it. ("At least the barbarians didn't shame us completely by taking our citadel!") Most likely, a ransom was paid to stop the fighting.

What we do know is the Romans immediately built a wall around their city, ten meters high in many places and three and a half meters thick at the base. Some of this wall still stands. There's a section of it outside Rome's main railway station, for example, and if you go into the station and enjoy a burger at McDonald's basement restaurant, you'll be sitting next to more of it!

That unexpected defeat revealed to Rome's Latin "allies" that the city was weaker than they'd imagined. Immediately, some ripped up the treaties of Latium and revolted, especially in the south, where Umbrian influences still lingered. For about thirty years, Rome's legions were aggressively putting out fires across the region, finally subduing the last Latin city in 338 BCE. From then on, it was Roman consuls who would come down and conduct the sumptuous religious ceremonies of Latium with dazzling splendor on the hill of Alban in the center of the region.

Rome was now secure in Latium and Etruria, but the Romans wanted more. Their consuls and generals gathered votes from the citizen assemblies, and from 343 to 290 BCE, they repeatedly marched south out of Latium from the Bay of Naples (then in Greek hands) and its brooding Mount Vesuvius, fighting their way into the hills and cities of the Samnite peoples. It was bloodshed for more than fifty years.

It began as a year or two of minor battles followed by a fifteen-year pause. Next, Rome provocatively planted a colony on Samnite land, and in 328 BCE, that triggered the armed response they were hoping for but not the result. In the fighting that followed, Rome's army was surrounded and forced to surrender!

The colony was dismantled, but Rome kept its aggressive ambitions intact. Roman armies were sent to hold the regions in the east and south of the main Samnite area in what was probably a long-term tactical maneuver. Legions took the area north of modern Naples and reestablished colonies there. In 312 BCE, engineers built the Appian Way from Rome straight down to the Samnite lands. There was no hiding their aggressive intent.

The Samnites, the remaining resistance in Umbria and Etruria, and the Gauls from the far north rose up. Years of fighting followed. Records are sketchy, but we know, for example, at one point, 35,000 Roman soldiers and the same number of their allies were in a battle against Umbrians northeast of Rome. Those are huge numbers, and they were sufficient. In 290 BCE, the Samnites signed a treaty with Rome and put down their weapons for good.

With this two-hundred-year record of independence, abandoned treaties, and revolts, we'd be forgiven for thinking the alliances with Rome were often not worth the parchment they were written on. But that would be wrong. When the Romans took a city, they didn't hold it with iron-like control and hardhearted magistrates brought in from distant Rome. Rather, they used a variety of agreements and treaties that benefited everyone involved. The city was brought into the Roman administrative system. Local matters, identity, and social policies remained in local hands, and a proportion of young men were conscripted into the legions.

This was a first. No one else was expanding on this model. For a time, it gave Rome reserves of army manpower that grew proportionately as its territories grew. It established largely appreciated relationships with conquered peoples in the Italian Peninsula, who generally remained loyal when Greeks and later Carthaginians invaded and marched on the Roman Republic. And when the model was exported abroad, it proved a reliable foundation for Romanization and loyalty around the Mediterranean and beyond for some years.

This treaty concept may have grown out of a set of rights traditionally enjoyed by Rome and the other cities of Latium. Commercial transactions and marriages in one of these cities were recognized in other centers, and a person moving to another Latin community could become a citizen of their new hometown. These were relatively simple to agree to because Latins were ethnically and culturally similar.

This early cooperative arrangement dominated the first one hundred years or so of the republic, a time when the Romans were entering into alliances with Latin cities and concentrated on fighting the more distant tribes living in small centers just beyond Latium. When conquered, those small foreign communities were simply made part of greater Rome, and their land was given to Roman citizens.

In 380 BCE, the large Latin city of Tusculum, near the Alban Hills and surrounded by Roman state lands, was formally incorporated into Rome. This was the first time a large center had been added to the state of Rome, and while the details of the merger have been lost, it seems the people did keep a degree of local independence, although they were not initially given the right to hold offices in the city of Rome itself. Here, we see an outline of what was to become a tried and tested treaty system.

Things got much clearer in 338 BCE. That year, the informal Latin League was dissolved, and Rome absorbed Latium. There was no frontal attack or demolition of towns and cities. But the unseen political structure of the region was replaced with a Roman vise grip.

Now, each Latin city was tied separately and individually to Rome by a treaty. The earlier commercial, military, and social treaties linking Latin cities were torn up. As at Tusculum, local magistrates looked after local matters, and a city's citizens were given rights and obligations nearly equal to those of Roman citizens. But young men were still conscripted into the legions. The old Latin interdependence and cooperation shriveled. Commerce and culture with Rome got stronger while greater Latium withered.

Beyond the southern edge of Latium, Rome made less generous treaties with the foreign, non-Latin cities. There, people were Romanized, but at first, they were considered not quite ready to be fully absorbed into the state of Rome. They had some independence, but local management was limited, citizens had no voting rights over the laws and regulations sent from distant Rome, and men had to be provided for the legions. This slowly changed under the force of new circumstances, and one hundred years later, these people had been given full Roman citizenship.

Farther from Rome, treaties were more uneven. Those conquered citizens had to "uphold the Roman people's greatness," which meant sending conscripts to the legions and accepting Rome's foreign policy. They were not absorbed into the Roman state unless Rome wanted to hold a specific city closer to its bosom.

Rome also put a lot of effort into planting colonies to control and influence distant regions of the Italian Peninsula. When the Latins were still united as a league, these new settlements were manned by formerly landless Romans and Latin peasants, who were given autonomy, their own generously sized farms, and citizenship of the new settlement. As elsewhere, Rome conscripted these colonists for her legions. But unlike other forms of influence, these Latin colonists were wholeheartedly Romans. They brought their culture with them, and local peoples in those far-away areas would have adopted some of their customs. Later, some of these settlements were set up abroad where Rome wanted influence but felt the citizens were not yet ready for full Roman rights.

Rome also experimented with a slightly different colony. There, members retained their Roman citizenship even though this was clearly impractical. (How would they perform their duties at such a distance? How could Rome-based magistrates know their needs and aspirations?) These citizen colonies were basically military outposts, and perhaps because of this, colonists were not required to serve in the legions. They were neither popular nor widely used.

Rome was not the only colonizer in Italy. Greeks were scattered in a network of colonies at the very bottom of the peninsula and through Sicily. In distant Rome, consuls, senators, and citizens were in favor of replacing them with Romans. In 282 BCE, they made the first move.

They attacked the Greek city of Tarentum. The Greeks called for help to Pyrrhus, the king of Epirus in northwest Greece, and he arrived in 280 BCE with thirty-five thousand men and twenty elephants. The elephants spread terror, and the Greek commander outmatched the Roman officers. Rome's legion was defeated. However, four thousand Greeks were killed, and their king made a comment that has stayed with us until today, placing his name in the English language. "Another 'victory' would have cost me the war," he is reported to have said. A Pyrrhic victory indeed.

The king applied sound military strategy: pursue and destroy a defeated enemy. He recruited local anti-Roman tribes and marched on Rome. But the tribes closer to Rome stayed loyal, and Pyrrhus couldn't deliver the killer blow he wanted. He withdrew south.

The following year, the Greeks marched north again and defeated the legion once more; however, 3,500 of his men lay dead on the field, making his win as Pyrrhic as the earlier one. Obviously, Pyrrhus's forces were superior to Rome's, but the consuls rejected his offer of peace in return for the independence of the Samnite region and the south of the peninsula.

Just then, a call for help came from Greek colonies in eastern Sicily. They were being overrun by an army from Carthage. Pyrrhus sailed to Sicily in 278 BCE, and this accomplished Greek pushed the North Africans back to the west of the island.

However, southern Italy was still his priority, and he brought his force back and attacked what he mistakenly thought was a single Roman army. To his surprise, a second Latin army suddenly appeared, and Pyrrhus was forced to withdraw to Tarentum. And he kept retreating. Leaving the colonists to their fate, he returned to his kingdom in Epirus. Over the next twelve months, Rome took over everything in southern Italy. Hostile Gauls were still entrenched and active in the north, but everything else in the entire peninsula was now firmly in Roman hands.

But could they hold it? Yes. The legions had now mastered the craft of self-sustaining warfare in the mountains and valleys of Italy, and the peninsular cities largely benefited from coming under the control of Rome's consuls and magistrates. So, was there any need to send generals and troops abroad, where much longer levers would be needed to control and integrate foreign people? That would depend on the ambition of the Roman elite, and we are about to see just how strong that was.

Chapter 4 – Launching the Boats to Glory

Rome's elite families had grown wealthy during those 250 years or so as they grabbed land and trading links right down to the "toe" of Italy. But this push south now brought them face to face with a foreign city-state expanding up in the opposite direction. If they were to keep their place and riches in the peninsula, Rome would have to fight the navies and mercenaries of Carthage across the Mediterranean. They chose to, little knowing the fighting would last 130 years.

Carthage was a city of successful traders built on the northern coast of Africa in modern Tunisia, a location that could hardly fail. From there, fast merchant ships sailed east to modern Lebanon, the original homeland of the Phoenicians (Punics in Latin), who founded Carthage around the turn of the first millennium BCE, as well as west to the promising new lands of Europe and the islands of Sardinia and Sicily. Those two large islands lay too close to Italy for Roman comfort.

In earlier times, Punic traders sailed to Rome itself and set up treaties between Carthage and the town on the Tiber. But now, the Romans tore up those agreements and allowed themselves to be drawn into the fighting in Sicily between settlers from Carthage and Greek colonists. The First Punic War had begun.

In 264 BCE, Roman soldiers put troops on the island and soon occupied the eastern half. The western side was not as yielding, so the generals came up with a remarkable alternative to standard military tactics. Instead of attacking on the land, they would build fighting ships, learn how to sail them, blockade the Punic outposts, and force a surrender.

This audacity was matched with ingenuity. Conventional naval battles of the day were won with clever ramming tactics, and Punic sailors had centuries of experience in maneuvering oceangoing war vessels. So, the Romans developed an alternative, a portable bridge that they threw onto the deck of an enemy boat, allowing boarding parties to storm across and take the ship with traditional hand-to-hand combat, at which the legions performed well. There is some question about how this apparatus worked and if there really was a heavy spike on the underside to fix it to the Punic boat when it crashed onto the deck. But the thing was called the corvus, and for some time, it worked.

It was a clever innovation, but Punic ships were quickly replaced after those losses. In addition, the Carthage settlements on Sicily remained supported and undefeated. So, Rome again switched tactics. This time, they would build a huge naval fleet, confront the Punic fleet, and land an invasion force outside the walls of Carthage itself, some 550 kilometers (about 340 miles) across the Mediterranean in North Africa. They did this in the summer of 256 BCE.

Again, their success was muffled. Carthage's fleet was beaten, and the Romans filled their ships with plunder. However, the city of Carthage did not fall. There were peace talks, but the fighting season was drawing to a close with winter approaching. Supplies were insufficient to keep the whole Roman army in North Africa until the spring, so a large section was taken home.

In the following spring of 255 BCE, the twenty thousand men who remained were not reinforced quickly enough and were slaughtered almost to the last man. Rome sent 264 ships to rescue the few survivors, but that fleet was caught in a storm, in which 184 vessels foundered. It is said tens of thousands of men drowned. This was a massive defeat on all levels.

But we are looking at the Romans. They have always exhibited doggedness and limitless reserves of self-belief and manpower. They built 140 new ships and attacked Sicily the next year, this time capturing a major port. At the end of that fighting season, the fleet was caught in another storm, and 150 ships went down. The losses and numbers are mind-boggling. But it gets worse. They built 120 new ships, launched one successful ground attack in Sicily, failed in another, were beaten in a sea battle, and lost a fleet when it was pushed against rocks by a clever Punic maneuver in 249 BCE. It was a hurricane of losses.

Census records show a decline in Rome's males of 17 percent in these fifteen years of fighting. These were body blows that not even Rome could sustain. So, they put a pause on things. But in 242 BCE, a new fleet of two hundred ships was ready, and the boarding bridge tactic was scrapped and replaced with seamen trained in standard naval strategies and tactics. The fleet defeated the Carthaginians in Sicily in a decisive engagement when the North Africans tried to relieve their final port stronghold on the island. Carthage had to let go of its dream of holding Sicily and was forced to pay Rome a huge fine over the next ten years.

To the north, of course, was Sardinia, and Carthage had mercenaries on it. But Rome also had eyes on that island and forced the North Africans to abandon it and pay another huge fine. This rankled the Carthaginians, and mutual bitterness festered. Then, in 218 BCE, a North African general stepped forward to avenge Punic honor and forge a military history every schoolboy knows. Hannibal took his elephants across the Alps and stormed into Italy.

He left his base in Spain with thirty-seven elephants and around sixty thousand men and crossed the Pyrenees into Gaul. Next, he released about fifteen thousand soldiers and moved into the impenetrable wall of the Italian Alps. Just two weeks later, he emerged intact on the other side! Hannibal had fought off fierce ambushes from local tribesmen, endured epic hardship, watched men die in accidents, and clambered over steep passes. This was truly astonishing, and it's no wonder the trek is still remembered.

Hannibal had shown his ingenuity, skill, and determination, and he fully unleashed it upon the Romans. In northern Italy, he enlisted local anti-Roman Gauls and routed a Roman army sent to stop him. He moved south into Etruria in 217 BCE, where he trapped and annihilated the second force of legions trying to stop him.

Next, he circled to the south of Rome, called on non-Latins to support him, and launched a third battle against the legions. He won the fighting; some fifty thousand Roman soldiers were slaughtered. But he couldn't get local support. The city itself was now exposed, but Hannibal had no siege machines to trundle to the walls, so he turned to the "heel" of Italy and had that southern region in his control by 212 BCE.

Rome responded by spending every spare denarius to raise twenty-five legions (the largest force it had ever gathered), and in the following fighting seasons, they waged small-scale battles for towns and cities occupied by Hannibal. There would be no more large-scale pitched encounters, which Hannibal had always won. This mired the Punic juggernaut.

Next, Rome set out to cut Hannibal's supply lines from Spain, which Carthage occupied. By 207 BCE, the Iberian Peninsula belonged to Rome. A small army of Carthaginians escaped from Spain and attempted to link up with Hannibal in Italy. It was attacked and annihilated. By 204 BCE, all of Italy was back under Roman control, and the Romans moved to strike their own killer blow against the city of Carthage across the Mediterranean. This forced Hannibal to leave Italy, but even with his experience and help, the Punic forces at Carthage were brought to their knees by 201 BCE.

The two cities signed a fifty-year treaty that essentially broke up the Punic empire in the western Mediterranean, ended this Second Punic War, and reduced Carthage to just another city that paid annual taxes to Rome.

For fifty years, this arrangement held. However, the old animosities remained alive, and when the treaty expired, the drums of war were sounded in the Roman Senate. Rome sent its navy and legions to North Africa. Carthage and the surrounding towns attempted negotiations, but Rome attacked in 149 BCE with some successes. Then, in 147 BCE, engineers and shipwrights brought pressure on Carthage again. It was assaulted and taken the following year after a week of street fighting. Survivors were enslaved, the city looted and burned, and the site of the once-great city was put under a savage curse. It was later said to have been plowed over and sown with salt, but that is almost certainly an urban legend. Rome had secured its first African province. It would not be the last, however, because Rome's expansion machine was being set up in the eastern end of the Mediterranean.

Across the blue Adriatic Sea from Italy, Greece must have bobbed like a mirage in the eyes of generations of Roman senators. They knew about the lofty cultural achievements of the Greeks and the tenacity of their colonists living independently in southern Italy. But Greece was not a neighbor, so why try to occupy it?

The answer became apparent when Philip V of Macedon agreed to help Hannibal in Italy and appeared ready in 216 BCE to invade the region, which ran approximately from today's Trieste to Tirana. On both counts, Rome had a strategic interest in confronting Philip, which it did with some half-hearted military interventions over a period of ten years.

The tempo rose in 200 BCE. Several Greek city-states in the Aegean were then under attack by Philip and asked Rome for military help. It was given, and in 197 BCE, the legions wiped out the Macedonian army.

However, this left the Senate with a quandary. How could Roman forces hold and control the many independent city-states in Macedon and the Greek mainland and those on the shores of modern Turkey, where the Seleucid king, Antiochus III, had his own designs on Greece?

The answer was to wear a cloak of generosity. Philip was left as ruler of a weaker Macedon, where he would be a buffer against the tribes to the north and the growing hostile Seleucid kingdom to the east across the Aegean. Further, at the great Isthmian Games of June 196 BCE, a Roman herald announced all of Greece south of Macedon would be free, untaxed, and unsupervised by any Roman soldiers. Some 150 years of Macedon shackles were broken! The stadium erupted in roars of approval.

Rome now had a tentative control on Greece and could wait to see what Antiochus might do from the other side of the Aegean. The Romans only had to wait four years. In 192 BCE, the Seleucid monarch was persuaded to support an opposition group in Greece, which told him the entire Greek mainland was seething with unseen resentment against Rome. Of course, it was not. When Antiochus landed there with ten thousand men, he quickly discovered the rebels he had teamed up with were being cut down in Macedon, Roman troops were taking over that region, and a Roman army more than twice the size of his was being assembled.

To his credit, the king took up a position in Thermopylae and faced his doom with honor. Like the Spartans before them, his army was massacred. Antiochus barely escaped with his life to Ephesus. The legions marched after him, defeated an army he raised there, and forced Antiochus to pay an enormous indemnity and retreat back to Syria in shame.

What happened next is something of a shame on Rome. For the next fifty years or so, the Romans tightened and strengthened their grip on Macedon and Greece by force of arms, treachery, cruelty, and fear. Much of it was driven by outrageous greed.

Powerful families in Rome and magistrates in Greece used military units to enrich themselves. The old Macedonian taxes were diverted to Rome, and Roman landholding citizens living in Greece were made tax-exempt. The entire economy of Rhodes was deliberately undermined and destroyed. Enemies were slaughtered in head-spinning numbers. For example, some twenty thousand lost their lives after one battle in Macedon in 168 BCE. One year later, 150,000 Macedonians were enslaved in one day and sold in the markets of Rome. Rulers were humiliated in triumphs, prominent people were exiled to Italy, and the old kingdom of Macedon was arbitrarily split into four ill-fitting sections that disoriented the Macedonians. Treaties were torn up when it suited the Romans. Distant senators micromanaged affairs in Greece, while local collaborators were encouraged to purge their countrymen on trumped-up charges of disloyalty. In 146 BCE, Corinth was sacked and razed to the ground as a chilling reminder of where the power lay. Greece was cowed into submission.

At the other end of the Mediterranean, the "primitive" tribes of Spain had been largely left to themselves for centuries, as Greeks and then Carthaginians set up colonies and conquered cities along the coast. The Romans changed that. As we have seen, they drove Punic settlers and mercenaries out of Spain as part of their tactics to defeat Hannibal. But instead of then pulling back to Italy, they stayed. The locals objected, and ragtag Spanish tribesmen took up swords. Rome's legions were impressive and victorious against massed armies, but they had no quick answers to the hit-and-run tactics of the ill-armed local Spanish militias.

It should have been easy to subdue Spain because the tribes and towns of Spain were not united and could be picked off one by one. However, that very disunity meant there was no central tribal leader who could negotiate peace across many towns at one time. Roman officers could also be brutal and rapacious. After one battle in 151 BCE, they slaughtered eight thousand prisoners. On another occasion, twenty thousand surrendered men were hacked to death. Rogue officers frequently attacked settlements simply for loot.

The Senate in Rome was not in sync with commanders on the ground. But some of the atrocities in Spain turned the stomachs of the Senate so much that there were several attempts made to set up courts in Spain to try officers and officials for excesses. Sadly, like all such arrangements, they had limited effect.

To the dismay of the army accountants in Rome, it took nearly one hundred years to subdue the interior of the Iberian Peninsula. Victory was declared in 134 BCE, but the embers of revolt remained. Taking and holding Spain had been messy, inglorious, and difficult.

This expansion at both ends of the Mediterranean generated a massive problem for everyone involved. Conquered foreigners were frequently mistreated and resented Rome. Army officers and Roman magistrates serving abroad became increasingly independent of the Senate and public assemblies in Rome. They were too far away to micromanage, and the spoils of war filled both Rome's coffers and the pockets of the distant military commanders.

With all this new territory under its control and liable for tax, Rome could now spend on larger administration systems and great public works. Tax collection contracts would go to the wealthy non-political classes, which turned their new wealth into great landholdings that they cultivated with huge numbers of slaves brought in from conquered lands to the markets of Italy.

Armies throughout history have drawn foot soldiers from poorer families. This was the case in Rome, where those people were often also small landholders. If the men who went to war stayed away too long or were killed on foreign soil, their wives and children were sometimes compelled to sell that land to the great estate owners and move into the city of Rome to survive. Over time, a large disenfranchised group of these people began demanding a voice and opposing the large landowners. This would be a major problem in the next one hundred years of the republic. In just one century, it changed everything. The Senate would be disemboweled, and the whole management apparatus of Rome would be brought to its knees, as we will now see.

Chapter 5 – Rome vs. Rome in an Age of Blood

If we had to pick a date for the start of the collapse of the Roman Republic, it could be 133 BCE, the year Tiberius Sempronius Gracchus was beaten to death by a mob using clubs made from broken wooden seats.

As a wealthy young man from an aristocratic family in his late twenties and fresh from successful military campaigns in Spain, Tiberius Gracchus became head of the plebeian assembly back in Rome in our fateful year. He knew firsthand the desperate lot of ordinary Romans and the particular troubles of returned servicemen, and he attempted to ride to the top of Rome's politics on the back of those deepening grievances and economic hardships.

A decent, practical young man by all accounts, he proposed the Senate pass a law giving returning soldiers small parcels of farmland illegally occupied by large landowners or in conquered regions. This sensible piece of reform would do three things, he said. First, the law would be honored. Second, the supply of soldiers to the legions would be maintained. This was a pressing need, as the armies drew fighters from landowners, men who could finance their own weapons and kit even if they only owned tiny parcels of farmland and were going to be foot soldiers. And third, it would help control the huge workforce of slaves imported to farm the estates of the wealthy and who were apparently teetering on the edge of armed revolt and uprising. (Spartacus's slave army would do exactly that just sixty years later.) Not to mention the hostility of poor Romans who said slaves were taking jobs they could have done.

The assembly of the common people shouted their approval. The senators opposed it, arguing that centuries of social order would be upended. So, Tiberius Gracchus performed some political sleight of hand and had a law passed in the plebeian assembly. The Senate refused to support or finance the legislation, and when Tiberius Gracchus made a grab for state funds, senators erupted in a fury. "Tiberius Gracchus was intending to become a king!" they cried. Wooden benches were torn up, and a mob of patricians and their supporters stormed from the Senate and attacked Gracchus as he stood among the plebs on the Capitol. As many as three hundred people were clubbed to death. For the first time in the republic's history, murder was used as a political weapon. A terrible mix of assassinations and executions quickly became the lethal norm. And in less than one hundred years, it would pull down the republic and destroy the senators, the very people who initially seemed to profit from it so conveniently.

Tiberius Gracchus had a younger brother, Gaius Sempronius Gracchus, who shared his brother's concerns over Rome's poor, state corruption, the power of the Senate, and land reform. After some years of military service abroad, he was voted into the leadership of the plebs in 123 BCE and used this powerbase to pass shrewd, meticulously researched, and carefully considered laws that built on his brother's legacy.

In his second year in leadership, he turned his attention to the Italian problem. He needed to figure out how to placate the increasingly discontented people who had lived in the peninsula as long as the Romans, people who shared the same language and culture and had been brought into the economic and military circle of Rome but who were always treated with disdain and as (very) poor cousins by the citizens of Rome.

The Senate wanted to maintain the status quo. No surprise there. Gaius Sempronius Gracchus wanted to give them a mix of full and partial citizenship. The traditionalists won the vigorous debate, and they declared martial law and ordered an army to be camped outside Rome to find Gaius Gracchus on the Aventine Hill and kill him. The troops killed thousands of his followers but were not able to strike their leader. He committed suicide.

Senators were becoming increasingly comfortable using their new political weapon of murder. But they would soon be made alarmingly insecure with the unexpected result of a small administrative change that set off a chain of unintended consequences that transformed the power of army generals.

The officer responsible was the low-born Gaius Marius, who, against all odds, became consul in 107 BCE and had fatal legislation passed, making it possible to recruit landless men for the legions if they were freedmen. Until this time, soldiers owned land and had the voting rights of landowners and a stake in Rome's system of assemblies and the Senate, as we have seen. Now, men without land and those rights would be dependent on their commanders for payment and rewards. Their loyalties would be with their officers, not a political system they had no part in. Chilling stuff.

Gaius Marius knew warfare. He was successful and efficient in battle at a time when the legions in Africa and Gaul were frequently defeated, and General Marius saved Rome from a huge barbarian drive into northern Italy in 102 and 101 BCE. His victories were sufficient to get him repeatedly elected as consul (he held the post an unprecedented seven times!), but the establishment never embraced and accepted him.

By now, the clamor for citizenship from non-Roman Italians was inciting riots and killings. Southern cities revolted. Gaius Marius was sent to quieten the uprising, and a law was passed finally granting limited citizenship to the Italians. It didn't silence every uprising, though.

To add to the Senate's problems, a local ruler in Asia Minor, King Mithridates, was unwisely attacked by ill-suited Roman troops. He pushed them aside and launched himself across the Aegean Sea onto the legions in mainland Greece. In 88 BCE, with Greek cities in his pocket, the king ordered the killing of all Romans living in Asia Minor, and it is said eighty thousand people died.

Consul Lucius Cornelius Sulla Felix prepared to deal with this, but he was delayed by political unrest and a proposal that Gaius Marius go to Greece instead of him. Outraged, Sulla took his troops into Rome and made sure he was sent to the battlefields of Greece and Asia Minor, which was ripe for looting. For the very first time, troops (many of them landless freedmen loyal to Sulla) were used for political ends. Gaius Marius fled to Africa and had to watch on as Rome was wracked with civil unrest and Sulla won victories in the east.

In 87 BCE, Marius returned and took control of Rome using troops loyal to him. He had fourteen senators executed, all of them his enemies and some of them high-ranking members, then got himself elected consul. These were remarkable events. What they might have led to, we don't know because, in 86 BCE, Gaius Marius died of natural causes.

More deaths were coming. That year, Sulla drove Mithridates from Greece, but instead of hounding the king to a resounding defeat, he negotiated a deal with him. Mithridates would keep his lands in Asia Minor as a vassal in return for money and ships so Sulla could attack Rome itself! Sulla landed in Italy in 83 BCE with vast wealth. He recruited troops, marched on Rome, unleashed thugs to slaughter hundreds of his opponents, got himself elected dictator, and passed laws that exonerated him. Five years later, he died of natural causes, leaving a terrible benchmark in political killings and a demonstration of the power now held by army generals over Rome's senators.

His replacements soon appeared. One was urgently needed by 69 BCE when pirates had become a Mediterranean-wide menace. Fleets of them voyaged almost at will, defeating Roman warships and even seizing Rome's own seaport, Ostia, and taking prominent captives.

In 67 BCE, commander Gnaeus Pompeius Magnus (better known as Pompey) was given three years to wipe them out. He took less than three months. A major administrative change helped Pompey. He was given the legal standing to appoint fifteen subordinates with the full powers traditionally only given by the assemblies back in Rome. In the past, a commander's authority to fight pirates only existed when he was present. Now, that command could be held at a distance. These fifteen, along with their commander, swept the Mediterranean in coordinated attacks that wiped out piracy in forty-nine days.

Pompey then invaded Asia Minor and defeated Mithridates. He pushed farther north and found himself overrunning cities so distant they could be ruled but not directly controlled by Rome. Pompey arranged for rulers to become clients until the region could be absorbed into the state. This pattern was used across the Middle East for the next one hundred years or so.

Pompey kept moving. By 63 BCE, he had occupied Jerusalem. In just ten years, the legions had moved from Asia Minor's Aegean coast to the south. The wealth generated in this great stretch of land doubled Rome's tax intake, and administrators strained to cope.

For his successes, the old elite treated Pompey like Gaius Marius before him. On his return in 62 BCE, they withheld land grants to his troops, refused to legally recognize his accomplishments in the east, and denied his entry to Rome's top social strata. What happened next is the stuff of Hollywood blockbusters, with characters including Mark Anthony, Cleopatra, and Julius Caesar.

Let's begin with Gaius Julius Caesar, a patrician and extraordinary orator who was elected consul in 59 BCE. He negotiated with Pompey and Marcus Licinius Crassus to form the Triumvirate, a gang of three powerful men. For six years, their loyalty to each other and their use of violence and influence would make them invincible in the corridors of Rome's government.

Julius Caesar then left for Gaul and spent ten years fighting wherever he had an opportunity. In 54 BCE, he landed in Britain, but he found it difficult to fight the communities there, as they simply retreated when his army advanced and made it dangerous to station garrisons on their land. He left, claiming to have taken the island. But the Romans didn't return for another one hundred years.

On the continent, however, he crushed all before him. Hundreds of thousands of people were enslaved or slaughtered. Caesar later claimed he had killed 1.2 million people in his lifetime. The land between the Pyrenees and the Rhine was secured for Rome, and Julius Caesar made himself and his leading officers immensely rich. In fact, he sent so much gold back to Italy that the value of the precious metal there fell 25 percent.

Marcus Licinius Crassus was also fighting. He'd been made governor of Syria and should have been content to strip it of its great wealth for the benefit of Rome and himself. However, he chose to also reach for military glory, and in 53 BCE, he crossed the Euphrates and attacked Parthia. Treachery and some unwise battlefield decisions left him and thousands of his troops dead.

The next year, the other member of the Triumvirate, Pompey, was elected consul. Politics in Rome were tumultuous, murderous, and dysfunctional. The traditional voting patterns were under strain. And although Pompey had married Caesar's daughter, Julia, this had not prevented him from steadily aligning himself with the enemies of her father in the Senate. She tragically died in childbirth in 54 BCE, along with their infant also, and he then married the daughter of a senior elite senator.

The pact that had held the Triumvirate together was obviously now irrelevant. Pompey and Caesar were on a collision course, and the clash came in 49 BCE. In March that year, Caesar's assignment in Gaul would end, and he would lose his command of the legions and the legal protection against charges of corruption brought ten years earlier. His enemies in court were strong, and he was almost certainly going to be banished and exiled. Caesar chose to fight outside the court. He chose to cross the Rubicon.

Town after town willingly went over to his advancing army. Pompey calculated Italy could not be held against Caesar and made a tactical withdrawal to Greece, along with many senators, to regroup. With the peninsula in his hands, Caesar went to Spain, and in six weeks, he had fought and disbanded the legions loyal to Pompey. In 48 BCE, he became consul and sailed for Greece for a fight to the death with his archrival. Caesar won the battle, although Pompey managed to escape and fled to Egypt, where he had influence with the ruler, Ptolemy XIII, having put him on the throne earlier and lent him money. Sometimes, though, gratitude wears thin because Ptolemy had Pompey killed upon his arrival.

Julius Caesar landed in hot pursuit and was welcomed by Ptolemy XIII, who gave the Roman general the head of Pompey on a plate. Caesar was disappointed in this. He then quickly became more interested in the pharaoh's young wife, the twenty-one-year-old Cleopatra. She was actually Ptolemy's sister and had become his queen as a teenager. She and the fifty-two-year-old Caesar had an affair, and the following year, it is believed she bore the Roman a son.

Around that time, the Egyptians under Ptolemy XIII turned on Caesar, and Ptolemy was killed in the fighting. Caesar had Cleopatra married to her younger brother, who became Ptolemy XIV. War called, however, and Caesar left for Asia Minor, where he defeated a renegade son of Mithridates in four short hours. His report to Rome included the equally short "Veni, vidi, vici," which we all know as the famous saying of "I came, I saw, I conquered."

Caesar then went on to Rome, where the economy and his personal debts were in crisis and his republican enemies were reinforcing armies against him in North Africa and Spain. He managed to keep his own war-weary troops loyal, and for the next two years, they swept away the last remnants of republican troops in North Africa and the Iberian Peninsula at the cost of tens of thousands of their opponents.

It was now obvious to everyone in the Roman world that Gaius Julius Caesar was a power and a superstar of unprecedented stature. The subdued Senate in Rome was obliged to heap on him honor after honor, linking him with gods and ancient Roman kings. It was completely over the top, and even many erstwhile supportive senators were repulsed. He received powers to personally appoint half of Rome's magistrates and made himself the dictator for life. Any fig leaf of the old republic, with its formal assemblies and consuls elected for one non-recurring tenure, was now removed.

A plot was hatched to assassinate the tyrant, and we all know what happened on the Ides of March, 44 BCE.

At this point, the elites were unable to endorse rule by a single strong man, as it signaled the return of the monarchy. But Sulla and Caesar had demonstrated the power of the autocrat, and eventually, the traditional republicans would have to accept that this was the future shape of government.

The age of the emperors was about to begin. It was to be ushered in by a nineteen-year-old, and the story will include a second appearance by Cleopatra.

First, a successor for Caesar had to be found. The lead was taken by the consul Marcus Antonius, who we remember today as Mark Anthony. He did try to find a middle ground between the two opposing sides, but he had not factored in Gaius Julius Caesar Octavius, Caesar's great-nephew and adopted son. Caesar named him his heir, and we remember him today as Octavian. Although he was still a teenager, Octavian was brimming with very adult ambitions. Mark Anthony could not push the young Caesar aside since the murdered Caesar's popularity remained sky high and Octavian was his son and heir. Neither could he take the side of the dead tyrant, as this would alienate the remaining republicans. Furthermore, a comet appeared that seemed to confirm the dead Caesar's acceptance by the gods.

Things became tangled and turned violent. For the next twelve years, commanders, magistrates, governors, and senators marshaled troops, led them in battle, forged unlikely alliances among themselves, raided and looted to pay their soldiers, betrayed each other, sent rivals into exile, butchered opponents, and drove a non-stop struggle for Julius Caesar's mantle that ranged from Sardinia to Syria. Thousands died. It ended when the last men standing came face to face in Greece in 31 BCE. Cleopatra was alongside one of them.

Mark Anthony had met Cleopatra in 42 BCE in the middle of campaigning in the eastern Mediterranean. Over the next years, they had three children, and Anthony increasingly based himself in Egypt with her, having sent his Roman wife back to Rome with their two daughters in 35 BCE. This played out badly in Rome. There, people began to think the general had been turned by a wanton, decadent Eastern queen, the complete opposite of the chaste, noble women of Rome. They believed he had become a drunk and degenerate, living like a Greek despot.

Of course, Mark Anthony remained a talented army commander, but he was to need more ability when Octavian approached him for a showdown in Greece in 31 BCE. Anthony sailed from Egypt to fight but got trapped by Octavian's ships in the port of Actium. His breakout failed, and his troops went over to the young Caesar. Anthony and Cleopatra only just managed to escape to Egypt. They lasted barely one year. In 30 BCE, the young Caesar attacked Egypt, and Mark Anthony committed suicide. Cleopatra did the same a few weeks later. Her son by Gaius Julius Caesar, Caesarion, was executed, although Anthony's three children were spared.

The republic was now a façade, but merely removing most of the opposition was not going to maintain the young titan in power. Others had tried that and failed. To stay on top for decades, Octavian must find a new, enduring model. He did this in a breathtakingly audacious and complete maneuver that maintained him and his successors for some two hundred years. Hail the Emperor!

Chapter 6 – Power and Excess in the Palace

Octavian's first move was to reduce the size of the army that had grown to an unmanageable and uncoordinated half a million men. He dismissed 300,000 of these, and with the brimming treasury of Egypt at his disposal, he bought land for these troops in Italy and in new colonies abroad.

Two years later, he had the eastern Mediterranean running more efficiently, so in 29 BCE, he marched into Rome in a massive triumph, dished out money to his troops and Rome's citizens, and ostentatiously began divesting himself of the non-republican powers his predecessors had accumulated. He knew Rome was in no mood to be ruled by another king, but he was keenly aware from recent events that if administrators or commanders had any influence over the legions, there would be an ever-present possibility one of them would challenge the Senate and stoke the bonfires of civil war. Something the Romans were also fearful might take place.

How could Rome get a king without getting a king? Octavian did this by making a hidden move in the Senate and some very public changes in the army.

He surprised the Senate by offering to turn over all his powers to the senators. Senator after senator, some of them no doubt already secretly briefed by Octavian, rose to their feet and spoke to this totally novel proposition. They all knew some central power was necessary to prevent the internal warring of the last twenty years. So, they voted to adjust and shrink the authority and independence of the Senate and give Octavian the power to appoint senators who would lead the foreign legions for short terms. They also gave him a brand-new title: Augustus. He was neither a king, dictator, nor politician. He was now august: the "lofty and serene one."

It seemed that the republic and its citizen-led, Senate-based government had been restored! But this was an illusion. For one thing, a man must be extremely wealthy before he could be appointed by Augustus to the Senate. Once there, he would find himself with great prestige, but he would only debate trivial matters, and all his decisions needed Augustus's approval. Administrators below him fared even worse; they served only briefly, and eventually, their position became largely honorary.

Compounding this, over time, the wealthiest families from across the empire moved into the Senate. They were people without a strong connection to the republic and its traditional values, and this made it easier for the empire to be accepted by the Senate.

Augustus gradually accumulated overarching legal and religious powers. He could interfere in the running of the Senate without seeming to be autocratic and nominate and appoint senators to the highest posts and administrative offices. He established a loyal bureaucracy that ran Egypt's grain supplies, the smaller provinces, Augustus's personal landholdings, and the greatly enlarged Praetorian Guard. He also became the head state priest.

This first emperor embarked on a large program of reconstruction and social reform. Rome was transformed with impressive new buildings, and Augustus was a patron to Virgil, Horace, and Propertius, the leading poets of the day. He promoted himself throughout his empire with statues and coins.

Augustus also restructured the army. Power came from the javelins and swords of Roman legionnaires, and now, he made them answerable to himself through the handpicked military leaders he plucked from a pool of loyal senators. As we have seen, in the past, soldiers were landholders, most of them small, who elected Rome's leaders and fought under them for short periods in specific campaigns, sharing the booty afterward. Rome's conquests and expansion had made this model unsustainable. There were not enough men willing to leave their land for long postings and campaigns, and back in Rome, everyone knew what happened when distant commanders were able to share the loot with their men. So, the army was turned into a professional force. A soldier's loyalty was now to Augustus, not his commander, and for this, he was given regular pay, fixed terms of service (twenty years for citizen-soldiers and twenty-five for others), and either a cash payout or land in Italy or a foreign colony after his service ended. Ambitious soldiers could only become centurions.

It was an enormously expensive force. But Augustus himself had the pulse of the legions and could accurately assess and provide for their needs without wasting money. And thus equipped, he secured the borders of the empire. He occupied northwest Spain, arranged for Asia Minor and Syria to accept a degree of Roman control, decided not to attack the Parthians on the east of the Euphrates, and pushed into the Balkans and along the length of the Danube. He did not expand into Germany, having seen three Roman legions there wiped out in a massive ambush and coming to know that northern Europeans were as difficult to capture and control as Julius Caesar had found the tribes in Britain some fifty years earlier. More expansion would have stretched Rome too far. So, Augustus wisely settled for what he had: a vast swathe of territory and peoples at peace and under his control.

A downside of this was that the garrisons across the empire were put on a sort of extended guard duty. Several hundred years later, when the time came for Roman legions to be aggressive in the face of unprecedented barbarian attacks, they were found to lack the essential tradition and training. But that is for later in our story.

Augustus left a memorandum for his successors to be content with the empire's boundaries as he'd left them, and for the next two hundred years or so, his advice was followed. He was a gifted administrator and also left behind a remarkable record of public achievements, including Rome's first fire brigade and police force, splendid new city buildings, a sweeping and effective civil service, an empire-wide administration system that rejuvenated the decrepitude of the final century of the republic, and, of course, decades of peace for Roman citizens.

But all the glory he had earned could not make up for one embarrassing deficiency. Augustus could not father a son to succeed him. His first alternative was to marry his daughter Julia to someone trusted and appoint the sons of that union as his heirs. His eighteen-year-old nephew obliged, but he died a year later without producing another heir.

Next, Augustus married the still-teenaged Julia to a war hero, who performed admirably in bed only to die while his sons were mere boys.

A now-desperate Augustus married Julia to his eldest stepson, the dour Tiberius. That union also failed because the couple disliked each other, and there were no children. In fact, Tiberius left her and went into voluntary exile in Rhodes. When the discarded Julia's wild living became too inappropriate, Augustus banished her.

Augustus had two grandsons, but both died of illness and wounds in adulthood. So, a disappointed Augustus adopted Tiberius as his son and forced Tiberius to adopt Augustus's great-nephew, Germanicus, who was married to one of Julia's daughters.

The heir was finally ready. Augustus could now be seen as the one who had brought decades of peace to Rome, and when he died in 14 CE, the grateful city enrolled him among the gods. He had made "emperor" an acceptable position.

Augustus was succeeded by a short-lived dynasty of four emperors who were all related to him. They are names we know well: Tiberius, Caligula, Claudius, and Nero. We're still fascinated by stories of wild hedonistic depravity, cold political murders, the grinding power of their armies, gladiators, chariot races, engineering projects, and learned histories commissioned and encouraged by these four. The excesses were occasionally so revolting that it takes a strong nerve to read the details.

The emperors who followed those four are less well remembered, but all of them tended to tap into the wealth pouring in from around the empire and lavished money on the infrastructure of Rome, more fabulous public games, and generous social welfare, just as Julius Caesar had once done.

They built temples and expanded the new administrative centers, the famous forums. When needed, they extended the snaking aqueduct systems and the large public baths. They also added to Rome's glorious fountains and improved her remarkable public sanitation system. Money was spent on Rome's port at Ostia, as well as on libraries, theaters, and sporting venues such as the Circus Maximus, where chariots had been raced since the days of the republic, and the Flavian Amphitheater (which we now call the Colosseum), where gladiators were forced to kill and fight each other as entertainment.

The emperors were careful to maintain the late republic institution of a system called the grain dole. Originally, this was discounted grain, but it eventually became a free handout. It was given to 150,000 specific people listed in a register. Great shipments of grain were needed to feed Rome and Italy's other main centers, and most of it was imported through an enormous, sophisticated supply chain from the breadbasket of the world, Egypt. The dole was not a service to the poor. For one thing, a name in the ledger was an asset that could be bequeathed or sold. But more metaphorically, it was a symbol of the emperor's relationship with his people, for the citizens in the register represented all Roman citizens, and they assembled annually to ratify magistrates previously elected by the Senate. Their vote legitimized the emperor (who ran the Senate), and in return, he managed and cared for his people.

It appears the empire only just managed to balance the books. Indeed, it may have never been able to entirely pay all its debts. We say this because the currency was regularly devalued either by making coins smaller, giving them a higher face value, or reducing the bullion content. But even this failed toward the end of the empire when the army was called to move from defense to a war footing. At that time, imperial finances collapsed, as we will see.

Governors in the imperial provinces maintained order, collected taxes, and let cities run their own affairs, with the exception that a Roman citizen could not be flogged or executed by a magistrate without the approval of the people of Rome. So, most people on the empire's edges had no reason to interact with officials back in Rome.

Those subjects did interact with the idea of Rome, however. For example, when a non-citizen soldier was discharged, he was given citizenship. It was also given in stages to the people of non-Roman cities brought under Rome's control, which encouraged a voluntary and almost unnoticed Romanization of those places. Eventually, under Emperor Antoninus Pius, citizenship was granted to every free person in the empire because, in practical terms, it was not realistic for a poor citizen to have more privileges than a wealthy, foreign non-citizen. It's a rueful fact that the rich are often given more rights than the poor in any society.

Emperors were generally managers. There are very few examples of emperors intervening in the social life of Romans, such as the time Augustus penalized childlessness or when Trajan set up a program in Italy to help poor families raise their children. Where an emperor took a more hands-on approach, things could go wrong. Trajan, for example, personally set out on a conquest that dragged the empire into ruin.

An emperor was divine because, in the polytheistic Greco-Roman world, anyone with supernatural powers was thought to be a god. There's a certain logic to this. A king could do things ordinary people could not. Julius Caesar saw the value of this and wanted to be known as a god. (He was awarded that status but was given it two years after his death.) Augustus declined the title and honors, but on his death, he was given them posthumously. Nevertheless, emperors were addressed as divine, and libations might be frequently made to them across the empire. This may have something to do with the need for people to worship something greater than themselves. Certainly, it was a way to express a personal relationship with the empire. However, a divine emperor still had to function as a man, and some of those who followed Augustus were not so good at that.

Tiberius first succeeded Augustus and held office from 14 CE to 37 CE. He lacked the finesse and extraordinary skills of the first emperor to control the Senate without appearing to do so, opting instead for violence. Before his rule, only slaves and foreigners could be punished with execution. Citizens guilty of capital offenses were permitted to go into exile. Tiberius had uncooperative senators executed and their corpses abused in public. They were dragged with hooks to the Tiber and thrown into the river. Tiberius was a poor communicator, and instead of actively managing his governors and key administrators, he tended to only respond if things went horribly wrong. In 25 CE, tired of his responsibilities, Tiberius left Rome for the island of Capri in the Bay of Naples, never to return, although he held the title of emperor until his death.

He was briefly succeeded by Gaius, the son of Germanicus and Tiberius's adopted grandson, who ruled from 37 CE to 41 CE. Nicknamed Caligula, meaning the 'little soldier's boot," this man was cruel, deadly, and insane. The new emperor quickly executed potential rivals in his family, including his own heir, took the wives of two men for himself, spent vast sums of money building a bridge in the Bay of Naples, dressed as a god beginning in 40 CE, ordered a statue of himself as a god to be put up in the temple at Jerusalem (the Syrian governor diplomatically delayed that order), and was only stopped when some of the Praetorian Guard stabbed him to death, along with his wife and two-year-old daughter in 41 CE.

The assassins had no succession plan. It was felt that the empire could not return to a republic since the magistrates had been made powerless over the years and since the army was now loyal to the emperor rather than senators or even military commanders. There were no direct male heirs of Augustus alive, so the guard took Gaius's uncle, Claudius, and hailed him as emperor.

Claudius was emperor from 41 to 54 CE, though some said his wives and freed slaves actually ruled. He was physically deformed, but he was an academic, and he wrote now-lost histories. He saw the need to be militarily successful, so early on, he pushed legions across Rome's borders in several places and was personally present for the first two weeks of a successful invasion of the lower part of Britain and Wales in 43 CE.

Back in Rome, his teenage wife bore him a son, whom he named Britannicus to mark this campaign. She appears to have done little else for her husband and was openly unfaithful. Claudius eventually had her executed.

In 48 CE, he married his niece, Agrippina the Younger, the sister of Gaius (Caligula). She had been married, and her son in that marriage was Lucius Domitius Ahenobarbus, the great-great-grandson of Augustus, who was four years older than Britannicus. She had Claudius adopt him in 50 CE, and his name changed to Nero Claudius Caesar. He became the heir to the throne.

Claudius had a daughter, and ideally, she would have married Nero, but the girl was engaged. Agrippina took the girl's finance to court and had him exiled. She also had a prospective wife of Claudius exiled and driven to suicide. She put loyal men in charge of tutoring Nero, then in 53 CE, she had Nero marry Claudius's thirteen-year-old daughter, Octavia, although neither spouse was attracted to the other. The next year, it is believed that Agrippina fed Emperor Claudius poisoned mushrooms at a banquet, and on his death, her seventeen-year-old son became emperor.

By almost all measures, Nero's reign, which lasted from 54 to 68 CE, was a collapse of Roman idealism. It started well enough, as his mother and tutors ran the state for the teenager. But after five years, that team fell apart, and Nero turned against her. One day, before Agrippina's son Britannicus achieved his majority and would have theoretically been able to replace Nero, Britannicus was mysteriously poisoned and died. When

Agrippina criticized an affair Nero was having, he attempted to have her drowned in the Bay of Naples. She escaped (because she was able to swim), but there was no evading Nero's second attempt. He had her accused of treason and executed.

Nero did get involved in war in the east for a few years, but his preoccupation was not the martial arts. Instead, he was unusually fond of cultural arts in a society where the elite despised it. Moreover, instead of keeping this to himself, he staged artistic "games" and forced the upper classes to join him. He either ignored or did not notice how this repulsed them. But astonishment and grudges were quietly being stored upon the benches of the Senate.

Then, in the hot summer of 64 CE, the central quarter of Rome caught fire. For six days, fire brigades battled the flames, but their water pressure was insufficient, and they were reduced to simply watching the blaze. We should give Nero the benefit of the doubt and discount the story that he played the violin during the inferno. And while he later built a palace on the spot that burned down, this alone does not prove he lit the match. He accused the Christians of doing that and had a number of them burned alive at the stake. This happened around thirty-five years after the death of Jesus, which indicates his followers had spread to Rome by then.

Dissatisfaction with Nero was spreading among senators and other elites. There were plots and treason trials. Nero tracked down and killed the descendants of Augustus, and he pushed members of the imperial family to suicide. He accused his young wife, Octavia, of adultery, but he failed to convict her, so he divorced her on the grounds of sterility. This sparked sympathy for the young woman from the Roman crowds, so Nero promptly had her exiled and murdered on a remote island.

In 66 CE, he traveled to Greece and took part in artistic competitions and pursuits for two years, all the while ignoring reports that opposition was growing back in Rome. When he eventually returned to Rome, he paraded into the city in a mock triumph, where celebrations of a victory in war were replaced with achievements in the arts. That confounded belief and was the last straw. Rome's effete emperor was deliberately trampling on Roman sensibilities! In 68 CE, legions in Gaul and Spain revolted. They were put down, but a rumor got out that a commander had declared himself emperor. Nero fled, intending to get to the safety of Egypt but was trapped in a villa near Rome by his Praetorian Guard, so he committed suicide.

The empire was suddenly leaderless because Nero had slaughtered every remaining descendant of the founder of the dynasty. How would a new emperor be found?

First, the governor of Spain, Galba, was handed the position. He made some unpopular initial decisions, but his appointment showed elite onlookers that if Galba could become emperor, they could also. So, we have "the Year of Four Emperors." During 68 and 69 CE, four men grabbed the title: Galba, Otho, Vitellius, and Vespasian. Only Vespasian was not murdered.

Vespasian remained as emperor until 79 CE. He was Italian but not Roman, and since he had no family link to Augustus, he formalized his position with a written document whereby Rome's citizens gave their emperor the authority to rule in their stead. This worked. Unfortunately, Nero had pretty much emptied the imperial coffers, so Vespasian's gifts and debt repayments were necessarily modest. He was seen as a skinflint. However, he was fair and benevolent, and he established colonies for large numbers of retired troops.

Titus, his son, took over after Vespasian's death in 79, but he died of an illness just two years later, in 81. Although he was likable and generous, he left no significant imperial legacy, although he does go down in Jewish history as the commander who razed Jerusalem in 70 CE.

He was followed by his younger brother, Domitian, who was emperor from 81 to 96. This ruler was suspicious, unfriendly, unliked, paranoid, perhaps insecure (he demanded to be given deference usually reserved for the gods), and distant. However, he was a competent administrator but chose to interact with the Senate through a small group of senators and lower-ranked officials instead of talking directly with the whole august body of elites. In socially conscious Rome, this was a mistake.

Like his older brother, he had experienced war. He sent legions across the Rhine and against an uprising along the Danube. He was sometimes defeated, but he also enjoyed successes, and at times, he was personally present at the front. Domitian saw conspiracy at every hand, so he humiliated and executed men on the slightest of suspicions, often unjustly. One of his last acts was to kill his heir, his own cousin. At that point, the family quickly moved against him before he moved against more of them. He was assassinated, perhaps by his wife, personal bodyguard, and/or his closest freedmen.

Rome's second dynasty ended with him and raised a serious question. How could the people peacefully transfer imperial power away from an unsuitable emperor? The Senate soon came up with its answer. It would smilingly approve and applaud an emperor's every action, no matter what, in return for retaining the baubles of office. In a clap or be killed environment, senators would clap.

Chapter 7 – Government by Soldiers and Assassins

The performances of the next emperors were a mix of intemperance and hubris.

In 96, the military immediately replaced the assassinated Domitian with an aging non-entity, the sixty-six-year-old Marcus Cocceius Nerva. He lacked popularity and authority, and he was unable to control a violent outburst of anti-Domitian executions and the systematic destruction of his statues. Nerva also lacked children, so he adopted a popular governor. The two never met, and the governor showed no gratitude or affection when he succeeded the old emperor after his unexpected death in 98.

The new emperor was the likable forty-five-year-old Marcus Ulpius Trajanus, who we better remember as Trajan. A successful military man with popular backing in the Senate, he expanded a social welfare program that must have won the favor of the poor. His plan was modeled on private assistance programs run by some wealthy, public-minded individuals in their cities. Like them, Trajan gave grants to cities, which then invested the money and passed on the interest to poor families as welfare grants.

Trajan was a soldier. For years, he led campaigns in Germany and across the Danube. This was counter to Augustus's advice to stay within the boundaries he had carved out years earlier, and although Trajan brought great swathes of barbarian land and booty into Roman hands, he couldn't hold it. A Jewish revolt also took place during his reign, which took legions and good commanders to Cyprus and the coast of Egypt. Undaunted by the strain that decades of war had put on resources, in 113, Trajan battled in Armenia, then Parthia, sailed down the Euphrates and dragged his boats overland to the Tigris River, taking all before him until finally washing his weapons in the Persian Gulf. But again, these were gains Rome could not hold. There just weren't enough resources. So, Trajan withdrew, only to die in 117 on the way back to Italy.

His heir was Traianus Hadrianus, the newly appointed governor of Syria and a distant cousin to Trajan. Although they were distantly related, Hadrian, as he became known, was Trajan's only male relative. Hadrian had not been openly sponsored by the dead emperor, but a report quickly surfaced that Trajan had adopted him on his deathbed, and Hadrian was proclaimed the successor in 117. There seems to have been some significant opposition to this in Rome, but four executions resolved that issue.

Hadrian was unpopular with the Senate, which he weakened by formally separating the bureaucracy from senatorial oversight. In doing so, he opened the way for an absolute monarchy at the heart of the empire. He could be cruel and vindictive, but he was an avid builder with a fond interest in the arts, design, and architecture, specifically the artistic and literary examples of Greece. In fact, he said he preferred to be in Athens more than Rome! As if to underline this, Hadrian governed his empire by personally visiting its many provinces and directing affairs face-to-face with his governors, an itinerary that had him outside the capital for half of the twenty-one years he ruled.

However, he did keep a reasonable relationship with his legions, deliberately rolling back virtually all of Trajan's military advances in the east, although it became necessary to put down a persistent Jewish uprising. This had been partly caused by his plan to rebuild Jerusalem, which the Romans had destroyed some sixty years earlier, and put a temple to Jupiter Capitolinus where the Jewish temple once stood. With one eye on resources and a general disinclination to go to war, Hadrian advocated a limit to the empire and physically marked long sections of its northern boundary with walls. We can still see the one he built at the top of Britain.

Equally visible was his beard. Emperors before him had been clean-shaven, with the exception of Nero, but from Hadrian on, they grew beards as a sign of imperial dignity. For some years, Hadrian had an intense relationship with a young man who toured with him to Egypt, where he accidentally drowned in the Nile. Eyewitnesses said the emperor "wept like a woman" at this. He recovered enough to establish a Greek-like religious cult around the youth. It remained popular long after his benefactor's death, which came in 138 after several years of ill health.

Hadrian left behind a dynastic problem; there was no son from his marriage to Trajan's closest female relative, and he had already executed a boy who could have been his natural heir. He had had his eye on fifteen-year-old Marcus Annius Verus, but he was too young to be emperor at the time. So, in his final months, Hadrian adopted Senator Titus Aurelius Fulvus Boionius Arrius Antoninus, who promptly adopted Marcus Annius Verus, renaming him Marcus Aurelius. Antoninus, also known as Antoninus Pius, became emperor on Hadrian's death in 138. After twenty-three years of harmony with the Senate and peace abroad, his dull and unremarkable rule ended when he passed away in 161. At that point, the boy Hadrian had favored years earlier was the obvious successor, and he was proclaimed emperor. Some things just take time.

We remember Marcus Aurelius for a small philosophical book he wrote, known to us as *Meditations*, but ironically, this intelligent, inquiring man spent almost all his time as emperor engaging in warfare. He first focused on the east, where the Parthians had become aggressive, sending in the legions in 162. They were somewhat successful, but in 165, soldiers near present-day Baghdad contracted an unknown, contagious illness. It spread through the ranks, and men began dying like flies to the point where those legions were too depleted to defend the lands they had just occupied. The troops withdrew, and the disease went with them to the centers of a defenseless empire, where it began spreading and gobbling up more Romans with ferocious appetite and speed. The greatest plague the ancient world ever saw was, at times, claiming the life of every fourth person it struck. Nowhere was safe. Then, to add to the imperial workload, in 167, Germanic tribes began pushing across the Rhine and Danube into the empire, and the emperor had to direct ongoing warfare against them until his death in March 180.

Marcus Aurelius had one surviving son, the nineteen-year-old Commodus, and this young man became emperor. Within a year, he had pulled the armies back from fighting in the north and enjoyed twelve years of peace in the empire (thanks to a string of lucky, unplanned coincidences) and debauchery in the palace (instigated and led by Commodus). Like an unrestrained madman, Commodus joined slaves and criminals in the arena to fight gladiators and wild beasts. And although he commissioned a major building program in Rome following a huge fire there, he also announced he had become the god Hercules. He had senators executed, brushed aside an assassination attempt by his sister and others in 182, and was only stopped when his mistress and close officials fed him poison and had him strangled to death in 192.

An heir existed, but he was pushed aside by the Praetorian Guard, who proclaimed the son of an ex-slave, Pertinax, as the new emperor. This new ruler was a former governor of Britain and was once loyal to Commodus. He reined in the state budget, demanded discipline, and improved the value of the currency. None of this pleased the Praetorian Guard, who made several bungling attempts to assassinate "their" man. Unfortunately for Pertinax, he had a son, which prevented him from adopting a powerful army commander and shoring up his position in the usual way. As a result, Pertinax fell in 193, as so many had before him, to an assassin's dagger.

Five men leaped to claim his seat. Lucius Septimius Severus managed to push aside the sitting emperor, Didius Julianus, and take the throne. By 197, this North African had killed or sidelined his rivals in desperate fighting in Gaul, Italy, and across the east. Superstitious and, at times, violent and vengeful, he instinctively understood how to rule without being restrained by the Senate: simply arrange for a successor and give money to the legions. An emperor's power came from the swords and javelins of the army—if the men were loyal. In Severus's case, they only supported him so far. Severus campaigned and led the troops until his death in Britain in 211, and during that time, he had to cope with an increasingly independent mood among the legions.

The number of disgruntled soldiers would grow when Severus's son, the unbalanced Antoninus (better known as Caracalla), murdered his brother, the other heir, and became the sole emperor in 212. This violent, moody man also fought beasts in Rome's arena to the dismay and disgust of his people. However, one thing they no doubt thanked him for was the formal recognition of citizenship to every freedman in the empire. This was the culmination of a sensible administrative change that had begun under Augustus some two hundred years earlier. However, it was one of the few clever moves Caracalla made. He seemed to lapse into dementia at times and presented himself as Alexander the Great. He also led troops to a humiliating defeat in Parthia and sacked the major Egyptian port city of Alexandria, which Rome actually controlled, because his murdered brother was still popular there, and the paranoid emperor felt the need to impose his iron rule on the restive Egyptians. Although he identified with the ordinary soldier and increased their pay by 50 percent, a group of officers killed him in 217.

They were led by a praetorian lawyer with little personal fame or importance, Marcus Opellius Macrinus. A seer had prophesied Macrinus would become emperor, and Caracalla had heard about it. It was kill or be killed, and Macrinus moved quickly to fulfill the prophecy.

At the time, a large Roman army was still camped in the east, so Macrinus led them against the Parthians only to find the easterners to be too strong, and he was forced to negotiate a humiliating peace. (Would Roman emperors never learn?) He also denied new army recruits the pay increase Caracalla had given them. None of this sat well with the legions, so in 218, when an eclipse announced the gods' disfavor and signaled an upcoming change of ruler, the troops turned against their unpopular emperor. He fled his base in Antioch in disguise but was captured and killed.

He was replaced that same year by Caracalla's fifteen-year-old Arab cousin, Varius Avitus Bassianus, the chief priest of a local Syrian mountain god, Elagabal. In 219, he arrived in Rome, where he changed his name to Marcus Aurelius Antoninus and set about changing the religion of the capital. Rome's main god, Jupiter, was replaced with Elagabal, who was represented by a tall black stone, and the teenager became known by the Latinized version of the deity's name: Elagabalus. He rejected Latin clothing, preferring his priesthood's silky robes. Administration held no interest for him, as the processions, music, and dancing of worshiping Elagabal took up his time and focus. His debauchery was said to be boundless, and while this may be an exaggeration, the strange Arab religious traditions and worldview he brought into the heart of Rome (such as "marrying" his god to the Roman gods, then himself marrying a resisting chief Vestal Virgin) alienated the elite, for whom these actions were depraved and bizarre.

They struck back. In 222, a riot broke out while the imperial family was visiting the Praetorian Guard camp. Elagabalus and his mother were mysteriously slain, and their bodies were thrown into the Tiber. His cousin, the fourteen-year-old Marcus Aurelius Alexander, was immediately proclaimed emperor.

Alexander was a Latin through and through. He cooperated with the Senate, and Rome liked him. In 225, at the age of seventeen, he married, but his mother quickly decided she did not like his bride. Thinking the girl was too influential, Alexander's mother exiled the young woman and executed her father. More chillingly, the Praetorian Guard did not like their emperor's mother and flexed their muscle by blocking Alexander on small things and humiliating some of his key administrators.

It is possible they were testing the water. When Alexander led the legions to defeats in the east and then along the Rhine-Danube frontier in 230 and 234 and responded to those losses with cowardice, his frustrated troops revolted and proclaimed their commander to be the new emperor in the spring of 235. This officer led them against Alexander and his now powerless mother and killed them both.

Plainly, this was no longer the secure, peaceful empire set up by Augustus some 250 years earlier. No longer was the emperor a Rome-based manager who controlled the Senate, collected taxes, paid the army, and added to Rome's magnificent public buildings. No longer were the borders static and watched by a sedentary army led by handpicked commanders loyal to the emperor. Importantly, no longer were those military leaders chosen from the wealthy classes of Rome; rather, they came up through the ranks on merit. In the army mess halls, peasants gave orders to less able sons of nobility and had no interest in retaining the traditions of the republic and early empire. Basic principles of governing had slowly changed without anyone really noticing. The next two hundred years saw the outworking of these changes, which were to break the entire Roman Empire in two. Rome had declined and was about to fall, as Edward Gibbon said so memorably.

Chapter 8 – Retirement and Rebranding Options

The breakdown of army loyalty that so easily ended the life of Marcus Aurelius Alexander (and his unfortunate mother) came at the wrong time for Rome. It coincided with a sustained burst of attacks by barbarian armies that flooded across the Rhine and the Danube, as well as aggression by the new power in the east, the disciplined Persians. The legions were stretched to their breaking point, and there just wasn't enough money in Rome's coffers to effectively support and sustain decades of desperate warfare.

Even more damaging, military morality continued to slide. The next fifty years saw a succession of army officers plot and murder their way to power. Generals would be proclaimed emperor by their troops, struggle against rival commanders, and then killed by disillusioned or disgruntled soldiers (sometimes from their own units). Several times, two or even three self-proclaimed emperors tried to govern at the same time. Insanity ruled, and inflation raged.

This was one of Rome's darkest periods. It appeared to end with a twenty-one-year rule of one thoughtful emperor, but on his departure, strong men again faced off against each other, and thirty years of civil war followed until Constantine secured the empire for himself and changed everything. Welcome to a century of mayhem.

Its opening five decades can be surveyed quickly by looking at just the first few emperors, as their experience became the pattern.

As we saw, in the spring of 235, in modern-day Germany, General Gaius Julius Maximinus Verus, the son of a peasant, was proclaimed emperor by his troops. He accepted the honor and quickly killed Emperor Alexander in a one-sided encounter.

Maximinus returned to his job: killing barbarians in the north. Then, in late 237, a revolt broke out at the southern extreme of the empire, in North Africa, where a leading father and son were proclaimed joint emperors in early 238. The empire now had three emperors! The two North Africans were killed three weeks later by troops loyal to Maximinus.

These events triggered rebellions against the former general in Rome by both citizens and senators. Two elderly high-ranking administrators in the city were declared to be joint emperors. Not everyone was happy with that selection, however, and riots erupted. Maximinus brought troops down to sort this out, but he could not force his way past northern Italy, and his own troops murdered him there.

Then the Praetorian Guard in Rome slaughtered the two new joint emperors and installed a thirteen-year-old boy as emperor. He was Marcus Antonius Gordianus, the grandson of the North African father who had been killed a few months earlier. Romans called these few months of slaughter the Year of Six Emperors.

From day one, the young Gordianus had his armor on. Germanic tribesmen, North African rebels, and Persian armies moved against him. In 242, he was in the east with his army. It was there that the nineteen-year-old was apparently murdered in early 244 by his own troops, perhaps manipulated by a recently appointed Arab administrator named Marcus Julius Philippus, who was then proclaimed emperor.

In 249, two other men were proclaimed emperors in opposition to Philippus. Philippus managed to kill the first but was killed in battle by the second, Trajan Decius. This new emperor, Decius, died in battle in the north not even two years later.

This tumult continued for another thirty-five years or so, as successive army commanders took power using the tried and tested instruments of the legionnaire dagger and political chaos. Multiple emperors were common. The senatorial establishment was sidelined, and even a peasant could become emperor. None of them contributed significantly to Rome or the empire, and all of them reigned briefly except for one. This man was Publius Licinius Egnatius Gallienus, and he was emperor for fifteen years. However, he was forced to spend it all battling tribal invaders and rival claimants as northern fighters poured through weakened Roman troop lines on the Rhine.

And the lines were weak. For ten of those fifteen years, Franks invaded and ransacked Gaul almost at will as far down as Spain and Africa. At one point, others breached the Italian Alps. On the Black Sea, armadas of Goths landed on the shores of Asia Minor itself. And all the time, Roman warlords established themselves everywhere the current emperor's reach was weak.

This splintered empire was reunited briefly under one command in 270 when a former peasant, General Lucius Domitius Aurelianus, was proclaimed emperor. He made himself stronger by voluntarily vacating the large province of Dacia on the northern side of the Danube, which had soaked up many occupying troops ever since it had been taken some 170 years earlier. Aurelian (our name for him) decisively subdued both Gaul and the east with his legions and marked his successes by replacing Rome's seven-hundred-year-old wall with a new one. However, he failed in an attempted currency reform and was murdered in 275.

In 284, another low-born army general, Gaius Aurelius Valerius Diocletianus, took the throne. He proved to be a remarkable reformer. We know him as Diocletian, and he decisively replaced the very structure of the empire that had been designed over 250 years earlier by Augustus for very different times and circumstances. Augustus's imperial system no longer supported the empire, so Diocletian reorganized Rome's provinces, the bureaucracy that managed them, its army, and the imperial taxes. He conjured up a completely new way of looking at the emperor by dividing imperial power into four and assigning a quarter of the empire to four emperors who ruled simultaneously in unison. It was deliberately not dynastic and became known as the Tetrarchy.

Diocletian also ran large, well-funded yet unsuccessful campaigns to exterminate the new growing religious competitor to the Roman gods: Christianity. And, uniquely, after serving twenty-one years as emperor, he retired!

Diocletian's idea of the Tetrarchy solved the problem of controlling the army. As we have seen, soldiers were no longer loyal to Rome's emperor, the Senate, and the elites. Rather, they followed their commanders. If an emperor sent legions to confront invading tribes on a distant front, their general might be tempted to allow himself to be proclaimed a rival emperor. And many did just that.

When hostilities broke out on multiple fronts, this problem became acute. So, Diocletian appointed a trusted general and two of his sons-in-law as co-emperors. These four were called tetrarchs and acted rather like the board of a large, powerful 21ˢᵗ-century commercial board of directors. They cooperated yet took responsibilities for various areas under their sole control to achieve a common goal. This system worked. By the late 290s, these four had led the legions into all sections of the frontier and secured peace throughout the empire.

Diocletian solidified this tranquility with some administrative changes. We can't help admiring his ability and audacity as an administrator, though scholars today may have questions about one tactic. To foster loyalty to the emperor, Diocletian ramped up the worship and awe of the man in charge. For example, he formally and publicly traced his legitimacy to the favor of the gods and added religious rituals and ceremonies to his court. He also greatly reduced his public appearances, made people prostrate before him, and only gave a favored few the ultimate new privilege of kissing the hem of his purple robe.

On the other hand, we would have few questions about his taxation system that replaced the messy, ad hoc revenue gathering of the past. He based it on flexible units of land and those who farmed them. So, for example, in less productive regions, a unit of land would be larger than those in rich agricultural areas, and where women traditionally worked the land, they would be registered as taxable farmers but not where men normally farmed. This system was fair and could be adjusted easily across the empire. However, it eventually led to some socially and economically unhealthy practices, such as binding poor farmers to the land and the tax-and-spend tendencies we recognize today.

Diocletian also doubled the number of Roman provinces and restricted the power of their governors to better suit the professionalism and efficiency of his provincial legions, which used to be open to local governors' influences. Diocletian also tried to force non-Romans to adopt Rome's customs and social norms, such as Italy's long-standing ban on marrying close female relatives.

This cultural leveling was partly the trigger for his fierce persecution of Christians, who were certainly not going to do in Rome as the Romans did. In 299 and again in 303, he demolished church buildings, burned books, arrested clerics, seized church treasuries, and closed the court system to Christians. He cut out the tongue of one church leader and executed others. Yet the vibrant new faith burned even brighter, and in a few years, Christianity would be declared the official faith of the empire by Emperor Constantine (Flavius Valerius Constantinus, the son-in-law of Diocletian's adopted son).

Before this, however, the peace and efficiency of Diocletian's empire fell apart in May 305 when he retired to his vegetable garden in his homeland, modern Croatia, where he died in 311. The remaining tetrarchs fell on each other with diplomacy and swords.

Constantine's father was one of these tetrarchs, and when the older man died in 306, the son grabbed the position for himself. Already an experienced general, the young Constantine secured the west and the north of the empire as a personal power base. There, he won the support of the growing Christian community by repealing persecution laws and returning state-confiscated property to the church.

Then, in the spring of 312, he took his army into Italy, fought his way down to Rome, and challenged a rival tetrarch, his brother-in-law, outside the ancient walls. That night, he is said to have had a dream encouraging him to fight under the protection of the Christian God. He did. Before the battle, his men marked their shields with a religious symbol, and they won. Constantine's brother-in-law drowned in the Tiber trying to escape. For the first time, Roman troops had fought under a Christian banner.

Unsurprisingly, Constantine was then hailed by Christians as God's instrument. North African Christians saw him as the natural head of the church and called on him to assist in a major controversy: what was the standing of church officials who had cooperated in the burning of religious texts in the persecutions in Africa under Diocletian a few years earlier? Constantine convened a council in Rome, which eventually decided in favor of mercy.

During this time, Constantine was also busy fighting the surviving tetrarch, who was another brother-in-law. In 316 and again in 324, the two battled. Constantine defeated him on his second attempt in the north of Greece, then pursued him to the ancient city of Byzantium. When that fell, he cornered his brother-in-law on the Asian side of the Bosporus, where the brother-in-law negotiated to keep his life with the help of his wife, Constantine's half-sister. Constantine was now the undisputed emperor, and only Augustus's forty-year reign was longer.

The next year, Constantine set up another council, which would decide he was the uncontested head of the growing church. A prominent priest in Egypt, Arius, was arguing a theologically explosive position that Christ was distinct from God; in fact, the idea had been created by him. This had split the African church (again!), and some three hundred of its thinkers went to Nicaea in 325 to have Constantine adjudicate. He didn't preside over the debates but often personally attended them and certainly made his opinions known. Eventually, a creed was drafted, which was binding on Christians everywhere, and it was accepted with some reluctance by both sides due to Constantine's diplomatic skills. This short document survived for centuries as a core statement of orthodox faith in the West and is still familiar to many today. Arianism was beaten in the council, but it remained popular on the streets of the East.

Constantine was theologically able, but was this "Christian emperor" sincere? Although openly cruel and brutal at times, he shows evidence of personal Christian allegiance. For example, he openly identified with the faith beginning in 312 when he had that dream outside Rome. Further, he often wrote about God, attempted (without success) to ban the unchristian gladiatorial games and old Roman sacrifices, changed the laws on marriage and divorce to suit the church, built churches and donated property to Christians, gave prominent converts generous cash gifts, and was baptized on his deathbed, by which time Christianity was recognized and supported by the state.

He also brought about change in the administrative corridors of his empire, making it possible for Germans to enlist in the legions and even become generals. A knowledgeable commander, he reinstated an earlier strategy of using the best troops as rear-stationed flying squads able to quickly respond to any incursions along Rome's long border. Senators were given status again and real relevance.

But the thing we best remember Constantine for is his building of the new city of Constantinople, present-day Istanbul. Emperors had long chosen to live outside Rome, so it was not strange he would build a city at the geographic center of the wealthy Eastern Empire and put his residence there. This place on the European shore of the Bosporus was a natural trading hub, handy to the fighting both along the Lower Danube and also in Persia, and located on a peninsula, which made it impregnable if a navy could hold the sea. Constantine gave attractive tax incentives to would-be residents and moved his bureaucrats there. It was a very Christian site. The earlier Greek city of Byzantium had been there, but no pagan temples had ever defaced it. When he had finished the huge defensive northern wall, he dedicated his new city in May 330 on the day of a martyred saint who died in one of Diocletian's persecutions. God had triumphed!

The divine did not assist with the emperor's succession, however. In 326, at the age of fifty-five, Constantine executed his eldest son and perhaps ordered the death of his second wife soon after. His other sons were too young to rule alone, so he put them and one of his nephews in charge of small parts of the empire with himself in overall control. This suggests he was hoping to establish a dynasty after the smash-and-grab years following Diocletian's retirement. Deep down, he must have known this arrangement would not survive after him, but that was all he could set up by the time he died in 337 following a short illness.

Chapter 9 – Barbarians at the Gates

After Constantine died, the first thing his three sons did was murder every other relative of their father they could find. Next, they set about pushing their Christian theology onto the empire's Christians and fighting each other. The last brother standing was the middle son, Flavius Julius Constantius, who spent his reign in frontier battles and died of sickness in 361 while marching with his troops to the Balkans to confront Flavius Claudius Julianus, a successful administrator and general, whose troops had proclaimed him a rival emperor the year before. Today, Flavius Julius Constantius is remembered as Julian.

Julian was related to Constantine and had somehow survived the 337 purge. Fascinated with the glory days of Greece, he became a staunch follower of Greek gods and religion but mixed Christian tolerance and asceticism into his beliefs. Julian was the only pagan emperor after Constantine, and he spent his short reign reopening temples of the old Roman religion and reducing Christian influence. He died along with thousands of his troops during a disastrous retreat from Persia in 363. The general who was quickly made emperor after him only managed to get the troops out to safety by surrendering cities and five provinces to the Persians before he died in mysterious circumstances a few months later.

This erosion of imperial greatness continued. Two middle-aged brothers, Flavius Valentinianus and Flavius Valens, became joint emperors with the blessing of the army in 364. They came from peasant stock, so they were suspicious of the cultured elites and recruited and promoted men like themselves.

Valentinian (as we call him) permitted long-serving officials to automatically become senators, even if they were uneducated German generals. Both brothers were Christians. But where the moderate Valentinian permitted pagan sacrifices, saying, "A man's tradition is not a criminal offense," and upheld the Nicene Creed, Valens's attitude and theology were totally different. He demanded his people believe Arianism and was heavy-handed with those who refused. Both brothers were said to be unpleasant, and Valentinian apparently died in a fit of apoplexy and rage when violently disagreeing with a barbarian envoy in 375.

Valens then made two bad decisions, and both involved these northern barbarians. First, in 376, the emperor permitted a large group of Visigoths to find refuge in Roman lands south of the Danube. In return, they agreed to send troops to the legions. Corrupt local imperial administrators badly mishandled this mass migration, and the Goths went on a furious rampage. Second, in 378, Valens moved to stop this pillaging and destruction only to have his entire army surrounded near the Black Sea and wiped out. He died in the fighting, although his body was never found. His nineteen-year-old nephew, Flavius Gratianus, was left as the sole emperor.

Known to us as Gratian, he was at first tolerant of pagan religions but was pushed around theologically by the bishop of Milan, Ambrose. In 381, Gratian called a church council in Constantinople where he made the Nicene Creed official and binding for Christians everywhere; thus, the Arian debate was formally ended by the young emperor. His life was also about to end. In 383, commander Magnus Maximus was proclaimed a rival emperor by his troops in Britain. Gratian rushed to face him in Gaul, only to be deserted by his legions. He was then captured and executed by Maximus.

Gratian's place was soon taken by Theodosius, whom Gratian had made joint emperor in 379. But there was also a third emperor, Flavius Valentinianus (we call him Valentinian II), who had been proclaimed joint emperor as a four-year-old by a group of powerful officials in 375 after his father had died in that outburst of anger.

There was insufficient room for all three rulers. At first, Theodosius was mostly occupied with trying to get a treaty with the aggressive Persians, but he did temporarily block the passes of the Italian Alps and stop Maximus from attacking Valentinian II in Italy. Maximus eventually managed to break through in 387, and the young Valentinian II fled. By then, the Persian negotiations had wrapped up, with Rome again conceding vast territory, and Theodosius confronted and killed Maximus in 388. The next to die was the now twenty-one-year-old Valentinian II, who was found hanged in 392. The officials who announced this called it a "much-regretted suicide."

Theodosius had another contender to deal with, which he did in 394, but he died the following year, leaving the empire to his two utterly inadequate teenage sons.

No one could have imagined what was to happen in the next eighty years. In just one long lifetime, Germanic tribes overran the whole of Gaul, Britain, Spain, North Africa, and the Rhine and Danube Basins, establishing permanent independent kingdoms there. The Western Roman Empire basically disappeared!

How this happened and why those same tribesmen were not able to simultaneously take over the Eastern Empire can be put down to four factors: migration pressures, geography, military recruitment strategies, and loyalty to the central government in Rome. Throwing petrol on this bonfire were warlords and generals who actually ran the empire in this period, although Rome and Constantinople were the seats of often-overthrown emperors.

Migrations increased from the time Theodosius died. The tribes of central Asia were on the move, and a gigantic, irresistible domino effect occurred, spilling wave after wave of migrants into Gaul and eventually down to Spain and North Africa. This had happened before, but now, it was made unstoppable by a vicious cycle, for these tribes took a swathe of Roman land. The empire had fewer resources to put into defending adjacent land, which then also went to the tribes, leaving Rome with even less manpower and finances to try to stop the slow-moving tsunami.

Geography played an equally significant role. It was less demanding to migrate into the Rhine and Danube, then on to Gaul (where the population had significantly shrunk, leaving vacant lands to grab) and south into Spain and beyond, than to traverse from central Asia toward Asia Minor. Further, the Eastern Empire only had to fight for the Balkans and could rely on the Black Sea and Bosporus for protection. In addition, the rest of the east was subdued. Also, Egypt and, to some extent, Syria were the wealthy breadbaskets of the Mediterranean, and from there, grain and taxes poured into Constantinople. The Eastern emperors could pay for mercenaries from the different ethnic groups they ruled and block any migration from the north.

Mercenaries had also been recruited into Western legions, as we have seen. In the past, they served the emperor as part of the total Roman army. Now, large bodies of Germanic tribesmen joined Roman armies as independent units taking orders from their own German commanders who fought alongside the Romans. Military resources shrank, and Rome's authority in the provinces weakened. Soldiers looked to their commanders rather than the emperor, and the legions became increasingly uncontrollable breeding grounds for ambitious would-be emperors, of which there were many.

The fourth factor is less visible, but it is just as relevant. Large landowners used to be the backbone of the empire. But by this point, their influence had been removed by the reforms of Diocletian and Constantine. The richest landowners had a say in small provincial matters, but they no longer automatically became the top officials, soldiers, and generals, so they tended to withdraw and focus on their own prosperity, which depended on keeping good relations with whoever ran their province. It didn't matter to the elite outside Italy whether that person was a German warlord or an emperor in Rome. They were independent.

The warlords were likewise independent. We will trace the influence and deaths of just a handful to get a flavor of these brutal eight decades where strong men frequently had more power than their emperor.

Flavius Stilicho appears first in the story. A half-German soldier, he claimed Emperor Theodosius had appointed him guardian of the young boys who became joint emperors in 395 on their father's death. This was contested, but with that claim, Stilicho became a powerful figure for some thirteen years. He based himself in Italy with one young joint emperor, Flavius Honorius, and from there arranged for a German to kill a rival guardian protecting Theodosius's eldest son in Constantinople. But that rival was immediately replaced by a court eunuch and former slave who, for four years until his execution, was able to protect and manipulate the Eastern emperor.

Stilicho had plenty to do anyway, as Goths under their king, Alaric, were marauding through the Balkans, Greece, and northern Italy. Rome's military resources were under great pressure, but Stilicho was consumed with his ambition to control both of the now-adult joint emperors. So, when a huge force of tribesmen invaded Gaul on the last day of 406, he pulled his troops out of the West and left that region to its fate. The tribes proceeded to raid there at their pleasure.

Stilicho arranged to keep them out of Italy by persuading the Roman Senate to pay a huge ransom, and for the next eighteen months, he turned his attention to Constantinople. He attacked his own people there until exasperated, anti-German officials executed him in 408 with the support of his ward, Honorius, back in Italy. Stilicho had made the fatal mistake of thinking he could trust that young joint emperor. The young adult was, after all, Stilicho's son-in-law! Honorius went on without the assistance of his guardian and reigned for thirty years, during which time the West slipped almost completely from the hands of Rome.

There was the killing of rivals everywhere. In Britain, three soldiers proclaimed themselves emperor in 407. Two were murdered, and the survivor took troops to Gaul and Spain, attempting to take that region for himself. The Goths were also killing people. Visigoths poured into Italy, and in 410, they breached the walls of Rome. They looted and ransacked the city for several days. The next year, Flavius Constantius (Constantius III) was commissioned to retake Gaul and Spain, which he did. A tireless and successful soldier, he married into royalty and became the father to Valentinian III (more about him soon). Constantius III would be made a joint emperor for a few months before he unexpectedly died of an illness in 421.

But the tribes were organized and militant, and by 413, a group established a kingdom in northern Gaul, which the empire was forced to officially recognize. As for Britain, no such attention was paid across the Channel, and although there are no records, it is clear that within one hundred years, imperial troops were no longer present. The Angles and Saxons were, though, and they raided and pillaged across England at will.

A capable, prudent Visigoth was elected as king by his tribesmen in Spain in 415. His name was Wallia, and although he only ruled three years, he secured a treaty with Rome and fought for the empire in Spain. For this, his tribe was granted an attractive semi-independent state in southwest France. Emperor Honorius required Roman landowners there to surrender two-thirds of their lands to the Visigoths and to be grateful that they were left with at least one-third. Wallia's grandson was the Romanized Flavius Ricimer, who came to control all Gaul and Spain for over ten years.

The next figure in our story only deserves a place because of the length of his reign. Placidus Valentinianus (who history knows as Valentinian III) was emperor for thirty years, starting as a six-year-old boy, and he achieved virtually nothing unless we count the steady loosening of the Roman grip on the Western Empire.

Overshadowing him were two generals, Aetius and Boniface, who had been appointed by the boy's mother but eventually grew to be very independent of her and her son. Aetius proved his military credentials in Gaul. Due to the strength of them, he was appointed general in 429. He then murdered his predecessor the following year and spent the next five or six years dealing with problems in Gaul and securing Italy for himself.

In the meantime, Boniface came to power by a series of military defeats and questionable alliances. He'd been appointed a local commander in North Africa but never gained the trust of senior imperial officials. When he refused their command to return to Italy, they sent legions against him. He beat them off, but he couldn't repeat the performance against the Goths, who the same officials sent the following year. The tribal army captured important towns and may have even taken Boniface, but he appealed to the Vandals occupying southern Spain, offering to divide North Africa with them if they helped him.

Their king, Gaiseric, agreed. In 429, some eighty thousand Vandals crossed the Mediterranean, but they quickly broke the agreement and helped themselves more than Boniface. They plundered the Algerian coast, besieged Boniface in Hippo for a year, overpowered a relief army sent from Italy (in this battle, Boniface slipped back to Europe, where he later died of illness), took Carthage, and even prepared to invade Italy itself. They also made and then disregarded another agreement with the Romans and avoided a serious naval attack sent from Constantinople.

By 440, the Vandals had secured an iron grip on North Africa that would last one hundred years. Roman landowners were expelled, the local aristocracy was sidelined, and Roman culture was rejected. The Vandals were Christians, but they championed the Arian doctrines and hounded followers of the Italian version of the faith.

Aetius outlived Boniface, so he now controlled Italy and the emperor. His power was tested by Germanic tribes in Gaul, however. For years, he struggled against repeated invasions across the Rhine. (He even had to deal with a proposal by Attila the Hun, who wanted to marry Emperor

Valentinian III's older sister and be given half of Gaul as the dowry!) But Aetius's hold on the emperor slipped in late 454, and Valentinian III himself murdered the commander who had dominated him all his life. A few months later, the emperor was assassinated by an ambitious, jealous senator, and chaos followed.

The empire tottered. The Vandals seized the opportunity and launched their ships from Africa. King Gaiseric arrived at the gates of Rome. The bishop of Rome met him and asked the tribesmen to refrain from killing. They agreed and actually kept their word. For two weeks, the city was methodically looted. The emperor's widow and two daughters were taken. One daughter, Eudoxia, was obliged to marry Gaiseric's son, but her sister and mother were eventually sent to safety in Constantinople. The word "vandal" may be unfairly besmirched.

The man who presided over the decisive and final loss of the Western Empire now appears in our story. This was Flavius Ricimer, a successful commander (no surprise there) and the grandson of Wallia, the Visigoth who had negotiated a secure, independent kingdom for his people in southwest France some forty years earlier. By 461, he had enough control of Italy and his troops to murder a fellow general who had been proclaimed emperor four years before. For ten years, Ricimer would install a series of weaklings as emperors.

The Visigoths, Huns, and Vandals continued to fight the legions for land in Gaul and on the high seas. The line of command and army discipline from Italy was weak, and field commanders could be overlooked or undermined. One Roman commander who had been humiliated in Sicily stormed off to the Balkans and set up an independent, hostile base protected by the Eastern emperor. The astute Vandal king, Gaiseric, continued to play a role, claiming the late Valentinian III's property as dowry for the marriage of his son to the former emperor's daughter, Eudoxia, and using the refusal as an excuse for more fighting. It would be laughable if it was not serious.

A hugely expensive Roman fleet attacked Gaiseric's Vandals at sea in 468. Rome's ships were sunk in a defeat that brought great debt and even more humiliation. The West was slipping out of Rome's grip. Visigoths now comfortably occupied Gaul and much of Spain, and the Vandals had North Africa. Only Italy remained "Roman," although most of the imperial generals were actually Germans. In 472, Ricimer fought off an attempt to oust him and occupied the city of Rome, but he then died.

Emperors were proclaimed and rapidly deposed until 475, when an Italian child was given the title. It was hollow. The Germans actually controlled Italy. The boy, Romulus, was sneeringly nicknamed. Instead of Augustus, the people used Augustulus, meaning "Little August One." Soldiers sent the boy to his relatives in 476. Ostrogoths swept into the confusion and took Italy as their own. By this time, the Western Empire was no longer united or Roman.

Chapter 10 – Descent to the Vanishing Point

Our drama is now at the point where the Western Empire has disappeared. From about 476, it was nothing more than a memory and the stuff of war stories told by the Germanic tribesmen who had conquered it.

However, the Eastern Empire was still alive. Emperors sat in Constantinople for another one thousand years, although their reach quickly shrank and weakened, and their empire morphed into a Greek-based entity we now call Byzantium. Apart from a handful of long reigns, there is almost nothing significant to tell until 1453 when Arab armies swept into the last corner of the Eastern Empire and snuffed it out, much like those Ostrogoths who plowed into Italy in that fateful year of 476.

Let's tell the story of Constantinople, however, beginning back in 395 when Emperor Theodosius died and his two sons were made joint emperors: Flavius Honorius ruling the Western part and Flavius Arcadius inheriting the East.

The new Eastern emperor, eighteen-year-old Arcadius, was unable to take charge. For the thirteen years of his reign, he was manipulated by a series of ambitious insiders, including a former slave and eunuch, Eutropius, who the emperor later called "a filthy monster" and had executed. Between them, these rival advisors did keep the Huns somewhat at bay to the north of the Eastern Empire. And they all turned a blind eye in 400 CE when the citizens of Constantinople attacked their

Christian Visigoth neighbors in the streets of the city in a frenzy of anti-German riots that left some seven thousand of these foreigners dead. Their puppet emperor was more interested in his own piety than border security, and in 399, he issued an order to demolish pagan temples. But he had accomplished little else when he died of natural causes in 408.

His only son, the infant Theodosius II, was quickly proclaimed emperor, and he ruled for over forty years. With the help of guardians and then on his own initiative, he used payments of gold to keep the Germanic tribes straining toward Constantinople at bay. Of course, this was never going to work long-term. The German demands steadily got bigger, and eventually, Attila the Hun simply took great swathes of territory. To his credit, however, the emperor made a peace treaty with Persia along his eastern frontier, sorted out a significant tax issue, and built a wall across the northern suburbs of Constantinople, which remained impregnable for a millennium.

Theodosius II had a sense of his empire. He commissioned a sweeping nine-year survey of all imperial decisions since Constantine and published the results in 438. This was the first comprehensive attempt to codify Roman law in some 150 years, and it formed the basis for the great work of Justinian I about 100 years later. He also presided over fierce theological debates over the nature of Christ. They were arcane but sufficiently important in the minds of the church bishops in dividing the East from what was left of the Western Empire and in alienating the large Christian community in Syria and Egypt. Ever since then, Latin, Greek, and Coptic congregations have been affected by this.

Theodosius II died unexpectedly in 450 in a riding accident and was succeeded by the military administrator Marcian, who had the support of a prominent German general and kingmaker, Flavius Ardabur Aspar, and the late emperor's sister, who went on to marry the new emperor.

Marcian had a short, popular, and successful rule, during which time he played hardball with the Huns and other Germanic tribes in the north and with the theologians and bishops of Syria and Egypt. Significantly, he formalized the earlier occupation of lands south of the Danube by Ostrogoths in return for military service, which brought peace to the region. Further, he made great cuts in government spending and corruption, and by these means, rather than simply increasing taxes, he left the treasury he'd found empty when coming to office overflowing when he died in 457 of an illness.

The astute German Aspar then became kingmaker again, putting a non-entity from among his military contacts onto the throne. That new ruler was Leo I, who became increasingly independent of the German who had put him into power. He eventually had Aspar and his family executed. Leo I died of dysentery in 474, having accomplished little of lasting note.

We will skip ahead slightly to the high point of this period. Flavius Petrus Sabbatius Justinianus, who we know as Justinian, seems to have been born in a peasant home. But his uncle was an upwardly mobile military officer, and he adopted the boy, took him to Constantinople, and made sure Justinian had every educational and military opportunity. When the uncle maneuvered to become emperor, Justinian found himself in the corridors of power. He may have even had his hands on some of the levers of the empire, for when the older man was slowly overtaken by dementia, Justinian became an increasingly close advisor. After nine years in power, the uncle died, and Justinian was proclaimed emperor in 527.

This capable, energetic new ruler hit the ground running, becoming known as the Emperor Who Never Sleeps. One of the first things he did was authorize the jurist Tribonian to lead a team of ten experts and thirty-nine scribes who would evaluate and organize hundreds of years of Roman law that had been haphazardly recorded in several thousand law books, collect extracts of the best legal opinions of the empire, and write a guide and textbook for judges, lawyers, and law students. This had never before been attempted, perhaps because it was such a daunting task. But tidying up and codifying the empire's thousands of imperial enactments, laws, and the best opinions of earlier jurists was definitely needed to clarify, harmonize, update, and correct existing laws and let courts work faster.

The first draft of the massive *Corpus Juris Civilis* was released in 529, and the completed project of almost one million words was unveiled in Latin in 534. Another section was added shortly after. (This second part was in Greek, the language of the common people.) This organized, systematic collection of laws and legal opinions became Roman law for the next one thousand years. The Arab Muslims discarded it when they took Constantinople, but eventually, medieval scholars and jurists in Italy and then up through Europe realized it was a better legal framework for their growing towns, cities, and churches than the ad hoc oral traditions they'd inherited when the Germanic tribes overran the Western Roman

Empire. Today, international law is greatly influenced by the work of Tribonian's team, and the *Corpus* is the foundational document of Western law.

While the scholars were bent over their books, Justinian was dealing with a war against Persia that he'd inherited. His commanders and ambassadors were busy from Mesopotamia to Yemen and even Ethiopia, and they secured peace in the east through modest military successes and a large payment of gold by the Romans in 532. (The agreement was soon broken, with the Persians declaring hostilities eight years later and fighting until 562 until realizing neither side was making headway and more gold changed hands.)

Then, in 533, Justinian sent his finest general to North Africa, which the Vandals had taken over one hundred years earlier. A fleet of nearly one hundred warships and five hundred transport vessels landed General Belisarius and fifteen thousand men unobserved. Caught totally by surprise, the Vandals were overrun, and their king was sent as a prisoner to Constantinople. The city of Carthage was retaken, and the North African coastline was secured by 534.

It took longer to reconquer Italy. Belisarius and another general, Narses, each attempted to take it back from the Ostrogoths with mixed success. The city of Rome was taken and lost and taken again. (It changed hands three times!) In the spring of 540, Belisarius had his troops massed outside the walls of the city of Ravenna, which the Goths had made their Italian capital. The Ostrogoths made an offer. They would proclaim the general emperor of the West if he would desert Justinian and let the Goths settle freely north of the Po River. So many generals in the past had leaped at offers like this. The wily general appeared to agree. He took his men into the city, but in a stunning turnaround, he announced he was claiming it for Justinian. Belisarius clamped the Ostrogoth king in chains and carted him and his wife back to Constantinople in disgrace. Still, the Goths fought to keep Italy, and it was not until 554 that Narses had the peninsula firmly under imperial control. This came at a huge cost, including the levy of heavy, unpopular taxes, and it was maintained with a garrison of sixteen thousand troops. Eventually, this would prove unsustainable. But before that, Justinian secured a great swathe of land in southeastern Spain in a straightforward, relatively inexpensive campaign in 552.

Although Italy would revert to the Goths after Justinian's death, these military campaigns did give the emperor control of the Mediterranean, prevented the Vandals from retaking North Africa, and boosted tax revenues to Constantinople. On the other hand, it stretched Justinian's financial resources to its breaking point. He had been fortunate to have two exceptional generals during these wars, but he did not understand that the West had irreversibly moved away from any reunion with the Eastern Empire; the future was a permanent division.

One of his endeavors has stood the test of time. Justinian built Hagia Sophia. This huge domed building, which towers magnificently over the old quarter of Constantinople, replaced churches on the same site that had been destroyed by rioting mobs in 404 and again in 532. Justinian engaged Anthemius of Tralles and Isidore of Miletus to design and build a replacement. In just five years, they produced the world's largest covered space, under a dome, 32 meters (107 feet) in diameter, seated on four very novel spherical triangular pendentives. It was opened in 537, and for the next nine hundred years, it was the biggest cathedral on Earth. Orthodox churches everywhere began to adapt its design. Western crusaders ransacked it in the early 1200s and briefly turned it into a Roman Catholic cathedral. It became a mosque when Muslim Arabs took Constantinople, a museum in the final years of Ataturk's life, and most recently was deemed a mosque again by his successors. None of this, of course, detracts from Justinian's marvelous achievement. For an outstanding example of Byzantine architecture, one should look no further.

Justinian died in 565. His successors were confronted with an aggressive Persia, whose armies eventually overran the empire's territories in Syria, Palestine, and Egypt. After eighteen years of fighting, Emperor Flavius Heraclius Augustus (r. 610–641) managed to regain those lands. But it was time and energy wasted. Arab Muslims began pushing out of Arabia in the early 630s, and in a few years, they swallowed up the gains of Heraclius and took over the Persian Empire itself.

The Roman Empire now extended only to the borders of Asia Minor. Constantinople was cut off from the rich ethnic diversity of the earlier empire. People spoke Greek, adopted Greek culture, and followed the Greek version of Christianity. Sometime in the 7th century, the Eastern Empire had become Byzantine, the name used centuries earlier for the Greek culture of the region.

For these reasons, a case can be made for stopping the history of the Roman Empire right here. We shall accept it, although technically, the empire survived until the Ottoman Turkish Muslim armies took Constantinople in 1453, a date that everyone agrees marks the end of a remarkable two thousand years.

Chapter 11 – The People of Rome

Rome teemed with people. By 140 BCE, an astounding one million of them were packed into forty square kilometers (just sixteen square miles), an area only a little bigger than Heathrow Airport in London or LAX in Los Angeles.

The super-rich lived in sumptuous, roomy villas, as close as they could afford to the senators and emperors who ruled the empire. Ordinary Romans made do with cramped rooms in multi-story apartment buildings, which were separated by narrow, twisting, unplanned lanes that might have only been about two meters (six feet) wide.

Yet, Rome was a vibrant, diverse city, and its people enjoyed magnificent public temples and grand government buildings. Immigrants were always arriving there for food, clean running water, and promises of work. This heaving urban center was a magnet at the center of the empire.

Step from your front door into the crowd, and it's likely the first person to pass you would be a slave. Actually, they were not thought of as people but as objects, like good pairs of shoes. They had been hauled to Rome as prisoners of war and sold in public markets to small businessmen or wealthy patricians. Slaves were at the bottom of the social ladder, yet they were vital to the functioning of Rome. At times, slaves made up 30 percent of the city's population.

Slaves had no rights, but surprisingly, they could purchase their freedom, which Caesar Caecilius Isidorus famously did, going on to apparently own some four thousand of his own slaves! But this was rare.

More realistically, manumission was a motivation for a slave to obey and work hard, and across the empire, tens of thousands of slaves toiled, died, and were forgotten in the cities and farms of Roman citizens.

The Romans justified this slavery with their religion. They prayed and sacrificed to a large group of Greek-like gods and divine heroes who were described in fantastic tales. From these stories, a Roman came to understand inequality and freedom and, therefore, slavery.

The leading Roman god was Jupiter, who was worshiped and consulted in Rome's main temple. But the city lanes were home to hundreds of small temples, housing statues and sometimes supposed relics of the gods. Worshipers didn't gather inside these buildings but rather offered prayers and sacrifices out on the street. For a Roman, those quick street rituals were much more important than any personal zeal.

However, one could find devotion if one looked. For example, six-year-old girls were regularly selected from wealthy families to become full-time attendants to the goddess Vesta. These Vestal Virgins served in her temple until they reached the age of thirty and returned to normal life. During that time, they were to keep a sacred fire burning and maintain strict chastity. Any failure and the women were whipped or executed. However, they had huge importance and status in Rome, and they were given front row seats at the arenas when the gladiators killed each other. Other women had to sit high up in the segregated, distant back rows of the bloody stadiums.

Vesta and the other gods were frequently consulted. On birthdays, weddings, festivals, and important meetings, augurs were called to examine natural signs, like the flight of a bird or animal entrails, and deduce a god's message. No legion marched out of Rome without the approval of the gods.

Ghosts and evil spirits swirled through Rome's lanes, and a family's best defense against them was said to be a pet dog. So, Romans kept dogs. Some were large and fast, like the Vertragus, the ancestor of today's Italian greyhound, but tiny, ultra-expensive lapdogs were also popular. Dogs kept owners warm on winter nights. They also might be put into organized dog fights or sacrificed to a god as an ultimate act of piety. Most wore collars, which were often studded or spiked and maybe golden.

Emperors and politicians spent money on Rome's crowded neighborhoods, with one eye on the political benefits. As a result, homes had access to several grades of water, which was brought to the city in those still-famous aqueducts. Fire brigades battled fires, albeit with low water pressure. The city also maintained public latrines. Small covered drains washed huge amounts of household waste and sewage into a network of large pipes that fed into even larger sewers that eventually disgorged into the Tiber River, although this didn't stop residents from casually tossing disgusting waste into the lanes from upper stories. Neighborhood street shops complimented big city markets, selling meat, seafood, and vegetables.

In Rome, employees generally worked a six-hour day, starting early and taking their main meal in the afternoon. The wealthy ate imported delicacies and a lot of meat, but meat was expensive, and Rome's masses had to make do with bread, cereals, vegetables, and olive oil. Even wine wasn't found on the poorer tables; oftentimes, people simply drank water. But everyone could pack into the arena in the afternoon to watch gladiators fight or chariot teams race at fever-pitch speed because the shows were heavily subsidized by ambitious politicians (these fights are detailed more in the next chapter).

If nothing else, Romans were practical people. Take marriage; a wedding could be lavish and very public or a quiet family affair. June was a popular month, but an augur would always be consulted on the date and the couple's compatibility. The state had no part in this. A couple was married or divorced if they said so.

On the happy day, the bride wore yellow. According to the law, she had to be over twelve years old. A priest was usually present, but he might not officiate. The girl's family produced a dowry, and a contract was signed before a ring could slip onto the third finger of her left hand (as we do today). Then, the couple went to the groom's home, where they would probably live permanently.

Any children were extremely vulnerable to disease, poor nutrition, and inadequate hygiene. It's said as many as 30 percent of Rome's newborns died before the age of one, and 20 percent of all children died by the age of five. Roman mothers were expected to accept this without showing grief. That might have had something to do with a woman's status; in Rome, they had property rights but very little power. A woman didn't even have a unique name but was called "the daughter of such-and-such a tribe." So, for instance, Mark Anthony's two daughters had the same name, Antonia.

Men held most of the power in the Roman Empire, even when it came to sex. A woman was supposed to be chaste and loyal to her husband, while her husband's sexual relations were moderated to some extent by shame and officials who occasionally removed men from public office for mind-boggling sexual misconduct. Brothels were also common and openly used. A man could be gay or take teenage boys without raising any eyebrows until the 3rd century when sex between males began to become illegal. Generally, a man could have consensual sex with anyone lower in a social rank than himself without censure.

The walls and books of Rome were full of pornography, descriptions of sex, magic charms, and potions to make it better. However, male nudity was not common, and a loincloth or skirt preserved a man's modesty if he had to take off his toga or tunic in public.

But both men and women enjoyed the theater, especially pantomime, and they filled the hundreds of semi-circular, open, tiered theaters built throughout the empire. At any performance, one would find musicians, plenty of speaking roles, lavish background scenery, and wealthy politicians on hand with sponsorships. Popular actors became rich and famous.

Just as widespread across the empire were the public baths. Even small towns and remote army camps had them. Rome itself boasted nearly four hundred bathhouses in 410 CE when the Visigoths sacked the city. These facilities were much more than simply places to sluice water over yourself and wash off grime and sweat. They were for meeting and relaxing in the afternoon and early evening, and they were free or inexpensive. After the pleasure of a soak and a wash in warm water (or hot if you wanted that), you could go to a gym, see a doctor, socialize with friends, discuss business, swim, eat, or be entertained.

Some bathhouses were huge architectural extravaganzas, with vaulted ceilings, magnificent mosaics, soaring columns, spacious gardens, and ingenious heating systems. Emperor Diocletian's baths needed twenty thousand cubic meters of water to function. Emperor Caracalla's bathhouse could accommodate eight thousand people and boasted a library, tall glass windows, and a waterfall.

However, bath water was changed infrequently. The dirt and cosmetic scum one stepped into when starting a bath had been left behind after earlier patrons had "cleaned" in the same water. So, bathhouses bred disease. Tapeworms and lice were everywhere. Doctors at this time were struggling to understand the human body and what medications and procedures would cure people. The best doctors were in the army (of course), and surgery was poorly understood and rare. The link between germs and disease was unknown, and pills were mainly herbal concoctions.

The Romans might have smelled better because of their piped water, sophisticated sewage systems, and baths. Yet, their city was a cesspool, and they were as unhealthy as their distant ancestors had been when Rome emerged from a cluster of Late Bronze Age villages on the Tiber.

But in spite of this, the great city was a place where dreams came true and prayers were answered. For nearly a thousand years, people arrived, rented rooms in the city's crowded neighborhoods, and noisily and proudly laid claim to being citizens of Rome.

Chapter 12 – Gladiators: When Murder Was Entertainment

From humble beginnings, gladiator fights became a dominating feature of the empire. At its peak, Roman crowds would flock to some four hundred gladiator arenas all over the empire to watch thousands of men (and some women) pair up and fight, with perhaps over seven thousand of them being killed in full public view each year.

Criminals were gruesomely executed, and animals were wantonly slaughtered. Slaves at the very bottom of the social ladder were cheered on to accept death as a perverse way of gaining honor. Volunteer gladiators hoped for wealth and fame, while elites displayed their wealth with preposterous, obscene sponsorships or subsidies.

The earliest record of a fight is more modest. Decimus Junius Brutus had three pairs of men fight to the death in 264 BCE as part of the funeral of his father. People liked it. Other wealthy elites began sponsoring gladiatorial events at family funerals, and just eighty years later, the sons of Publius Licinius had sixty pairs of gladiators fight in honor of their father.

Then Julius Caesar took this to an entirely new level. He blended filial piety and political advancement by honoring the death of his father (twenty years after he'd been buried!) with 320 pairs of gladiators fighting in silver armor for all of Rome to see. It was all about self-promotion. Other ambitious politicians saw the benefits and got involved.

The state did too. At one point, emperors tried to cap the size of private fight events, but no one listened. So, the government itself began staging gladiatorial contests, often alongside religious festivals. Emperor Trajan, for example, showcased around 10,000 fighting gladiators and 11,000 doomed animals in 123 blood-soaked days of military celebrations. Gladiator games eventually permeated Roman society. They were wildly popular for some three hundred years and proved hard to stamp out.

The empire provided some of the best arenas for this entertainment. The first emperor, Augustus, built one in Rome partly from stone. It burned down in 64 CE, but a fully stone replacement was started by Vespasian and finished by Titus in 80. This was the Amphitheatrum Flavium (Flavian Amphitheater), the massive venue that seated fifty thousand people and which we today call the Colosseum.

The fights in this and all other arenas were not simple hack-and-slash, brute force affairs. The crowds in the seats paid to watch professional, evenly matched fighters toiling on the edge of death. There were referees with long staves, rules of engagement, and many owners. A gladiator was the expensive property of a syndicate, rich individuals, or army units. For them, the fights were investments.

Gladiators were methodically prepared for this in special schools. Rome had four, and the largest housed two thousand gladiators. The men were fed a high-energy vegetarian diet, required to train for hours each day with blunt or wooden weapons, and harshly punished for lapses until they had perfected all the classic military sword and spear thrusts. It was a hard life, and for many, it must have ended in death just minutes after they first stepped into the arena.

Amazingly, some fighters were women who were owned and trained like men. From about the middle of the 1st century CE, they were being advertised (perhaps salaciously) as exotic and thrilling.

Even more strikingly, some emperors fought. The most powerful man in the whole empire became a totally despised slave-gladiator! Caligula, Titus, Hadrian, Commodus, and others did this. Claudius harpooned a giant fish imprisoned in a harbor outside the gladiator arena. Of course, the fights were rigged, and the ruler would win, but for onlookers, it must have been an extreme, titillating, and emotional rollercoaster.

In the early days of gladiatorial games, organizers matched the same type of fighters. Later, uneven but complementary types of fighters were put against each other. This means a lightly clad man with his trident would face a massively armored shock trooper with a heavy sword and shield.

For the winner, there was a palm branch and prize money. If a sponsor with an eye to publicity threw him a substantial gift, it also belonged to the fighter. When a condemned man won his fight, he might be given his freedom and, with that, a symbolic wooden sword. But winner or loser, the gladiator was always scum. Even if he won his freedom, he could not leave a will, and decent society would always associate fighters with the lowest castes.

Their fights were promoted by slick marketing teams. There was gladiator merchandise with names and pictures on jewelry, ceramics, glassware, and silver. Billboards listed the fighters by name and, for the gamblers in the audience, the track record of each. The public was drawn in with advertisements offering prizes, shaded areas, music, and food; it was a big day out, and ticket scalpers were as active then as now. The night before an event, a gladiator would have a banquet and perhaps attend to any business or loose family ends.

On the day itself, with men and the Vestal Virgins occupying all the front seats and other women relegated to the distant top tiers, the game would start with animal hunts or men pitted against animals. Next, criminals would be publicly executed, often as doomed actors in a reenactment of a Greek legend. Some events would include comic acts. Gladiators might also warm up in the arena with wooden weapons.

Then the professional killing would take place, in fights that would last between ten and twenty minutes. A gladiator would fight perhaps two or three times a year. Most would only survive for around ten appearances, and their average age was somewhere in the twenties. In Sicily, the headstone at a gladiator grave records his time in the arena: "Flamma, secutor, lived 30 years, fought 34 times, won 21 times, fought to a draw nine times, defeated four times, a Syrian by nationality. Delicatus made this for his deserving comrade-in-arms."

Not all were as successful as Flamma. If a gladiator suddenly refused to fight, he would be whipped, branded, or goaded into action. And with most fights, there was a loser whose life depended on what the referee decided. The roaring crowds with thumbs down did influence the referee, but it did not always dictate a fallen gladiator's death. Indeed, as time passed, fights to the death became less frequent. Some gladiators made a career out of never killing their opponents.

If he was to die, though, a defeated gladiator was supposed to calmly accept a quick death from a sword blow to the neck. This was a fitting penalty for an ignoble death in Roman eyes and could be an example for those who watched. Some perhaps even saw it as redemptive. Here was a man obedient to his owner, accepting of his fate, dignified, standing above his own humanness and defeating death by facing it. Gladiators who died this way were carried out with honors to the arena's morgue, where their throat would be cut to make sure they actually had been killed.

A gladiator who died ignobly, however, was shamed. He was given a slow death in the arena, dragged out like a dead animal, had his head crushed with a mallet, and was most likely thrown into a river, doomed to an eternity of wandering. There are crushed skulls on some skeletal remains in gladiator cemeteries.

The gladiatorial games slowly shriveled up as the message of human worth and love preached by Jesus in Palestine was adopted in Rome and Constantinople. Tertullian in the 3rd century CE condemned the killing as murder, pagan sacrifice, and a moral blight. The great Augustine wrote against them. Emperor Constantine prohibited forcing criminals to fight to the death as gladiators. And while the fights lingered and were popular with some, the last gladiator eventually hung up his sword and went looking for more respectable work in the legions.

Chapter 13 – Roads: Moving Legions and Imperial Letters

An absolute essential of any empire is information and communication. For these, Rome depended on its roads.

Whole government departments were set up to build and maintain the 372 major roadways that serviced Rome at its peak. Emperors, armies, messages, and merchants sped along some 400,000 kilometers (that's a quarter of a million miles) of smooth, weather-proofed, often laser-straight roads from the top of Britain, all through Europe, across North Africa's deserts, and to the eastern edges of Syria. Some 20 percent of these roads were paved with stones. These highways are a majestic achievement.

Engineers building a Roman road were meticulous. For example, there was a standard width for a carriageway. Originally, the width of straight sections was eight Roman feet (which would have been close to our modern "foot" of twelve inches, or thirty centimeters) and the corners sixteen feet. The eight later became twelve feet, wide enough for two carts to pass and still leave room for pedestrians. Having said this, width did vary where 12 feet (or 3.5 meters) was impractical or unpopular.

Roads were always a top priority in the empire. The army itself was responsible for building the long inter-city roads, for which the empire paid. Towns and cities were ordered to build local roads. On all of them, tolls were collected, perhaps at bridges but certainly at city gates. The first emperor, Augustus, pushed through changes to the administration of the empire's road construction program. He brought it under the direction of his own office and demanded greater efficiency from his officials.

Roman roads were straight where they could be. To survey an unbending line, the engineer used a set of four plumb bobs hanging on a special frame. He lined up two of the bobs with a marker on the road behind him. Then he sighted forward along the other two bobs and put a marker ahead where the next stretch of his road should run. If a hill or river was in the way, he had to negotiate with the terrain. Early engineers were reluctant to bend their roads, so they often punched tunnels through mountains or pushed roads up almost impossible 20 percent gradients to keep moving straight ahead. But traveling merchants and farm wagons needed fewer slopes, so over time, engineers curved their roads if that would avoid the worst of the hills.

A section of Roman road started as a ditch. Men would dig down perhaps 1.5 meters (that's 5 feet) to solid earth, then systematically fill it with layers of rubble, rocks, small stones, and maybe sand. When the ditch was almost full, gravel was laid down and very firmly pounded into a flat hard surface called "pavement." On 80 percent of Roman roads, there was nothing more to do. But where the carriageway was to be covered with stone, engineers went one step further. They spread coarse concrete on the "pavement," then a layer of finer concrete on that, and into this set flat paving stones. A finished road surface was cambered and remarkably smooth.

The emperor's carriages and his postal carts could race across a road like this at breathtaking speeds. Horse-drawn vehicles routinely made forty kilometers (that's twenty-five miles) in a day. Postmen on relays of horses could deliver mail twice that distance in that time.

These distances were known. From the early days, when the only roads were in Italy, the miles were precisely marked with solid two-ton columns sunk two feet into the ground and rising five feet above it. They were one thousand Roman paces apart. A pace was standardized to five Roman feet, so one thousand paces would be five thousand Roman feet. Since their foot was slightly shorter than the modern foot, their 5,000 feet is only 4,841 of our feet, but it is still close enough for us today to use their word for this 1000-pace measurement. The *mila passuum* is now our "mile."

What's more, all roads radiated out from an elaborate marker set up by Augustus near the Temple of Saturn in Rome itself. The empire's main cities were carved on it, along with the distances to them. When the center of the empire shifted to the east, Constantine set up a similar marker in Constantinople.

The roads had names. Many carried the name of a city, but the officials who built them might also name the road after themselves. The very first road, the Via Appia (Appian Way), running south from Rome, was named after Appius Claudius Caecus, who developed the first section as a military highway in 312 BCE.

A traveler could step onto this or any road with the aid of detailed regional "maps." These guides used roughly drawn parallel lines to represent roads and then symbols to mark towns, rivers, distances, and hotels on those lines. They were compiled from a hugely detailed central record of roads, which emperors updated from time to time. Julius Caesar produced the first register with the help of three Greek geographers who worked on it for twenty-five years. Commercial mapmakers copied parts of this massive collection of facts and sold them in local marketplaces.

Our traveler could set out assured of accommodation along his way. If he was on official business, he could use one of the villas set aside for him every twenty-four to thirty-two kilometers (fifteen to twenty miles) along the main road. Not a government man? No problem. Near most villas, he could find private rest houses with rooms for rent if he did not mind sharing with thieves, prostitutes, and the lower classes. But what if he was a little more genteel? In the early days of the roads, private homes were required by law to give shelter when it was demanded. These *tabernae* eventually morphed into something much more like our modern taverns, which use the same name. For the drivers and carriage attendants, another sort of resting place could be found at regular intervals where wheels could be fixed, horse tack mended, animals cared for by veterinarians, and so on.

We take highways for granted today. For people living along the Roman roads, however, this network probably inspired awe and gratitude. Fast-moving, merciless legions marched on them to the edges of yet-unconquered territories. Heavily guarded carriages sped along them, distributing the wealth of the empire. And innovative new ideas from the commercial and political center of the civilized world were delivered to distant doorsteps.

Chapter 14 – Urban Rome: Managing the Largest City on Earth

For nearly two thousand years, Rome was the biggest city in the world. Eventually, London grew larger, but that was not until the 1800s. In the time of the emperors, one million freedmen, elites, and slaves lived in Rome. It's remarkable that they were all housed, organized, and fed.

Some people lived above or behind their shops, but most lived in cramped, multi-story apartments. These could be as high as eight floors, but more than 85 percent of the apartments were half that height or less. And like today, the owner of one floor might not own the floor above him.

Engineers often made the load-bearing walls on the ground floor particularly thick, and they frequently designed the footprint of each floor a little smaller than the one it sat on, like a tiered wedding cake. Where the side of an apartment block went straight up, buildings could be close and privacy at a minimum. There are reports of residents complaining they could actually shake hands across the narrow lanes between these apartments! There were no services to the higher floors, so it's likely the rents up there were lower and attracted poorer people. They'd often get up there on external stairs. Some apartment roofs were built with Rome's famous concrete, while others used wooden joists and presumably used lighter top cladding.

Romans knew the delightful benefits of courtyards. A single-story apartment would be built around a private courtyard. But on ancient maps of Rome, many multi-story apartment blocks are shown built in clusters enclosing a public courtyard the occupants shared. The homes of the elite would have several courtyards, plus reception rooms. They were modeled on the large, sumptuous villas of wealthy landowners in the countryside, but because Rome was built on hills, flat land was scarce, and the average size of a leading family's home in the city was between 1,300 and 1,500 square meters (1,550 to 1,800 square yards), which limited courtyards. In the 4th century CE, about 1,800 of these residences housed Rome's elite. There were twenty-five times as many apartments for the ordinary, less fortunate people of the city.

Rome's planners imposed few zoning restrictions. The city was a bustling warren of narrow lanes, tiny factories, and shops mixed up with apartments, arcades, retail outlets, magnificent elite villas, bazaars, schools, and gardens.

Yet there was order. As early as 378 BCE, there were four magistrates, each managing a quarter of the city's streets, food supply, and water. In 8 BCE, Augustus surveyed the city and the next year divided it into fourteen regions, probably on the basis of population as each had the same number of firefighters. Again, a magistrate was put in charge of each region.

At first, they were completely independent. They took care of their region's many neighborhoods by removing encroachments; judging disputes; overseeing water, food, street repairs, and sewers; investigating fraud; maintaining weights and measures; and seeing to the cult of the emperor.

One supreme official was set over this administration. He generally left the magistrates to run the daily business of the neighborhoods as they saw best, but by the 2nd century, the inefficiency of this system came to a head. This officer was then made supreme, and the fourteen magistrates were replaced by supervisors who were responsible to him.

The neighborhoods were protected by spirits. They were respected and taken care of at cult altars set up at the crossroads, which were usually the focus and center of each neighborhood. Then, each winter, neighborhood leaders organized wildly popular local cult festivals and games. Of course, these celebrations could be exploited by politicians, and because of this, rulers frequently tried to put a lid on them. It is thought this was partly behind Augustus's reform of the neighborhoods in 7 CE. He also tried to blend the neighborhood cult festivals with emperor worship and donated a statue of the emperor cult to each neighborhood to be paraded annually by the magistrates.

Over time, these cult festivals and games dwindled, but so did the social cohesion of Rome's neighborhoods and the condition of neighborhood roads and infrastructure. Due to this, ambitious politicians found other ways to retain regions as their power bases.

The Tiber River was another focus for Rome's tumultuous people. They were extremely dependent on it. This is Italy's third longest river, and it protected Rome from warships and pirates because it allowed for the city to be away from the coast yet linked to the sea. It was big enough to take all the wastewater and sewage Rome's people could throw in. (And Rome's sewer networks were big. Just one of them alone had 1,600 kilometers—1,000 miles—of pipes!)

The Tiber also flooded. There were truly massive floods every twenty years or so, and in some of these, the river would burst its banks and sweep 2.5 kilometers (1.5 miles) into the city right up to the Appian Way. Officials did their best with frequent protection work, but that was often breached. The river had to be propitiated. So, once a year, priests and the Vestal Virgins went in a procession to the water and, with great ceremony, threw an effigy of a man into the torrent. There's a suggestion this was a remnant of actual human sacrifices made long before.

Boats must have plied the river since the Stone Age. The mouth is twenty-five kilometers (fifteen miles) away, and even a large vessel could navigate to Rome in the early days. In fact, in 167 BCE, after a battle in Macedon, a huge ship with eight banks of oarsmen (it might have even been sixteen banks!) was brought up as a prize of war to the city's southern docks. Much later, Emperor Caligula floated a huge obelisk to Rome on a 100-meter (3300foot) barge with a 7,000-ton displacement.

But the main cargo on the river each year was grain from Egypt. Half a million tons of it was brought on ocean-going vessels to Rome's seaport and manhandled into a flotilla of privately owned specialty riverboats. The Tiber was constantly moving with boats, and at any one time, something like one hundred of them would be these grain delivery craft.

Moving heavy-ladened boats upstream was difficult, and there were risks. However, it was desperately important, so the city gave grain boat owners tax incentives. Their vessels were sixteen meters (fifty-two feet) long with small sails that were used when it was possible, but the main power came from oarsmen or lumbering oxen that towed from a path on the river bank. The seamen were mostly freedmen who were unionized and working for wages. We can imagine how they felt tying up at the south dock at the end of a trip. Home again to the big, busy center of the empire!

Conclusion

It's head-shaking stuff to look at how Rome's roads spread like tentacles across so much of the known world, the huge water-bearing aqueducts that snaked into their busy cities and towns, the jaw-dropping temples, arenas, and monuments, the gloriously soaring Hagia Sophia in Istanbul, and the sumptuous country villas of the fortunate, cultured elite.

The sheer power of the Roman military leaves us sobered. For one thing, the best of Rome's politicians and army generals devised a system that, for centuries, supplied increasing numbers of trained soldiers to the most distant fields of an expanding empire. There were sensational defeats but also breathtaking victories. In military academies today, students still read about innovative tactics devised by the Roman commanders, who were informed with accurate intel and backed by a competent emperor. On the ground, time and time again, non-Romans experienced just how hard it was to resist the brute power of thousands of Romans moving in disciplined groups with lethal force in their hands.

For almost unbelievable stories of excess, these Romans shock us. Do you want murder and passion? Look no further than Emperor Nero, who came to the throne as a teenager in 54 CE with his mother's help. A few months later, a potential rival, his half-brother Britannicus, was poisoned, apparently by the new ruler. At the time, Nero was married to Octavia, but he had an affair with another woman, Poppaea, who became pregnant. The emperor then divorced his wife, banished her to a spot near her birthplace of Pompeii, and later had her killed in exile when it became obvious she remained popular in Rome. He married Poppaea, who died in 65, pregnant with her second child to Nero, seemingly at his hands. Unbelievably, Nero ordered the drowning of his own mother, Agrippina, and when that failed because she could swim, he had her executed in a more conventional manner.

Prefer something more salacious? The adopted grandson of Emperor Tiberius, Caligula, provides us with more than enough of this. He was the son of a popular soldier and became the emperor as a young man only because the Romans insisted on power being passed through the bloodline. Totally out of his political depth, Caligula fell into legendary debauchery and is said to have regularly had incest with his sisters in public, with his wife looking on and others forced to take part. It's all hearsay, and there is more, but you get the drift.

Then there is the geographic spread of the Romans. At its peak, it was huge. In the cold north of the British Isles, Emperor Hadrian left a wall that still stands. And some 6,400 kilometers (4,000 miles) to the east, in the sands of Egypt, Roman emperors and generals ran the eastern end of the empire. Everything in between, around the top of Africa and from western Europe along the Rhine and Danube into what is now Turkey, Roman legions and colonies imposed taxes and exported Italian culture. For centuries, all roads led to Rome.

Roman intellectuals produced work we struggle to better. How does one small group of senators and military commanders support and command a vast empire? Their taxation systems (of which there were several) and administration somehow did exactly this. The iron grip of tradition and the courts kept millions of slaves hewing wood and carrying water until they dropped dead. Roman philosophers, poets, and playwrights are still being published in dozens of languages. One basis of European law remains an ancient collection of Roman legal decisions and commentary codified in the final days of the empire in what is now Turkey.

In short, the Romans leave us inspired. For two thousand years, they stayed intact due to a sense of cultural identity and self-belief. Supremely confident, the Romans ruled their world for well over a millennium, and it is not possible to forget them.

Part 2: The Roman Games

A Captivating Guide to the Gladiators, Chariot Races, and Games in Ancient Rome

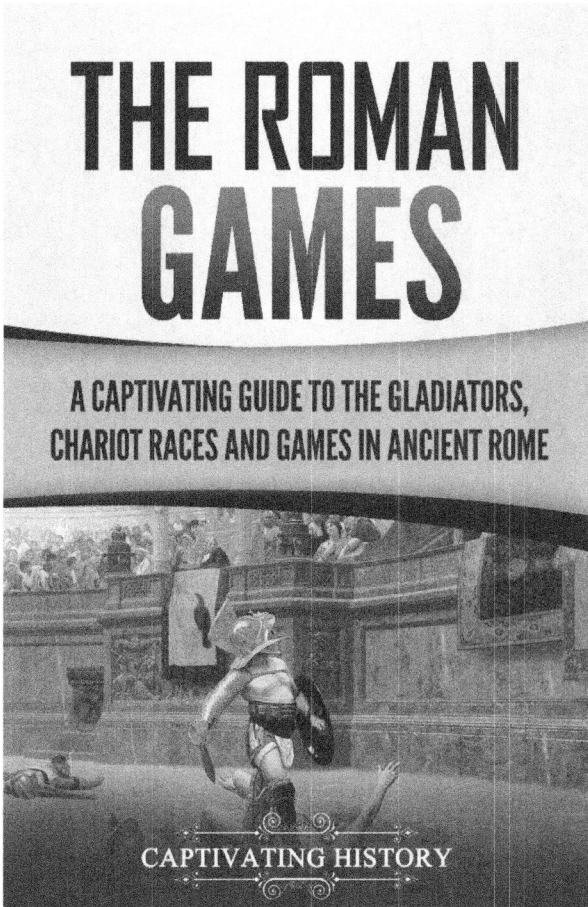

THE ROMAN GAMES

A CAPTIVATING GUIDE TO THE GLADIATORS, CHARIOT RACES AND GAMES IN ANCIENT ROME

CAPTIVATING HISTORY

Introduction: Cruelty of the Ages?

It has long been hard for historians to reconcile the greatness of Rome with the cruelty of the arena. On the one hand, the Romans were clearly intelligent empire builders. They could conquer just as easily as they could establish sensible laws and practice virtuous philosophies. Yet, these highly civilized people had no problem at all with two men killing each other to the excited shouts of their fellow Romans in the arena.

Gladiators have been in vogue since the early days of the Roman Republic, and once you throw in a few lions, tigers, and bears (oh my!) inside a huge colosseum, you truly have a spectacle on your hands. Those condemned to fight in the arena were considered criminals of the state, but one must remember that what Rome considered to be criminal behavior is something we might not today.

Christians, after all, were considered criminals simply for their religious beliefs, partly due to their refusal to offer sacrifices to the prosperity of the emperor. As writer and historian Alison Futrell put it, the Christians were condemned simply for "refusing to participate in public religion." Romans publicly offered sacrifices to both their gods and their emperor; Christians were, therefore, quite conspicuous for their refusal to do so.

In fact, they were considered unpatriotic zealots, and they were made to pay a heavy price for their religious convictions. Emperor Nero of Rome would famously blame the Christians for Rome's "Great Fire" in 64 CE, and for the next few centuries or so, Christians would be widely perceived as treacherous enemies of the state.

But besides the Christians and other religious and political dissidents who were thrown to the lions, others condemned to participate in the games were most likely criminals as we would classify them today. Murderers, robbers, rapists, and the like were routinely trotted out into the colosseums to be publicly executed in the trappings of an elaborate game.

But even if some of those slated for death were mass murderers, most today would have a problem with using their execution as a source of amusement. If someone were to take a modern-day killer on death row and throw him in the ring with a lion, there would most certainly be a public outcry against it. For example, the US Constitution has built in safeguards against cruel and unusual punishment. In the days of the Roman games, however, there was no such thing.

If you were condemned by the government of ancient Rome, your life was forfeit, and the state could do anything it wanted with it. In some instances, prisoners were even forced to act as mythological characters before being cruelly snuffed out in the final scene. Just imagine someone forcing an inmate to play a character for a modern-day film only to have them killed at the end of production. For most of us, such a thing would seem unimaginably monstrous, yet it was considered standard fare in Rome.

Even if the Roman games did not involve direct combat, certain elements of cruelty were still in place. Chariot races, for example, forced drivers to compete on a track at high rates of speed, and the main draw for spectators was the last lap when the charioteers would try to literally drive each other off the road. Charioteers were often flung headlong from their chariots and were killed or terribly maimed as a result.

One of the only peaceful pastimes of the early Roman games was the presentation of exotic animals in the Circus Maximus. In the early days, just the sight of an elephant or a lion or two was enough to get the crowds excited. But eventually, bloodshed was required here as well. And so, large-scale hunting was demonstrated before the masses, and in time, complete beast matches were arranged. Wild beasts were made to fight each other, as well as hapless humans.

Roman spectators could watch a crocodile take on a lion one moment, then see a bull charge a defenseless prisoner the next. The Roman public is said to have had a compulsion for entertainment. So much so that the Roman poet Decimus Junius Juvenal, better known simply as Juvenal, famously declared that "bread and circuses" were all that was needed in order for the Roman populace to remain content.

Juvenal proclaimed this in bitter sarcasm at the state that Rome had found itself in. He, like many of his contemporaries, felt that Romans had become so blinded by their need for entertainment that they had developed a complete disregard for their civic duties as citizens.

This callous disregard for the feelings of others, even the feelings of the condemned, stands in stark contrast to today's much more sensitive stance on both human and animal rights. Today, neither a bad crook nor a big cat would be sacrificed for the sake of the public. Such things would be considered incredibly cruel. So, having said that, the question remains—why didn't it seem that way for the Romans? Were the Romans just exceptionally cruel?

Considering what the Roman games came to consist of, it would be hard to argue anything different. But, of course, there is often more to a story than first meets the eye. So, let's examine the full history of the Roman games to gain a better understanding of what may have motivated ancient Rome to routinely host these incredible spectacles.

Chapter 1 – Where Did the Games Begin?

"It was the wont of the immortal gods sometimes to grant prosperity and long impunity to men whose crimes they were minded to punish in order that a complete reverse of fortune might make them suffer more bitterly."

-Julius Caesar

Although there isn't a clear starting point as to when what we call the Roman games began, the practice is generally believed to have evolved from various religious festivities. Grand religious extravaganzas that celebrated Roman deities and religious rituals were indeed at the heart of the early Roman games. It became standard fare to have the public participate in games and activities sanctioned by the Roman state that were meant to foster solidarity while seeking divine blessings for continued prosperity.

The games followed a well-regulated routine in which everyone knew their part and moved in procession to celebrate Roman religion and culture. It is believed that the very first instance of the official Roman games—that is, when they were observed as an annual event—may have occurred as far back as 366 BCE at a festival held in honor of the Roman god Jupiter.

However, more sporadic celebrations may date all the way back to a man named Lucius Tarquinius Priscus—the fifth king of Rome. Tarquinius's rule of Rome began in 616 BCE and ended in 579 BCE. This was long before the Roman Empire and even before the founding of the Roman Republic. It was from this basic city-state of Rome that the very first Roman games can be traced.

These festivals became known as the Ludi Romani, which literally translates into the "Roman Games." The festivals lasted for several days at a time. The events often consisted of the following formula: a parade, ritual sacrifices, and then finally, the Ludi Romani, or as we like to call them, the "Roman Games." During the pomp and circumstance of the parade portion of the festivities, observers were reminded in an elaborate fashion of the power of Rome and what Roman society expected of them as citizens.

And in order to magnify this feeling of obedience and civic duty, the parade followed predictable, highly orchestrated patterns, with participants put in place according to their rank or importance and with the significance of individual members being conveyed by the costumes they wore. On cue, these participants sang and gave oratory to commemorate important aspects of Roman religion, politics, and tradition.

Sacrificial animals often marched in the parade, and their distinction was also often designated by the wearing of ceremonial flowery garlands or special bows and ribbons tied around them. This was done to distinguish special ritual animals from regular pack animals, as well as to create the perception that these beasts of burden were voluntarily allowing themselves the honor of being made a sacrifice.

Obviously, animals do not have the wherewithal to make such decisions on their own, but the fact that a well-fed calf was decked out in garlands, wreaths, and bows sure made it seem like it was happily marching off to slaughter. The parade of the Ludi Romani was always followed by an official sacrifice of ritual animals. Like many ancient peoples, ancient Roman religion centered around the sacrifice of animals.

The custom of sacrificing a prized animal to a deity was meant to convey the sense of humanity giving up something it could have used for itself to their god. It's not that the gods needed a fatted calf, but rather, it represents the notion that a human being would be willing to give up—*to sacrifice*—something that they needed as a gift to the gods.

In exchange for this sacrifice, it was hoped that the gods would look favorably upon human beings, ensuring that they were healthy, protected, and well cared for. In the order of events at such a Roman festival, after the sacrifices were made, priests would then specifically pray for the gods to help meet the needs of the community. On some occasions, Roman priests might even take individual prayer requests.

Although pagan in its backdrop, such things are not all that different from Christian prayer requests for church members. In church, Christians often mention requests for prayer in the belief that the power of the unified faith of the church members would help to pull them through their difficult times. Romans did very much the same thing. And it was only after the sacrifices were complete and the prayers had been made that the Roman games would officially begin.

The early Roman games were more akin to their immediate predecessors in Greece. Yes, many of the traditions of Greece eventually found their way to Rome. It's for this reason that Roman civilization is often referred to as Greco-Roman, as the two cultures are intricately linked together. And in the early days of the Roman games, Greek influence is very evident. At the inception of the Ludi Romani, the main focus was on games of athletic skill and endurance, similar to the Olympic Games in Greece.

There were also games involving music, as well as theater, the latter of which was most definitely imported from Greece. The Romans, of course, would later put their own spin on these things by having condemned prisoners fight to the death. Perhaps even more disturbingly, the Romans would have the condemned act as "mimes," having them mime the actions of famous figures from Greek tragedies, essentially turning them into the ancient world's equivalent of "snuff films."

Yes, it's one thing to act out a tragic play in which the main character pretends to be killed or pretends to commit suicide; it's a whole other thing to force the main character of a production to actually lose their life. And shockingly enough, that's what the Romans would eventually do. Indeed, all manner of horrid entertainments awaited those in attendance at the Roman games.

Initially, however, the Roman games were a much tamer affair in comparison to the lethal nature that they would one day adopt. Rather than throwing people to lions, the early Romans were more likely to simply display lions for curious spectators at their circuses. In the early days of the Roman games, the main draw was not gladiatorial combat, as would later be the case, but rather chariot races.

In these games, the winning charioteer could win fame and renown for their exploits on the Roman race track. They could also win a whole lot of money. Charioteers received regular pay for their services in addition to prize money. And depending on the situation, that prize money could bring in a fortune. If a charioteer played his cards right, he could end up being quite a wealthy man.

Roman writer Juvenal said as much in his epic *Satires*, comparing the net income of Roman lawyers with that of prize-winning charioteers. Juvenal remarked, "How about advocates then? Tell me the sum they extract from their work in court, those bulging bundles of briefs. They talk big enough...Yet if you check their incomes (real, not declared), you'll find that a hundred lawyers make only as much as Lacerta of the Reds." For those unfamiliar, Lacerta was a famous charioteer for the Romans "red team" of racers (teams consisted of reds, blues, greens, and whites).

There were also basic athletic forms of entertainment, such as foot racing, wrestling, and boxing. In these halcyon days of yore, the games were the playground of the people, where they could enjoy a mild-mannered spectacle in their downtime. The main shift in the early Ludi Romani and the later Roman games was an increasing emphasis on regional and other political leaders of the Roman state.

In the beginning, the festivals were primarily dedicated to the Roman gods, but as time progressed, the festivities were increasingly used to emphasize specific rulers and the governmental systems of the state. It was during these massive celebrations that Roman leaders found the best opportunity to convey their directives to the masses. It was for this reason that what was initially a religious festival took on the trappings of a political rally or military parade, the latter of which became important, as Rome's military generally used the parade portion of the Ludi Romani to showcase their latest triumphs against neighboring rivals. It was quite common for the spoils of war to be held high in glorious triumph by Roman soldiers as they marched in lockstep during the elaborate procession. Even the famed Roman general Scipio Africanus, for example, first displayed his prowess before the early Roman Republic during one of the Roman games held in 213 BCE. Scipio would hold much grander games several years later in 206 BCE in commemoration of his victories he helped score in the Second Punic War.

Over time, three distinct types of Roman games began to emerge. First of all, there were the more standard games, which were controlled and organized by a civic magistrate known as an aedile. One of the most famous of these so-called aediles was the Roman historian and politician Cicero, who masterfully organized several Roman games.

The more excessive Roman games, which typically featured a special military triumph over one of Rome's enemies, were typically held by Rome's elite class of leaders. The top echelon of Rome's hierarchy was also responsible for the establishment of gladiatorial games, which pitted men against each other in what was often more or less mortal combat. It was the latter that quickly gained in popularity for a variety of reasons, with the most obvious reason being the general public's fascination with the spectacle of watching scenes of bloody combat. Such things might be shocking for us today, but for the ancient Romans, it was their equivalent of watching a football game. These blood sports developed into a profitable attraction with a high turnout.

Seizing on its popularity, the Roman elite began to host gladiatorial combat in commemoration of events. Even funerals were sometimes commemorated by the hosting of gladiatorial combat in the arena. Not very many of us today would commemorate our loved one's passing by going to watch a wrestling match, but for the ancient Romans, rather than sitting down to eat a meal with mourners, they just as well might sit in the arena to watch gladiators. This funerary practice was actually borrowed by the Romans from the Etruscans.

The Etruscans lived in northwestern Italy prior to their annexation by Rome and had borrowed much of their culture from the Greeks. The Etruscans valued athletic games just like the Greeks, but it was their habit of having elaborate "funeral games," in which gladiators competed against each other in memory of those who had passed, that really caught the attention of the Romans.

Early Christian writer Tertullian, who, due to his Christian faith, quite understandably condemned the practice, stated that before gladiatorial games were in vogue, there was a practice already in place of occasional human sacrifice. This was due to a belief among the masses that the "souls of the dead are propitiated by human blood." If the sacrifice of another person was believed to satisfy restless spirits, it really begs the question of who was going to satisfy the restless spirits of those who were sacrificed.

At any rate, as Tertullian put it, "The ancients thought they were performing a duty to the dead by this sort of spectacle after they had tempered its character by a more refined form of cruelty. For in time long past, in accordance with the belief that the souls of the dead are propagated by human blood, they used to purchase captives or slaves of inferior ability and to sacrifice them at funerals. Afterwards, they preferred to disguise this impiety by making it a pleasure. Thus, they found consolation for death in murder. Such is the origin of gladiatorial contest."

As Tertullian explains it, the gladiatorial games were used as an elaborate mask of what would otherwise have been viewed as cold-blooded murder. Just like the fatted calf dressed up in wreaths, garlands, and bows, the gladiators, dressed up in armors, helmets, and shields, were a distraction from their true purpose as a sacrificial lamb for the recently deceased.

Having said that, it was Scipio's grand gladiatorial games of 206 that perhaps demonstrated this practice best. These games were not only held in commemoration of the recent victories against Carthage but also in remembrance of both Scipio's father and uncle who had recently passed. Roman historian Livy captured Scipio's dramatic festivities quite well.

Livy tells us, "Scipio returned to [New] Carthage to pay his vows to the gods and to conduct the gladiatorial show which he had prepared in honor of his deceased father and uncle. The exhibition of gladiators was not made up from the class of men which lanistae are in the habit of pitting against each other, that is slaves sold on the platform and free men who are ready to sell their lives. In every case the service of the men who fought was voluntary and without compensation."

Livy made mention of *lanistae*, which was a kind of team owner who made it his business to buy, sell, trade, and train gladiators in the hopes of reaping considerable profits from their matches. Under the guidance of the *lanistae*, many of these gladiators were placed in special teams or "troupes," which were termed *familia gladiatorum*. This was basically a family of gladiators, who were prepped and primed to make as much profit for the *lanistae* as possible.

The Roman historian then went on to state, "In addition to this gladiatorial show there were funeral games so far as the resources of the province and camp equipment permitted." While the actual start date of the Roman games may be a bit murky, they seem to be intrinsically tied to Roman religion and views on the afterlife. The Romans, it seems, very much enjoyed a good show, and they were under the impression that the dearly departed would like one as well.

Chapter 2 – Political and Religious Implications of the Games

"Be prepared, when you speak before an assembly of men, to study their tastes, not, of course, everywhere and by every means, yet occasionally and to some extent. And when you do so, remind yourself that you are but doing the same as you do when, at the people's request, you honor or enfranchise those who have slain beasts manfully in the arena; even though they are murderers or condemned for some crime, you release them at the people's request. Everywhere then the people dominate and prevail."

-Roman orator, Marcus Cornelius Fronto

An indisputable aspect of the Roman games was the fact that they eventually came to fuse both religion and politics. And this fusion was often exported to client states of Rome when it was deemed desirable to put on a full demonstration of the "Roman brand," if you will. This was precisely the case in 168 BCE when the last of the long line of kings in Macedonia—King Perseus—was defeated.

In the wake of the Roman administrative takeover of Macedonia, Roman authorities wished to project not just Roman military might but also Roman political power, and this was often done through the extravagant spectacle of the Roman games. Roman General Lucius Aemilius Paulus Macedonicus was on the scene, and he staged Roman games at the Macedonian city of Amphipolis in order to demonstrate to the Macedonians just how cultured their conquerors were.

Roman historian Livy documented this moment of excess, writing, "The serious business was followed by an entertainment, a most elaborate affair staged at Amphipolis. This had been under preparation for a considerable time, and Paulus had sent messengers to the cities and kings of Asia to give notice of the event, while he had announced it in person to the leading citizens in the course of the Greek states. A large number of skilled performers of all kinds in the sphere of entertainment assembled from all over the world, besides athletes and famous horses, and official representatives with sacrificial victims; and all the other usual ingredients of the great games of Greece, provided for the sake of gods and men, were supplied on such a scale as to excite admiration not merely for the splendor of the display but also for the well-organized showmanship in a field where the Romans were at that time mere beginners."

Livy then goes on to state, "Banquets for the official delegations were put on, equally sumptuous and arranged with equal care. A remark of Paulus himself was commonly quoted, to the effect that a man who knew how to conquer in war was also a man who would know how to arrange a banquet and to organize a show." Yes, the Romans of those days were eager to show their subjected people that they really knew how to put on "a show."

And other regional kings did indeed take notice. The infamous Greek ruler of Syria—Antiochus IV Epiphanes—for one, began to introduce his own version of the Roman games at home. Perhaps even more infamously, Antiochus tried to enforce his own version of the games on the Jews of Judea, whom he had been attempting to subjugate. This led to the Maccabean revolt that overthrew the forces of Antiochus, and Antiochus himself died shortly thereafter in 164 BCE.

This event, which is recorded in the apocryphal First and Second Books of Maccabees, left a lasting impression on the Jewish people. Antiochus, in his lust for Hellenistic-styled games, tried to shove Greco-Roman culture down the Jews' throats—in some cases quite literally since there are accounts of Jews being force-fed pork. In his ruthless belligerence, he even went as far as to have his troops storm into the Jewish temple and sacrifice a pig on the sacred altar. This event would become known as the "abomination of desolation," and it would be mentioned by Jesus himself in the New Testament in both remembrance and as a foreshadowing of potential ill omens to come.

Antiochus IV Epiphanes's attempt to force the Jewish people into Greco-Roman gameplay was ultimately defeated by the Jewish Maccabean revolt, and the holiday of Hannukah was established in remembrance of the event. At any rate, by the 1ˢᵗ century BCE, powerful Romans, such as Roman General Pompey and Roman statesman Julius Caesar, used the Roman games to enhance their own image and standing.

As early as 73 BCE, a young statesman named Julius Caesar was attempting to impress his political rivals by putting on elaborate gladiatorial games. Caesar apparently outdid himself, however, and unleashed the backlash of an alarmed Roman Senate. As the Roman historian Suetonius put it, Caesar had "collected so immense a troop of combatants that his terrified political opponents rushed a bill through the House, limiting the number that anyone might keep in Rome; consequently, far fewer pairs fought than had been advertised."

Suetonius also gives us a vivid description of just how elaborate the Roman games under Caesar could be. At one point, he says, "His [Caesar's] public shows were of great variety. They included a gladiatorial contest, stage-plays for every Roman ward performed in several languages, chariot-races in the Circus, athletic competitions, and a mock naval battle."

Suetonius then goes on to reveal some of the political implications, mentioning, "At the gladiatorial contest in the Forum, a man named Furius Leptinus, of praetorian family, fought Quintus Calpenus, a barrister and former senator, to the death." He fought a former senator to the death? Just imagine a feat like this carried out among some of the political hacks of today!

Caesar's eventual rival, Pompey, in the meantime, used the games to commemorate everything from military conquests to the opening of theaters. This was the case in 55 BCE, which was documented by the Roman statesman Cicero. In a letter to an associate, Cicero spoke of the event. "To be sure, the show (if you are interested) was on the most lavish scale; but it would have been little to your taste, to judge by my own. To begin with, certain performers honored the occasion by returning to the boards, from which I thought they had honored their reputation by retiring. I need not give you further details—you know the other shows. "

Cicero then went on to say, "They did not even have the sprightliness which one mostly finds in ordinary shows—one lost all sense of gaiety in watching the elaborate productions. These I don't doubt you are very well content to have missed. What pleasure is there in getting a Clytemnestra with six hundred mules or a Trojan Horse with three thousand mixing bowls or a variegated display of cavalry and infantry equipment in some battle or other? The public gaped at all this; it would not have amused you at all. Or perhaps having scorned gladiators, you are sorry not to have seen the athletes!"

Cicero then acknowledges, "Pompey himself admits that they were a waste of time and midday oil! That leaves the venationes, two every day for five days, magnificent—nobody says otherwise. But what pleasure can a cultivated man get out of seeing a weak human being torn to pieces by a powerful animal or a splendid animal transfixed by a hunting spear? Anyhow, if these sights are worth seeing, you have seen them often; and we spectators saw nothing new."

Cicero mentions the *venationes*, or skilled hunters, who were sent out to hunt wild animals in the arena. While these kinds of spectacles certainly did draw crowds, many event managers, including the great Pompey himself, held a dismal view of them. You can even see Cicero's negative viewpoint of them in the above passage. Many considered them to be a "waste of time."

Julius Caesar was a man intricately linked to Pompey, both through the elite power circles in which they operated and through their own personal families. Caesar's daughter Julia, you see, had been joined in marriage to the general. Tragically, Julia passed away of sudden illness. Upon her death, Julius Caesar oversaw public festivities that included a banquet, games, and even a gladiatorial show for the masses who attended.

Such extravagance was simply part of the routine for prominent Roman figures such as Pompey and Caesar. But as one might imagine, holding these lavish and complicated extravaganzas wasn't cheap. They cost their hosts quite a bit of money. And the fact that one couldn't get much traction in the Roman political world without the ability to host these lavish games made it increasingly difficult for the less affluent to gain a foothold in Roman politics.

Cicero notes as much when recalling the political campaign of one Titus Annius Milo. Milo was attempting to become a Roman consul, but according to Cicero, he spent a fortune simply trying to hold more elaborate Roman games than his opponents had. In 52 BCE, Milo's campaign ended in scandal, and he was put on trial for the murder of his political rival, Publius Clodius Pulcher, during which he became Cicero's very own client. Milo was ultimately exiled for his actions, yet the public would long remember his generous extravagance in hosting public games and festivities.

Another Roman politician, one Publius Sestius, gained notoriety in relation to the Roman games under very different circumstances. For, in 56 BCE, Sestius had been hit with a charge of "irregular campaigning tactics." Part of this "irregular campaigning" apparently involved the utilization of his own personal goon squad of gladiators, which was used as hired enforcers while he was in office as a tribune. Another famous political scandal of the 1st century BCE involving the Roman games occurred in 62 BCE when Lucius Licinius Murena was accused of bribery when he supposedly attempted to swap expensive seats in the arena in exchange for political benefits.

The previous year, Cicero himself had attempted to codify into Roman law a prohibition on using the Roman games as a perk when campaigning. This bit of lawmaking stipulated that those actively campaigning for public positions should not be allowed to host any games to prevent candidates from using the games to curry political favor. Yet, the Roman games and, in particular, the cobbling together of gladiators as personal guards continued to be the norm during political campaigns.

And the games would continue after the Roman Republic transitioned into the Roman Empire. According to writer and historian Roland Auguet, the very first Roman emperor, Emperor Augustus, was known to have as many as "625 pairs of gladiators for each spectacle." Needless to say, that was an awful lot of gladiators, and it made for quite an elaborate and ostentatious display.

These displays were meant to convey Roman power to both the average Roman citizen and any foreign visitors who just happened to be in Rome at the time. Under Augustus, the events were streamlined even further, with special efforts made to assign seating to different segments of Roman society. Roman soldiers sat in one section, the commoners in another, and, of course, the upper crust had seats of their own.

Augustus's successor Tiberius had an incredible disdain for the Roman games and felt that while it might have been fun for the plebeians (commoners) and other lower classes, it was well below his station as emperor. But although he didn't care too much for it, his sons, Germanicus and Drusus, did. This imperial father was still occasionally appalled, even by the passions that his own children had, for the games.

As the Roman historian Tacitus explained, "A gladiatorial display was given in the names of the Emperor's adopted son Germanicus and his own son Drusus. The latter was abnormally fond of bloodshed. Admittedly it was worthless blood, but the public was shocked and his father Tiberius was reported to have reprimanded him." It's interesting to note Tacitus's words, "worthless blood," which demonstrates the contempt that Romans had for the lower classes who performed in the games.

At any rate, Tacitus then went on to state, "The Emperor himself kept away. Various reasons were given—his dislike of crowds, or his natural glumness, or unwillingness to be compared with Augustus, who had cheerfully attended." It was Tiberius's disapproval of the games that often caused his subjects to seek out games elsewhere. This led to more underground venues popping up by the same lower classes that Tiberius seemed to so despise.

Sadly, the ramshackle arenas that were often created by amateurs led to terrible collapses. On one occasion, a man named Atilius had a wooden amphitheater built only for it to collapse and kill some fifty thousand people. It was tragedies such as this that led to Rome building one of its greatest architectural wonders—the Roman Colosseum.

By the time of the Colosseum, the Roman games were ritualized and infused with religious and political Roman imagery. When a gladiator perished, for example, a man dressed as Charon—the deity representing death—stepped forward and proceeded to hit the defeated gladiator's corpse with a mallet. This apparently signified death's grip on the fallen.

After this bit of theatrics, another man dressed as the Roman deity Mercury would poke the fallen gladiator with a red-hot iron. Along with the religious imagery this invoked, the striking of the fallen with a hammer and prodding with an iron were done just to make sure the defeated gladiator really was dead. If the gladiator didn't get up after being hit with a hammer and burned with an iron, it could be safely assumed that he was no longer among the living.

As the customs mentioned in this chapter well indicate, the Roman games became an intrinsic part of both religion and politics for the average Roman. They felt that their gods needed blood, and the gladiator was the sacrificial lamb to satiate them. The Romans also sought to use the game to project political and military power. He who could throw the most elaborate games was considered a real statesman. It was bread and circuses that made the Roman world go round.

Chapter 3 – The Gladiators of the Roman Games

"What beauty set Eppia on fire? What youth captured her? What did she see that made her endured being called a ludia [gladiator's woman]? For her darling Sergius had already begun to shave, and to hope for retirement due to a wounded arm. Moreover, there were many deformities on his face; for instance, there was a huge wart on the idle of his nose which was rubbed by his helmet, and a bitter matter dripped continually from one eye. But he was a gladiator: this makes them Hyancinthuses. She preferred this to her children and her country, that woman preferred this to her sister and her husband. The sword is what they love."

-Roman poet, Decimus Junius Juvenal

The notion of throwing two people into an arena to fight to the death first became popular in the Roman Republic sometime around 264 BCE. Gladiators were first used as a gruesome means to honor the dead, and gladiatorial combat was often done to honor the very rich dead since the average Roman could not afford such excess at their funerals. It was in that fateful year of 264 BCE that a noble Roman named Junius Brutus had his death commemorated by having enslaved men do battle against each other in what would become standard gladiatorial fashion.

These gladiators were not men who wanted to fight but rather men who were forced to fight. This first wave of gladiators in Rome was referred to as *bustuarii* (singular: *bustuarius*), which is a word related to death and the grave. The name seemed fitting since the gladiators first performed as part of the last rites ceremony to honor deceased Roman elites. In the early days, many of these memorial matches didn't occur in an arena or the Colosseum but rather took place in the "cattle market" or, as the Romans called it, the Forum Boarium.

It wasn't quite so glamorous to have gladiators duke it out at a cattle market, but the backdrop of a forum for such an event set the general standard of things to come. In these early days of Roman gladiatorial games, there were no stands in which spectators could sit. Instead, they simply gathered around in the background, claiming whatever spot they could find to watch the match. Just imagine regal Romans after a funeral procession standing on the sidelines of one of these bloody events, supposedly carried out in honor of the dearly departed.

The closeness of the spectators to the fighters created an intimate, if disturbing, connection. During these games, the gladiators typically battled in pairs and were outfitted with the same minimal armor, small shield, and short sword, known as a *gladius*. The fighters began the match in single pairs, but this number could multiply as the match progressed. In some cases, there could be as many as one hundred gladiators locked in combat at one time.

Gladiatorial fighting after funerals was also often accompanied by a banquet. It probably seems rather sinister to the modern reader to imagine the ancients literally wining and dining themselves after watching a gladiatorial bloodbath, but this was apparently the custom. As indicated, rather than the Roman gladiatorial games being an event held in the middle of an arena with thousands of fans in attendance, gladiatorial fighting was initially viewed as being part of the last rites of the deceased.

Some have suggested that this Roman concept of gladiators—which was borrowed from the Etruscans—also stems from an older Roman tradition of committing human sacrifice over the graves of the deceased. If true, the smokescreen of gladiatorial combat was simply a dressed-up form of the same habit of human sacrifice. Roman writer Festus seemed to confirm this when he remarked, "It was the custom, to sacrifice prisoners on the tombs of valorous warriors; when the cruelty of this custom became evident, it was decided to make gladiators fight before the tomb."

As Festus seems to indicate, gladiators were an offshoot of an older tradition, and they had simply been given a facelift for more modern Roman sensibilities. Rather than simply tying up a hapless victim at a stone idol or before a funeral pyre, they would force two men to fight to the death instead. If true, either way, the end result of spilled blood as a sacrifice for the recently departed remained in force.

The ancient Romans believed that the spirits of their dead required certain rites to be conducted, and if they were not, they feared that the ghosts of these dead men just might come back from the grave and haunt them. It might sound absolutely ridiculous to us today, but this was a real concern for the ancient Romans. And the spilled blood of gladiators as a sacrifice for the supposed appeasement of restless spirits was still part of Roman funeral customs in the days of the Roman Republic.

Christian writer and apologist Tertullian would easily make this very connection in the 2nd century CE when he wrote, "The ancients thought that performing this spectacle was a duty to the dead, after they tempered it with a more humane atrocity. For, once upon a time, since it had been believed that the souls of the dead were propitiated by human blood, having purchased captives or slaves of bad character, they sacrificed them as part of funeral ritual."

Tertullian then went on to explain, "Later they decided to mask the impiety as entertainment. And so those they had purchased and trained in what arms and in whatever way they could, only that they might learn to be killed, they soon exposed to death on the appointed day of the funeral. Thus, they sought consolation for death in homicide. This was the origin of the munus." *Munus* is a word that means "obligation," as in the obligatory duty to have gladiators perform at a funeral.

The games would become much more elaborate over time, of course, and most especially as it pertained to gladiators. The gladiatorial fighters evolved into set categories of warriors. Although the fighters may have hailed from all over the empire, they were usually forced to act out the part of specific stereotypical caricatures of Roman adversaries. There were four basic types of gladiators—the Samnites, the Myrmillo, the Retiarius, and the Thraex.

Those who were selected to represent the Thraex group were outfitted in traditional weapons and armor used by the warriors of old who hailed from the region of Thrace in the Balkans. The gladiator playing the role of a Thraex wore the infamous high-crested helmet of a Thracian, which would come to symbolize gladiators as a whole. Thraex fighters were also equipped with a small square shield, greaves to protect their arms, and a short, curved dagger with which to attack their opponents.

The games created special strategies for the gladiators involved since each category of fighter had its own strengths and weaknesses due to the weapons and armor with which the gladiators were equipped. Although a Thraex gladiator was nimble and fierce with their dagger, they could be captured with a carefully aimed net by an opponent. That iconic, high-crested helmet, in fact, was quite easily snagged by the nets wielded by the Retiarii gladiators.

The Retiarii were known as the "fishermen" because these lightly armored fighters carried fishing-styled nets, as well as a three-pronged trident. These gladiators were highly effective against Thraex fighters. Other gladiators, however, who wore smooth, low-crested helmets to which nets were unable to attach, were a different story. Some helmets also had narrow visors, which the trident-hurling Retiarii were unable to penetrate. Different helmets might allow better vision while also rendering the head more vulnerable.

Another gladiator variation to appear later during the Roman games was the so-called "Secutor," who were heavily armored and wore a "bullet-shaped" helmet, the latter of which would be the favorite of Roman Emperor (and part-time gladiator) Commodus. Some other forms of gladiators have been discovered that seem to be much rarer. According to writer and historian Roland Auguet, there is an unknown variant that was later discovered by archaeologists who happened upon two separate bas-reliefs memorializing gladiatorial combat that depict the same unknown category of fighter.

In these depictions, the gladiator is paired with a Retiarius and seems to be equipped to do battle with the Retiarius's net. The character has a special cone-like contraption on his arm, with a rod protruding out of it, topped off with a hook. It seems that this hook was used by the gladiator to snatch up and rip away the net wielded by the Retiarius. At the end of the day, every aspect of a gladiator's dress had its strengths and weaknesses, and it was up to the gladiators who fought each other to make the best of both.

One of the most interesting aspects of these games was how well versed and interactive the spectators were with the battling gladiators. If fans found themselves close enough to the action, they would proceed to shout directives from the stands. Just like a modern-day fan at a basketball game shouting at a player to make a basket or pass the ball off to another player, Roman spectators shouted out completely unsolicited advice to the gladiators below.

It was entirely up to the gladiator whether they heeded such advice, however, and in the heat of the battle, it's likely little attention was being paid to a bunch of loud-mouthed fans. But if the gladiator ended up on the losing end and was bested by his opponent, they couldn't help but notice. For it was the fans up in the stands who played a role in a defeated gladiator's fate.

If the spectators felt that the gladiator had fought bravely, they could be moved to call for them to be spared. The means with which they did this is debated, although it is popularly believed that the sign from fans to spare a gladiator was a thumbs up, whereas the signal for them to be killed was the infamous thumbs down. For the sake of speculation, let's stick with the most common perception. Thumbs up, the gladiator lives, and thumbs down, he dies.

It wasn't the spectators who ultimately decided the fate of the gladiator, though; that decision belonged to the so-called "editor" of the Roman games. The editor was the one who orchestrated the whole series of games and oversaw how they were carried out. Much of the time, the editor was actually the Roman emperor or some other high-up official. But even though the editor was the one who ultimately made the decision, they almost always followed the whims of the public.

Let's just imagine for a moment that the crowd is ready to signal with a thumbs down, meaning they wish for a defeated gladiator to be killed. Now picture the gladiator defeated, his opponent standing over him with his sword in hand. This man's life is now in the hands of the audience and the editor. Almost immediately, the crowd shouts, "Finish him!" and soon, nearly everyone in the audience presents an outstretched hand with their thumb pointed down.

The editor, in the meantime, watches all of this very carefully, and not willing to go against the wishes of the crowd, he stands up and dramatically turns his own thumb down as well. The victorious gladiator below sees this cue and immediately slits his defeated opponent's throat, thereby ending his life. This was typically how gladiators met their end. If the audience, however, felt that the gladiator showed spirit and fought well, they just might call for him to be spared, causing the editor to rule likewise.

Interestingly enough, the more years one remained a gladiator, the greater the chances were of survival. You see, whereas veteran gladiators may have developed a solid fan base, it was the new gladiators who faced the most hostile audiences. If a gladiator was well known and had developed a reputation as being a good and honorable fighter, the audience was more likely to demand that they be spared so that their beloved gladiator could be seen performing again in future games.

If, however, after everything was said and done and the audience and editor ruled that the gladiator was to die, the defeated fighter was expected to stoically accept their fate. As part of their training, it was always drilled into the gladiator's mind to face death as bravely as they had fought for life. In defeat, they were trained to not struggle and simply wait for the final blow from their opponent.

And incredibly enough, it seems that most gladiators did just that. These warriors, for the most part, accepted the hand that fate had dealt them and stretched out their necks to make it easier for their assailant to cut. This was the final curtain call for many gladiators in the Roman games.

As bad as it might seem, in some ways, perhaps those who died early on in their career were better off. Those gladiators who continued to fight and survive certainly didn't have a very good go of it. The Roman physician Galen gives us a startling window into what the life of a veteran gladiator was like.

After several years of fighting in the ring, it shouldn't be too surprising that these men would develop all manner of physical and mental ailments by the time that they got out. Galen took note of these deficiencies and even seemed to diagnose something that persistently plagued these veteran gladiators. This diagnosis would be similar to the modern-day diagnosis of "PTSD" (post-traumatic stress disorder). As Galen describes to us, "In the amassing of [the athletes'] great quantity of flesh and blood their mind is lost in the vast mire. Receiving no stimulation to develop, it remains as stupid as that of brutes...They fatigue themselves to the limit and then gourmandize to excess, prolonging their repast often into the middle of the night."

Galen then goes on to state, "Analogous rules to those guiding their exercise and eating regulate also their sleep. At the hour when people who live according to the laws of nature quit work to take their lunch, the athletes are rising...While athletes pursue their profession, their body remains in this dangerous state [of hyper development]. When they quit it, they fall into a state even more dangerous."

The state that we might call PTSD is what Galen refers to as a "dangerous state" of alertness. The gladiator is accustomed to a life of adrenaline, yet when they suddenly stop and try to break away from this life of blood-rushing adrenaline, they find themselves a nervous wreck.

As Galen puts it, "Some [gladiators] die shortly after, others live a little longer, but never reach old age...Their bodies enfeebled by the jolts they have received, [they] are predisposed to become sick on the least provocation. Their eyes, ordinarily sunken, readily become the seat of fluxions; their teeth, so readily injured, fall out. With muscles and tendons frequently torn, their articulations become incapable of resisting strain and readily dislocate. From the standpoint of health, no condition is more wretched."

After coming to this determination, Galen then warns, "Many who have been perfectly proportioned fall into the hands of trainers who develop them beyond measure, overload them with flesh and blood, and make them just the opposite...[Fighters] develop a disfigured countenance hideous to look upon. Limbs broken or dislocated and eyes gouged out of sockets show the kind of beauty produced. These are the fruits they gather. When they no longer exercise their profession, they lose sensation, their limbs become dislocated, and, as I have said, they become completely deformed."

In other words, after a life serving in the Roman games came to an end, the wrecked shell of a human being would find themselves entirely unable to live a normal life. They had become used to being under the spotlight and glare of the arena, violently living for the moment. How in the world would someone who had been subjected to such intense conditions suddenly pack everything up and live a quiet life on a farm?

Yet, this is indeed apparently what some gladiators did. Although it surely must have been a struggle, some successful gladiators managed to retire and use the money they earned to retire in peace. But after the trauma a gladiator had been subjected to, just how peaceful their retirement might have been is anyone's guess.

Chapter 4 – Spartacus Fights for Freedom

"He's young still, physically fit to bear arms, and hot-blooded. Gossip claims that with no official compulsion, but no ban either, he'll sign his freedom away to some tyrant of a lanista, take the gladiator's oath...They'll hock the family plate, or pledge poor Mummy's portrait, and spend their last fiver to add relish to their gourmet earthenware: thus they're reduced to the gladiators' mess-stew."

-Roman poet, Decimus Junius Juvenal

The most famous participant of the Roman games to come down to us through history is, without a doubt, a gladiator known simply as Spartacus. Spartacus hailed from a little-known place called Thrace. The ancient region of Thrace comprised sections of Greece, Turkey, and Bulgaria. As it was a rich agricultural area, the Thracians were initially known as farmers.

As time passed, however, inner turmoil among the Thracians began to develop. Petty factions and rivalries led to constant infighting that managed to weaken the Thracian state. Neighboring nations took notice and used the vulnerability of Thrace to literally enslave its people. Greece lorded over the Thracians by the 7th century BCE before the Persian Empire rose in the east and swept the Thracians into their orbit.

Despite the fact they were a conquered people, the Thracians had retained a reputation for being fearsome fighters. Even under Persian dominion, they were widely used as mercenaries to field Persian armies.

The Persian Empire soon went into decline, however, and its borders retreated beyond the land of Thrace. Left to their own machinations, for a time, the Thracians forged their own kingdom.

But it was short lived. In 335 BCE, the armies of a Macedonian king named Alexander the Great decimated what was left of Thracian independence and brought the region firmly under Macedonian control. The situation for Thrace then changed once again in 169 BCE when Thrace, as well as Macedonia itself, was absorbed into the Roman Republic. Despite the shifting political powers that ruled over them, Thracians still had a vibrant culture of their own.

And their martial abilities as fighters were still in demand. So much so that Romans were quick to pick up on it. Soon, Thracians were being imported into Roman arenas to perform as gladiators in the Roman games. The man named Spartacus, of course, would become one of the most famous of these warriors. It seems that Spartacus began his career as a mercenary and fought in the ranks of the Roman army. It was indeed quite common for Thracians like Spartacus to serve in Rome's so-called "auxiliary troop" detachments.

Although the details are a bit murky, it seems that Spartacus eventually grew weary of the life of a Roman soldier and decided to go AWOL (absent without official leave). Abandoning a military post always has severe consequences, and this was especially the case for the Romans, who viewed such negligence as being treacherous and beyond the pale. Most of the time, those who abandoned their assignments were killed right on the spot if they were unlucky enough to be tracked down by the Romans.

Spartacus apparently realized that his actions had made him persona non grata among the Romans. And knowing that he was now an enemy of Rome, he made the best of it, joining homegrown resistance efforts against the Roman occupiers. He knew that the Romans were coming for him eventually, so he figured that he would at least go down fighting.

But Spartacus did not die on the battlefield against Rome (at least not this early in his life); instead, he was captured by his former Roman taskmasters. The big question, which historians haven't quite figured out, is why such a rabble-rouser wasn't simply killed outright for his trespasses against Rome. Could it be that he was such a daring and bold fighter that he impressed the Romans enough to spare his life? Whatever the case may be, he was soon taken captive, and once the Romans connected to the gladiatorial games took one look at this tough Thracian, it was determined that he would make a great addition to the arena.

Now a man forced into slavery, Spartacus would be a forced participant of the Roman games. He began his career under the auspices of one Gnaeus Cornelius Lentulus Batiatus. Lentulus Batiatus was in charge of a gladiatorial training center in Capua, Italy. During the course of his training, Spartacus, like all other gladiators, was carefully guarded and monitored. All he was allowed to do was eat, sleep, and train while being under constant surveillance and the threat of death should he defy his captors.

The gladiators were locked up in stalls, little better than what one might expect an animal to be held in. They were heavily guarded and only allowed out to train or to be led to the arena. Being a gladiator was a brutal business, and most tossed into the ring would have a short lifespan. Even if matches were not always lethal in outcome, the likelihood of sustaining severe injuries was extraordinarily high.

The fact that Spartacus lasted as long as he did bears testament to just how good of a fighter he really was. Spartacus was such a good gladiator that it was the person who was unfortunate enough to be matched against him who would face terrible repercussions. No doubt many men died by Spartacus's hand. Most didn't want to have to fight in the ring like this, but they had no choice.

All gladiators, when the time came, were forced out of the stockades that held them and made to burst forth into the arena so that these vicious Roman games could begin. If a gladiator was a little too slow to emerge, one of their handlers would be there ready and waiting to hit them with a whip or prod them forward with a flaming torch. These gladiators usually did not wish to do battle with one another but rather were forced to do their handlers' bidding.

Nevertheless, even under these brutal conditions, Spartacus began to get to know some of his fellow gladiators. And after the roar of the crowd had ceased and Spartacus and those who had survived that day's events were herded back into their living quarters, they would converse with each other. It was during these private moments that he and his fellow gladiatorial peers of the Roman games began to plot their escape.

It's not entirely clear how Spartacus and his comrades broke out of their confinement, but it's known that once they did, they made a beeline for the mess hall where their food was usually prepared. They didn't do so because they were hungry and needed a snack, mind you; they simply knew the kitchen was a place they could grab knives and other implements with which to defend themselves.

You see, when the gladiators were not battling it out in the arena, they were denied access to weapons. Since these weapons were locked up and out of reach, the next best thing was to grab kitchen utensils that could be wielded as basic weapons. After this, they then proceeded to cut through the men who guarded them. Slashing and hacking their way out of the compound, the runaway gladiators were able to hide out in the wilderness while they planned their next move.

It took the leadership of that star gladiator of the Roman games—Spartacus—to hold the band of gladiators together. Shortly after Spartacus and his comrades escaped from their confines, their old taskmaster Lentulus Batiatus lodged a complaint with Roman authorities, resulting in an all-out manhunt for the renegades. Leading this charge was a Roman praetor by the name of Gaius Claudius Glaber.

Fortunately for Spartacus and his group, Rome's crack troops were way too busy fighting the various wars and insurrections that had recently erupted than to deal with a slave rebellion of gladiators. The Roman Republic had entered a period of tremendous upheaval and couldn't expend its best military resources just to take down a group of gladiators.

As such, Glaber was forced to put together a rather motley crew of his own, utilizing fresh recruits who were not the most experienced of fighters. Even though these men would be well armed, their lack of experience would be clearly evident upon facing off with the battle-hardened gladiators. Compounding Glaber's challenge of rounding up Spartacus and the other escaped gladiators was that Spartacus's rebellion had become a kind of movement that had gained steam with the enslaved masses of Rome. Soon, several other slaves from the surrounding area had escaped to join up with Spartacus's roving band.

These escapees that flocked to Spartacus were mostly domestic workers and field hands—not exactly skilled warriors ready for combat—but the fact that Spartacus's main group of gladiators was able to add auxiliary troops of any kind made the task of putting down what was initially a minor rebellion a much more difficult task. Spartacus had also created his own mountain fortress atop Mount Vesuvius, making it exceedingly difficult for any force to go on the offensive against him.

Initially, his pursuers attempted a war of attrition, thinking that they could starve the rebels down from their mountain stronghold. Glaber parked his forces around the mountain and simply waited for the gladiators to come down. This proved to be a big mistake since Spartacus and company, who were well versed in how to ambush their enemies, were able to launch a sneak attack in the middle of the night against the enemy camp.

They descended the mountain right in the midst of Glaber's forces and, catching them unaware, absolutely decimated them. Their opponents were forced to flee, and it seems that Praetor Glaber either perished in the struggle or simply gave up the fight, as his name is not brought up in association with Spartacus thereafter. The Roman enforcers, who were forced to flee, left behind food, armor, and other important supplies at the base of the mountain.

This proved to be a much-needed resource for the desperate gladiators, who quickly nourished their bodies with Roman rations and armed themselves with Roman armaments. Authorities in Rome were furious about what had happened at Mount Vesuvius, and unable to tolerate the notion that a ragtag group of gladiators would be able to best Roman power, it was arranged to have proper Roman legions—the best Roman troops available—to take on the renegades.

Despite the inclusion of the powerful legionaries, the first battle between these Roman troops and the rebels was a decisive failure for Rome. An entire detachment of troops was defeated. Spartacus then went on the offensive and led a portion of his fighters to assault another Roman legion nearby, and it, too, was defeated. With Roman legions smashed before them, Spartacus's gladiators were, at least for the time being, able to take to the countryside unopposed.

Before their oppressors could regroup, Spartacus took the initiative and attempted to put distance between himself and Rome. Roman troops were soon in hot pursuit, however, and the gladiators would have to often take to rearguard attacks to fend them off. The gladiators were fierce fighters, but the Roman soldiers were relentless, leading to several back-and-forth exchanges between the two.

Spartacus's large group of followers had become divided in the meantime, with one portion overseen by Spartacus himself and the other portion by a fellow gladiator and escapee of the Roman games named Crixus. In 72 BCE, the gladiator rebellion was struck a terrible blow when the forces manned by Crixus were defeated by a Roman legion.

Crixus was in command of tens of thousands of rebels at the time, but after the Roman legion tore through his ranks, he was only in command of a small fraction of that number. Spartacus was both enraged and alarmed at what had happened, knowing that it wouldn't be long before the hammer dropped on him as well. As such, he finally decided that it was time to take the battle to the Romans themselves.

A wealthy and noble Roman by the name of Marcus Licinius Crassus, in the meantime, took charge of the efforts of ridding the Roman Republic of the menace that Spartacus and his rebels posed. Spartacus's roving band, after all, was now regularly raiding Roman settlements for supplies, and such transgressions could not continue if the Roman Republic was to stand. Crassus led a resurgent Roman army against the rebels and steadily pushed them southward.

Reaching the coast of southern Italy, the group realized that they would have to find a means of passage across the waters lest they be driven into the sea. It was then that Spartacus concocted a scheme involving Cilician pirates (another brand of hunted outlaw) to ferry them to the island of Sicily. Here, Spartacus believed he could bolster his forces and prepare for a final showdown with Rome.

Spartacus was double-crossed by the pirates (apparently, you just can't trust pirates), for after taking an advance fee for transport from Spartacus, the pirates simply took the money and ran. This left Spartacus and his group stranded in southern Italy with no means of leaving the Italian Peninsula. With the forces of Rome closing in, out of sheer desperation, these escapees from the Roman games began to build makeshift crafts out of whatever wood they could find.

Little better than rafts, these treacherous vessels were now the only means of escaping certain death at the hands of a resurgent Roman army. This proved futile, however, since these makeshift crafts proved unable to tolerate the strong current of the four-mile strait that separated mainland southern Italy from Sicily. Cunning Crassus, in the meantime, had actually built a walled fortification zone spanning the entire forty-mile width of southern Italy, essentially locking the rebels in place. Now Crassus could simply starve the gladiators into submission without having to even fight them.

Spartacus wasn't willing to give up without a fight, though, and in 71 BCE, he sent his men smashing into the Roman fortifications. These tough gladiators actually scaled the walls and took the fight to the Romans. Utilizing their hard-honed skills and toughness learned during their stint in the Roman games, these warriors managed to overrun the walls that were built to keep them caged in, and once again, they made a mad dash to the north.

Hunted and hounded by the Romans, Spartacus and his remaining followers ended up making their last stand shortly thereafter. The Romans were able to make short work of the tired and weary gladiators, killing tens of thousands of them in one battle. Spartacus—that great champion of the Roman games—was among the number to have died that day.

Chapter 5 – Christians and the Roman Games

"Too mad with passion to defer or check his wrath, [the judge] appoints that they shall be burned with cruel fire. They, rejoicing, bid the throng not weep...By this time, they were entering a place enclosed by tiers of seats in a circle, where frenzied crowds attend and are drunk with much blood of wild beasts, when the din rises from the bloody shows, and as the gladiator, whose life is being held cheap, falls under the stroke of the stark sword there is a roar of delight."

-Roman poet, Aurelius Clemens Prudentius

The image of Christians being thrown to the lions at the Roman Colosseum seems to be seared into the memory of Western civilization. Christianity, a religion born in the Middle East, collided with Greco-Roman culture with explosive results. The first great persecution of the Christians of Rome occurred in 64 CE in the aftermath of the so-called "Great Fire" of Rome.

Historians still do not know for sure what happened, but for centuries, it has been widely believed that the depraved Nero set the fire himself, only to blame it on Christians. Even though no one can conclusively say that this is what happened, there are a lot of factors that make this scenario seem feasible.

The Roman emperor, it seems, had a strong—although entirely insidious—motive for setting Rome alight. Nero, as it turns out, wanted to demolish large parts of the city to make way for new construction. And after the fire leveled several structures to the ground, that is, in fact, exactly what he did.

Many have pointed to these events as an indication that the whole thing had been planned by Nero in the first place. But even if he hadn't, the Christians were a convenient group to blame these horrible crimes on. Even though today, it might be hard for us to understand it, the Romans felt that the Christians were the absolute worst of the worst.

For one thing, the average Roman grossly misunderstood the religion and believed that Christians were a part of a warped secret sect that practiced abominable things. For example, Romans commonly misunderstood the practice of communion, likening it to cannibalism. But why would they do this? It is because they misunderstood the words of Jesus that Christians quoted in regard to the practice of communion.

Just consider the Bible verses from Luke 22:19-20, which read, "And he took bread, gave thanks and broke it, and gave it to them, saying, 'This is my body given for you; do this in remembrance of me.' In the same way, after supper, he took the cup, saying, 'This cup is the new covenant in my blood, which is poured out for you.'"

For the average Roman who knew nothing of Christianity, hearing Christians quote such passages could be startling. Non-Christian Romans thought that Christians were actually commemorating the eating of Christ's body and the drinking of his blood. Today, we are fully aware of the symbolism involved, but back when Christians were an obscure sect, such things were easily misunderstood.

Furthermore, there were certainly those who did understand the symbolic nature but chose to exploit the confusion over it to make Christians look bad. For those that didn't like Christians, the easiest way to publicly shame them would be to point and shout, "Hey! Look over there! It's Christians! They're nothing but a bunch of cannibals!"

Christians were also believed to be weird because they frequently met in graveyards. Ironically, the main reason for Christians meeting in graveyards was due to the fact that they were so persecuted. The cemetery was simply a safe place to meet away from prying eyes. But one can only imagine that this habit only added to Christian strangeness.

Some of the more zealous followers, however, may very well have also preferred standing around graves due to the Christian belief that the dead would be resurrected in the last days. It was these more apocalyptic visions of Christianity that Nero and others latched onto after the Great

Fire of Rome.

Christians continually spoke of how Rome and everything else would soon go up in flames, so it wasn't hard to claim that perhaps some Christian provocateurs set Rome on fire in an attempt to trigger the very Armageddon of which they spoke. Some modern historians, in fact, have since taken a good second look at the Great Fire of Rome and seriously considered the possibility that Nero was telling the truth after all and that the fire really was started by Christians.

But even if the fire was initially ignited by some misguided Christian or Christians, it certainly didn't give Nero the right to persecute every single Christian in the Roman Empire as punishment. Such a thing would be akin to punishing every single Muslim for 9/11 just because the hijackers happened to be Muslim. Obviously, today, we know that such collective punishments are wrong, but in Nero's day, they were fair game.

And so it was that massive numbers of Christians were crucified, thrown to the lions, and lit up as human torches, all to supposedly teach the members of this mysterious sect a lesson. At any rate, it was the Great Fire of Rome that would lead to the greatest construction the Roman Games would render—the Roman Colosseum.

Prior to the Colosseum, temporary wooden structures were used for the Roman games. Many of these were burned to a crisp in the Great Fire of Rome. Immediately after the devastation, the Roman public's desire for the Roman games was satiated once again through temporary structures, which were erected just for the purpose of the main event before being taken down.

It wasn't until Emperor Vespasian came to power in 69 CE that Rome began work on a permanent place to hold the Roman games. This grand structure, which was partially built with a large labor force of thousands of slaves and prisoners of war, would become known as the Roman Colosseum. It should be noted that many of those prisoners of war were taken from Jerusalem.

Jewish freedom fighters who had struggled with the Romans during the great siege that resulted in the destruction of their sacred temple in 70 CE ended up being forced to lay down stones for the Colosseum. The more cynical among us might be tempted to think that the whole assault on Judea in 70 CE—the very same year that construction on the Colosseum began—might not have been a coincidence. It is a fact that much of the funding for this construction project was achieved by way of the treasures stolen from the temple in Jerusalem. But could it also be that Rome saw a prime opportunity to create a massive slave labor force by attacking Judea? At any rate, it is rather chilling that Jewish prisoners of war, who were pulled from the wrecked rubble of their sacred temple, were forced to lay the stone foundations of the Roman Colosseum, in which so many of their descendants—both Jewish and Christian—would be persecuted.

According to Roman Jewish historian Josephus, just prior to Titus becoming emperor, he, as the general of the Roman army in Judea from 66 to 70 CE, made sure that many Jewish captives from the conflict in that region were brought back to Rome. Before the Colosseum was opened, several other Roman games were held by Titus in various locales, in which these captive Jews were forced to participate.

In fact, it is said that as many as 2,500 of these condemned prisoners of war died in just one Roman game. The inaugural games of the Colosseum, in the meantime, would be held in 80 CE during the last year of Titus's reign as emperor. But the Colosseum would not be fully operational until Emperor Domitian's reign in 81 CE.

Domitian was fascinated with grand architecture, and he would end up launching many feverish building projects during his reign. As the Roman historian Plutarch once wryly noted, Domitian seemed to be afflicted with "a disease of building and a desire, like Midas had, of turning everything to gold or stone."

It was Domitian who added the finishing touches of the hypogeum, which consisted of underground passageways in which animals and gladiators could be held until trap doors were opened, allowing them to walk out into the main stage of the arena. Just imagine Rome's religious and political dissidents helplessly huddled together in fear when a trap door was suddenly released, allowing several wild and hungry lions or a bloodthirsty group of gladiators to emerge.

Rome had a long history of throwing dissidents of all kinds into the arena. Anyone who disagreed with Roman rule, whether militarily or simply philosophically, ran the risk of being condemned to a grisly fate in the Colosseum. Ever since Judea (southern Israel) was incorporated into the Roman Empire, Jewish religious and political dissidents were frequent fodder for the Roman games.

The whole idea of feeding folks to lions was certainly not a new one for the Romans when the Colosseum was built. And at the very first inaugural games for the Roman Colosseum in 80 CE, among the main events was indeed a showing of *Damnatio ad bestias,* which is Latin for "condemnation to beasts." During this routine, the criminally condemned, whether the reason for their condemnation was theft, murder, or simply refusing to bow down to the emperor, were strategically placed in the arena so that they could be rushed by lions, tigers, bears, and other wild beasts.

The condemned were often tied up or otherwise rendered unable to defend themselves so that the animals could feast upon them with abandon. Such spectacles were often advertised for several days in advance, with special placards put in place along roads in and out of the city. These advertising campaigns made sure that the seats in the Colosseum were packed with visitors, from both near and far, who wished to feast their eyes upon the destruction of the condemned.

One of the most famous Christians who were condemned to be destroyed in the Colosseum was supposedly none other than the Apostle John. John, also known as John the Revelator due to his contributions to the Book of Revelation, was one of the original twelve disciples of Jesus Christ. John stands out as the only disciple who managed to die of natural causes and live a long life. In fact, John is said to have lived all the way until 100 CE (although some sources say 98 CE), passing at the ripe old age of ninety-four years old.

But according to Christian tradition, it was only with God's help that this apostle managed to do so. Other biblical sources on John allege that during the reign of Domitian (r. 81–96 CE), the Romans attempted to execute this long-lived apostle right in the middle of the Roman Colosseum before thousands of screaming spectators. In their gruesome excess, his executioners had concocted a scheme in which John would be dunked into a vat of boiling oil.

The oil was fired up to a super-hot temperature. John was hauled out, and a couple of Roman soldiers picked him up and threw him right in. But according to tradition, once submerged, John remained miraculously unscathed. He simply stood there in the midst of the boiling cauldron, none the worse for wear. It's said that the thousands of Roman spectators who bore witness to this event were so touched by it that they began converting to Christianity on the spot.

This was most certainly not what John's Roman persecutors had in mind! It was supposedly after this failed attempt on the Apostle John's life that his captors gave up the idea of killing him and instead simply exiled him to the Greek island of Patmos. And according to Christian tradition, it was on Patmos that John had his vision and wrote what would become the final chapter of the Christian Bible: the Book of Revelation.

There is no hard evidence that John was miraculously spared death in the Roman Colosseum. And as such, whether or not it actually happened is more or less a matter of faith. At any rate, one Christian martyr whose demise is clearly documented is one of the Apostle John's very own disciples—Saint Ignatius.

Ignatius was, at one point, chosen to be the bishop of Antioch in Asia Minor. Although the details are not clear, it appears that he, too, was caught up in Roman persecution, as he was arrested and hauled off to Rome to await his fate sometime during his tenure as bishop. It is said that Ignatius was taken into Roman custody during the reign of Domitian's successor, Emperor Trajan, who reigned from 98 to 117 CE.

According to tradition, during the journey to Rome, Ignatius was able to write many letters, which were sent to local churches along the way. These letters provide some historical documentation for what may have actually happened to Ignatius. Some are skeptical of the letters, however, insisting that it wouldn't make sense for the Romans to allow Ignatius the privilege of writing them. Furthermore, these detractors contend, the Romans would have taken Ignatius by boat directly to Rome rather than overland. If this were the case, he wouldn't have had the opportunity to drop off letters.

At any rate, around the year 108, he ended up being condemned to the Colosseum, where he wasn't exactly thrown to lions but was rather left standing in the middle of the Colosseum as lions were *thrown at him.* Traditional accounts tell us that Saint Ignatius was attacked by at least two lions, which promptly began feeding upon the martyr. It's said that Saint Ignatius did not panic and run from the beasts but stoically accepted his fate, offering no resistance as the lions tore him apart.

It was a fate, in fact, that Ignatius had apparently already anticipated. He even mentioned it in one of the letters he is said to have left for Roman Christians. The letter read, in part, "I am writing to all the churches and am insisting to everyone that I die for God of my own free will—unless you hinder me. I implore you: do not be unseasonably kind to me. Let me be food for the wild beasts, through whom I can reach God. I am God's wheat, and I am being ground by the teeth of the wild beasts, that I may be found pure bread of Christ."

If the letters attributed to Ignatius are indeed authentic, it would seem that Ignatius successfully foresaw the grisly fate that would await him when he was forced to participate in one of Rome's warped games. Decades after Ignatius was martyred, one of his previous associates, Polycarp, the Bishop of Smyrna, was martyred, dying around 150. Polycarp, an esteemed church father at the time of his demise, was widely admired for the bravery and courage that he showed in the arena.

In the Christian text, *The Martyrdom of Polycarp*, these feelings take center stage. In it, the Christian writer proclaims, "We are writing to you, dear brothers, the story of the martyrs and of blessed Polycarp who put a stop to the persecution by his own martyrdom as though he were putting a seal upon it...Just as the Lord did, he too waited that he might be delivered up, that we might become his imitators...Who indeed would not admire the martyrs' nobility, their courage, their love of the Master? For even when they were torn by whips until the very structure of their bodies was laid bare down to the inner veins and arteries, they endured it, making even the bystanders weep for pity."

After these words of encouragement and exultation, the writer then goes on to state, "As Polycarp entered the amphitheater, a voice from heaven said: 'Be strong, Polycarp, and have courage.' No one saw who was speaking, but those of our people who were present heard the voice. Then, as he was brought in, a great shout arose when the people heard that it was Polycarp who had been arrested. As he was brought before him, the governor asked him: 'Are you Polycarp?' And when he admitted he was the governor tried to persuade him to recant, saying: 'Have respect for your age'; [and other similar things that they are accustomed to say]; 'swear by the Genius of the emperor. Recant. Say, "Away with the atheists!"'"

The account then goes on to state, "Polycarp, with a sober countenance, looked at all the mob of lawless pagans who were in the arena, and shaking his fist at them, groaned, looked up to heaven, and said: 'Away with the atheists!' The governor persisted and said: 'Swear and I will let you go. Curse Christ!' But Polycarp answered: 'For eighty-six years I have been his servant and he has done me no wrong. How can I blaspheme against my kind and savior?'" Polycarp had been a Christian for decades, and even when threatened with force, he was unwilling to bend. His persecutors, infuriated at his refusal to recant, had Polycarp set on fire and burned alive in the arena.

Another famous Christian martyr to face death in the Roman games was a young woman by the name of Vibia Perpetua. Vibia Perpetua came under Roman scrutiny around 202 CE when she refused to pay homage to the Roman emperor. Quite contrary to the image of aged Christian saints, such as the Apostle John or even Saint Ignatius, facing off against Roman persecution, Perpetua was a newlywed young mother in her early twenties when she faced Rome's wrath.

As the story goes, this young Christian's life was interrupted when she and her local group of Christians came to the attention of Roman authorities in her hometown of Carthage. Upon being confronted by Roman officials, she refused to perform the obligatory sacrifice to the emperor. Even though her own father begged her to renounce her faith so she could live, Perpetua steadfastly refused.

Perpetua was from a rich and well-educated family. And the fact that she was secretly practicing Christianity was a deep embarrassment to them. However, the fact that Perpetua was an educated woman from the 3rd century proved to be a great gift for Christian literature due to the fact that she was an epic diary writer and documented many of her own thoughts and experiences.

She continued to write even after her arrest, at one point making the vivid entry, "Oh bitter day! There was a great heat because of the closeness of the air, there was cruel handling by the soldiers. Lastly I was tormented by concern for my baby." Yes, perhaps the worst part of Perpetua's confinement was the fact that she had been separated from her child. She documents how her father pleaded with her until the very end to simply renounce her faith.

If she had simply given up being a Christian (or simply pretended to do so) and then paid the traditional respects to the emperor, she would have been allowed to live and would have had all of her previous freedoms restored. She noted in her diary how her own father had so desperately sought to persuade her of such.

She recalled one such attempt, in which her dear old dad pleaded, "Have pity, daughter, on my grey hairs; have pity on your father, if I am worthy to be called father by you—don't give me over to the scorn of men. Think of your brothers; your mother, your aunt. Consider your son, who will not live long if you die. Give up your resolution; do not destroy us all."

Think what you will about her father's efforts to dissuade her, but this is quite obviously a man who loved his child and sought to bring her back from the brink of destruction. Yet, Perpetua was resolute in her decision, and she refused to back down. During her trial, her father continued to plead with her. At one point, he even held up her little son, urging her, "Perform the sacrifice! Have mercy on the child!"

This, of course, was done to remind her of how much of a hardship her son would have, to grow up without his mother, if she refused to recant and offer sacrifice to the emperor. Nevertheless, Perpetua continued to refuse, simply stating, "I am a Christian." In the end, the Roman procurator—a man named Hilarian—brought down the final verdict as it pertained to Perpetua's fate. She would be fed to the lions in the Roman Colosseum.

The night prior to her execution, Perpetua had a strange dream. She dreamed that she was in the arena, forced into gladiatorial combat against an "Egyptian opponent." Moments later, her clothing fell away, and she found that she had been transformed into a man. She then proceeds to wrestle the Egyptian to a standstill until she is declared the winner and led through the gates of the arena, victorious.

Despite what one might interpret from such a dream, Perpetua did not view it as an indication of a worldly victory in the ring but rather a spiritual victory over the devil. Perpetua interpreted her Egyptian opponent as being the devil in disguise (as Egypt was often Israel's enemy in the Old Testament) and that her passing through the gate was an indication of her arrival in heaven after being martyred.

Her dreams were indeed prophetic. She and her fellow condemned Christians were taken out into the arena on the day of their condemnation, and wild animals were set loose upon them. The beasts only managed to kill two among the group, however, so a gladiator was called in to dispatch the rest. This man was able to quickly kill all of the condemned, but when Perpetua's time came, it's said that, for some reason, he lost his nerve and accidentally botched her execution.

Instead of slitting her throat, he cleaved right into bone, causing terrible pain and suffering. Nevertheless, Perpetua gathered what remained of her dwindling strength and directed her killer's knife back to her throat, aiding him in the very act of cutting her down.

Even though Christians often met a grisly end in the Roman games, it would be Christians who would play a major role in eliminating them. For it was after the Roman Empire became predominantly Christian in its makeup that the blood sports of the past were eliminated entirely. Centuries of persecution made it clear that the Christian faithful could not be dissuaded from their beliefs by way of force. If anything, it only emboldened the Christians even more. The Roman government wanted to eliminate Christianity as an alternative belief system, yet Christians were becoming all the more militant in the face of persecution.

In the mid-3rd century, Cyprian, the Bishop of Carthage, captured this sense of urgent militancy well. During one of the great persecutions of the day, he wrote his so-called "Letter to the Martyrs" to address this very notion.

Cyprian declared, "The multitude of those who were present saw with admiration the heavenly contest, the contest of God the spiritual contest, the battle of Christ, saw that his servants stood with free voice, with unyielding mind, with divine virtue—bare indeed, of weapons of this world, but believing and armed with weapons of faith. The tortured stood more bravely than the torturers; and the limbs, beaten and torn as they were, overcame the hooks that beat and tore them."

He then elaborates, "The scourge, often used again and again with all its rage, could not conquer invincible faith, even though the membrane which enclosed the guts were broken, and it was no longer the limbs but the wounds of the servants of God that were being tortured. Blood was flowing which would quench the blaze of persecution, which would overcome the flames of Gehenna with its glorious gore. Oh, what a spectacle was that to the Lord, how sublime, how great, how acceptable to the eyes of God in the allegiance and devotion of his soldiers!"

The Christian leader then goes on to urge his fellow Christians, "If the battle shall call you out, if the day of your contest shall come, engage bravely, fight with constancy, knowing that you are fighting under the eyes of a present Lord, that you are attaining by the confession of his name to his own glory...He only looks on his servants, but he himself also wrestles in us, himself is engaged, himself also in the struggles of our conflict not only crowns, but is crowned."

Christian persecution in the Roman Empire would only end with the Edict of Milan in 313 CE. This edict, issued by Roman Emperor Constantine and his co-emperor Valerius Licinianus Licinius, stipulated that Christianity would be recognized as a legal religion and forbade any further persecution of the faith. The influence of Christianity would continue to grow in the meantime, and by 380, it would be made the official state religion of the Roman Empire under Roman Emperor Theodosius.

By this time, the old Roman games of the arena looked more and more like pagan relics of the past. For Christians, these vestiges of Rome's pagan roots would soon become an intolerable eyesore. Saint Augustine, a contemporary of the time, even went as far as to say that the practice of these old traditions was akin to conjuring up demons.

An excerpt from Saint Augustine's *Sermons* tells us, "For such demons are pleased with misleading songs, with worthless shows, with varied foulness of the theatre, with the frenzy of the games, with cruelty of the amphitheater, with the violent contests of those who undertake strife and controversy provocative even of hostility in their support of noxious characters, for instance, of an actor in a mime, a play, or a pantomime, of a charioteer, or of a venator. By acting in this way that, as it were, offer incense to the demons within their hearts. For the deceptive spirits rejoice in seduction they feast upon the evil customs and the notoriously vile life of those whom they have misled and entrapped."

The Roman games did indeed spring from religious practices, and Saint Augustine, now speaking as a leader of the newly Christianized Roman Empire, reinterpreted the games as nothing short of the worship of demonic influences. To Augustine, the spectacle of violence, lust, and all the other vices of the arena could only be seen as an offering of "incense" to the demonic forces that thrive on such negative energy. Whether demonic entities were literally hovering around the arena to lap up the negative emotions that were unleashed is anyone's guess, but Augustine's words certainly struck a chord with his audience.

And the newly Christianized Rome was most certainly finding the old Roman games to be a source of embarrassment and shame rather than something to celebrate or be proud of. Christian thinker Aurelius Prudentius Clemens, more commonly known as simply Prudentius, was even more explicit when he directly drew a connection between the deaths of gladiators in the colosseums with human sacrifices to pagan gods.

In the text *Books Against Symmachus*, Prudentius proclaimed, "Look at the crime-stained offerings to frightful Dis, to whom is sacrificed the gladiator laid low on the ill starred arena, a victim offered to Phlegethon in misconceived expiation for Rome. For what means that senseless show with its exhibition of sinful skill, the killing of young men, the pleasure fed on blood, the deathly dust that ever enshrouds the spectators, the grim sight of the parade in the amphitheater?"

Invoking the name of the Roman god of death, who was so often portrayed in the Roman games, Prudentius then rails, "Why, Charon by the murder of these poor wretches receives offerings that pay for his services as guide, and is propagated by a crime in the name of religion. Such are the delights of the Jupiter of the dead, such the acts in which the ruler of dark Avernus finds content and refreshment. Is it not shameful that a strong imperial nation thinks it needful to offer such sacrifices for its country's welfare and seeks the help of religion from the vaults of hell?"

As Christianity became more entrenched in Roman society, the Roman games were becoming increasingly out of step with many. As the old traditions became more and more marginalized, they were soon cast aside entirely, and as Prudentius would say, they were eventually consigned to the vaults of hell.

Chapter 6 – Extravagant Military Reenactments

"A noble man compares and estimates himself by an idea which is higher than himself; and a mean man, by one lower than himself. The one produces aspiration; the other ambition, which is the way in which a vulgar man aspires."

-Roman emperor, Marcus Aurelius

Along with gladiatorial fighting, wild beast hunts, and even throwing prisoners to the lions, the Roman games often boasted extravagant military reenactments. The arena could be flooded for naval reenactments, or flora and fauna from faraway lands could be inserted into the sands to imply a foreign battlefield. It was on these backdrops that grand military dramas for the masses were orchestrated.

Interestingly, the wild and untamed lands of Britain were a favorite backdrop at the Roman games. In particular, the rapid-fire fighting of Celtic tribes on horseback and chariot were emulated on a grand scale. Celtic warriors were even imported to participate in the battles. During the days of the Roman Republic, military triumphs such as these were standard fare.

Roman historian Livy leaves us an excellent record of what they were like. Livy recorded, "It was the custom in those days, before the introduction of the modern extravagance of filling the arena with wild beasts from all over the world, to seek out spectacular performances of all kinds; for one race with quadrigae [chariot drawn with four horses] and one bareback display scarcely took up an hour for the two events. In one of these displays, groups of about sixty young men [sometimes more in the more elaborate games] entered the arena under arms."

He then goes on to state, "Their act was to some extent an imitation of army maneuvers, but in other respects it demanded a more sophisticated skill than that of ordinary soldiers, and it had more in common with the style of gladiatorial combats After performing various evolutions they would form in order of battle, with shields massed together over their heads, the front rank standing, the second stooping a little, the third and fourth increasing their stoop, and the rear rank kneeling, the whole forming a 'tortoise' with a slope like the roof of a house.'"

What's being described is actually a classic Roman battle formation, in which shield formations in the front, with the shields raised tightly over the Romans' heads, created an impervious barrier. Romans would use this famed "tortoise" formation to essentially create a human tank that could march toward enemies even under a heavy onslaught of enemy arrows.

Livy then goes on to explain, "From this, two armed men would rush out, about fifty feet away from each other, and, after making threatening gestures at one another they would climb up from the bottom to the top of the 'tortoise' over the close packed shields. They would then perform a kind of skirmish along the outer edges of the 'tortoise,' or engage in combat in the center leaping about just as if on solid ground." This testimony bears perfect witness to the pomp and circumstance of military reenactments during the Roman games.

Emperor Claudius, who reigned from 41 to 54 CE, was an emperor particularly keen on celebrating Rome's military prowess by staging massive triumphal displays. During these events, which recreated Rome's triumph over Britain, Claudius ditched his traditional imperial garb for the dress of a grand general of the Roman armed forces in an effort to further solidify his image as the most powerful man in the Roman Empire.

However, it was the naval battles that seemed to have captured the Roman public's imagination like no other. Many of these mock naval battles, or as the Romans called them, *naumachiae*, were held at Fucine Lake (also known as Lake Fucino) in central Italy. In 52 CE, Emperor Claudius held a grand affair on the lake in which two whole fleets, consisting of some twenty-five ships each, waged war against each other.

Although these are referred to as "mock naval battles," the fighting was real since tens of thousands of condemned prisoners were forced to do battle with each other across the decks of these crafts or even on wooden bridges erected over the waters. To make sure that these naval gladiators put on a good show and didn't try to run off, the whole lake was ringed with Roman troops.

Some of the troops even actively manned catapults at the perimeter of the lake, more than ready to bombard a craft with stone boulders if the pilots of that craft were to go off script and attempt to race to the shore to escape. During Claudius's exercise in 52 CE, the condemned men apparently put on a very good show for the masses in attendance of the Roman games that day.

And the preparation for all of this was immense in scope. Roman historian Tacitus described it as thus, "Nearly at this date, the tunneling of the mountain between Lake Fucinus and the river Liris had been achieved; and, in order that the impressive character of the work might be viewed by a larger number of the visitants, a naval battle was arranged upon the lake itself."

Tacitus then goes on to say, "Claudius equipped triremes, quadriremes, and nineteen thousand combatants: the lists he surrounded with rafts, so as to leave no unauthorized points of escape, but reserved space enough in the center to display the vigor of the rowing, the arts of the helmsman, the impetus of the galleys, and the usual incidents of an engagement. On the rafts were stationed companies and squadrons of the praetorian cohorts, covered by a breastwork from which to operate their catapults and ballistae: the rest of the lake was occupied by marines with decked vessels."

Tacitus then concludes, "He and Agrippina presided, the one in a gorgeous military cloak, the other—not far distant—in a Greek mantle of cloth of gold. The battle, though one of criminals, was contested with the spirit and courage of freemen; and, after much blood had flowed, the combatants were exempted from destruction." Yes, Claudius was so pleased with the efforts that pardons were in order.

Claudius's successor, Nero, held even more extravagant mock military games. He was known to start off his games with an animal hunt before flooding the entire arena so that reenactments of great naval battles could be displayed. After this, he would then drain the arena and host gladiator matches on the dry ground before flooding it once again just so he could invite the spectators to a lavish banquet held on board a huge floating craft.

As mad and deranged as Emperor Nero has been characterized to be over the centuries, he certainly knew how to please Roman audiences when it came to the Roman games. But not everyone appreciated his efforts.

Later, the Roman historian Tacitus in his *Annals* criticized the emperor, writing, "Nero himself now tried to make it appear that Rome was his favorite abode. He gave feasts in public places as if the whole city were his own home. But the most prodigal and notorious banquet was given by Tigellinus. To avoid repetitious accounts of extravagance, I shall describe it, as a model of its kind."

Tacitus then further elaborated, "The entertainment took place on a raft constructed on Marcus Agrippa's lake. It was towed about by other vessels, with gold and ivory fittings. Their rowers were degenerates, assorted according to age and vice. Tigellinus had also collected birds and animals from remote countries, and even the products of the ocean. On the quays were brothels stocked with high ranking ladies. Opposite them could be seen naked prostitutes, indecently posturing and gesturing. At nightfall the woods and houses nearby echoed with singing and blazed with lights."

Emperor Titus later inaugurated the Roman games at the Roman Colosseum in 80 CE with some rather extravagant reenactments of his own. He began the show with the slaughter of animals in massive beast hunts, which was quite common at the time. But what really galvanized the masses was the military reenactments at the end. As the Roman writer and historian Cassius Dio recorded, "There was a battle between cranes and also between four elephants; animals both tame and wild were slain to the number of nine thousand; and women [not those of any prominence, however] took part in dispatching them. As for the men, several fought in single combat and several groups contended together both in infantry and naval battles."

Dio then continues, "For Titus suddenly filled the same theatre with water and brought in horses and bulls and some other domesticated animals that had been taught to behave in the liquid element just as on land. He also brought in people on ships, who engaged in a sea-fight there, impersonating the Corcyraeans and Corinthians; and others gave a similar exhibition outside the city in the grove of Gaius and Lucius, a place which Augustus had once excavated for this very purpose. There, too, on the first day there was a gladiatorial exhibition and wild-beast hunt, the lake in front of the images having first been covered over with a platform of planks and wooden stands erected around it. On the second day there was a horse-race, and on the third day a naval battle between three thousand men, followed by an infantry battle. The 'Athenians' conquered the 'Syracusans' [these were the names the combatants used], made a landing on the islet and assaulted and captured a wall that had been constructed around the monument. These were the spectacles that were offered, and they continued for a hundred days."

All of these grand displays of raw power that Cassius Dio describes were meant to demonstrate the greatness of Rome in general and Titus in particular. Probably the most infamous Roman "triumphal" display over an enemy came in the aftermath of the so-called "Jewish War" that destroyed the Jewish temple in Jerusalem and brought countless Jewish freedom fighters, who were now prisoners of war, directly to Rome and its Roman games. Roman Jewish historian Flavius Josephus recorded how these prisoners of war eventually became fodder for military-inspired Roman games under Titus.

Josephus relates, "During his stay at Caesarea Maritima, Titus celebrated his brother's birthday with great splendor, reserving for his honor much of the punishment of his Jewish captives. For the number of those destroyed in contests with wild beasts or with one another or in the flames was more than two thousand five hundred. Yet to the Romans, notwithstanding the myriad forms in which their victims perished, all this seemed too light a penalty. After this, [Titus] Caesar passed to Beirut, a city of Phoenicia and a Roman colony."

He then furthers stresses, "Here he [Titus] made a longer stay, displaying still greater magnificence on the occasion of his father's birthday, both in the costliness of the spectacles and in the ingenuity of the various other items of expenditure. Multitudes of captives perished in the same manner as before. Leaving from Beirut, Titus exhibited costly spectacles in all the cities of Syria he passed through, making his Jewish captives serve to display their own destruction."

It's interesting to note that along with the famous Colosseum in Rome, the Romans were in the habit of building temporary amphitheaters in far-flung corners all over the Roman Empire. These amphitheaters were often built on the frontiers, and for the Romans, they had militaristic as well as entertainment value. These constructions were often built by the soldiers themselves and doubled as training grounds for the troops stationed in those frontier regions.

The structures proved to be great propaganda platforms for the Romans as it pertained to demonstrating Roman power to subjected peoples. Newly conquered groups would even be invited to attend martial demonstrations of Roman military might. These served not only as a means to entertain and pacify the locals but also to clearly demonstrate to them the power of their overlords.

The structures were also important as a backup fortification should the local populace of the frontier regions get restless and turn aggressive against the Roman occupiers. Such military-styled amphitheaters can be found in Britain, France, and many other frontier regions held by the former Roman Empire.

Chapter 7 – Commodus: The Emperor Turned Gladiator

"While all Greece honored an Olympic victor and to go onstage as a spectacle for the people was held in no way shameful to them, all these things are considered by us to be infamia, humilia—and far from honorable."

-Roman biographer, Cornelius Nepos

Roman Emperor Lucius Aurelius Commodus came into this world on August 31ˢᵗ, 161. Upon becoming emperor in 176, Commodus is said to have boasted that he was "born both man and emperor." This was in reference to the fact that he was the son of Marcus Aurelius, with whom he co-reigned from 176 to 180, the year Aurelius perished. Afterward, Commodus would continue to rule Rome on his own, with his reign only coming to an end in the year 192.

Interestingly enough, however, his political enemies long whispered that Commodus wasn't the son of an emperor at all but rather was the product of an illicit union between his mother, Faustina, and a gladiator. The gladiators (at least those who truly tried to compete in the ring) were the heartthrobs and bad boys of Rome, and some of them really did have affairs with noble Roman women.

But it has not been determined if Commodus's mother was one of them. Nevertheless, it is rather astonishing how fascinated Emperor Commodus would become with the Roman games and gladiatorial combat. In fact, he would insist on throwing himself personally into the ring. It seems that Commodus's first taste of Roman spectacle occurred as a child when his father's co-emperor (and Commodus's namesake), Lucius Aurelius Verus, held a military triumph to commemorate Rome's recent victories over the empire's eastern enemies, the Parthians.

This triumphal event imbued much of the past pageantry of the Roman games, with sacred white bulls being marched by the spectators as they were led to their ultimate destination—to become a sacrifice to the Roman deity Jupiter. These were followed by the spoils of war, the various goods and treasures pilfered from the enemy, which were paraded before all. Next, actual prisoners of war were showcased, all of them marching off toward the games held in the Roman Colosseum.

Co-emperors Marcus Aurelius and Lucius Aurelius Verus were both in attendance, and more than likely, so was little Commodus. And if so, it was likely this event that heralded his first exposure to the excitement of the Roman games. His father, Marcus Aurelius, was not a fan of the games, especially detesting the blood sports that often took place. In one incredible instance, it is said that Marcus was so disturbed by the pain inflicted on an acrobatic performer who accidentally fell to the ground that he had specially cushioned matting placed on the floor of the arena to soften any such future falls. He is also said to have occasionally ordered the gladiators to fight with blunted weapons to prevent the spilling of blood.

Marcus Aurelius, a man known for his stoic philosophy and moderation, did not wish to see violence in the ring. Commodus, on the other hand, would grow incredibly fond of the Roman games and all of its bloody trappings. It wasn't long before he himself began to train his body in anticipation of participating in the games himself.

In fact, history tells us that it was while Commodus was training at a "wrestling school" as a young man that he faced his first brush with death. It wasn't due to the strong arms of a fellow wrestler that Commodus nearly perished but rather the sudden onset of illness. He was said to have been "seized by a hot fever." Fortunately, for Commodus, he had one of the best doctors at his disposal—the Roman physician Galen.

As young Commodus's health seemed to rapidly deteriorate, Galen quickly took charge of the situation, having the future emperor "gargle" a concoction of "honey and rose water." The treatment seemed to do the trick, and to the amazement of everyone, Commodus's health was restored. And in that fateful year of 176, when Commodus first became co-emperor with his father Marcus Aurelius, he got to see firsthand how important the Roman games were to the people and to Roman political governance itself.

For it was that fall that he joined his father for an appearance at the games in Rome, in which his father gave a public speech about Rome's political state. Not only did Aurelius speak, but the crowd also answered back, requesting gratuities from the emperor. Even though the Roman Empire was cash-strapped at the time, Marcus Aurelius obliged, generously handing out gold coins to the crowd.

Commodus learned a valuable lesson that day as to both the power of the Roman games and the power the spectators had over the emperor. Shortly thereafter, on December 23rd, 176, a special "triumphal chariot race" was held, in which Commodus played a part. Here, Commodus paraded around the track in grand display. He also handed out gold coinage and other prizes to the spectators. Just a few years later, in 180, Commodus's father and co-emperor, Marcus Aurelius, passed, making Commodus the sole ruler of the realm.

Commodus had a lot on his plate, but he still had time to indulge in gladiatorial contests. In addition to that, he also began heavily training for them himself. Fascinated with the Roman games, Commodus took on the trappings of a gladiator known as the Secutor. These gladiators were heavily armed with solid helmets that granted limited vision. They also came equipped with an oblong shield, otherwise known as a *scutum*, as well as a short sword known as a *gladius*.

This type of gladiator was often paired with the Retiarius, who wielded a net and a trident and usually attempted to poke, prod, and parry their opponents, all while attempting to ensnare them in their net. Before ever going into the arena himself, Commodus quietly trained in private, competing with a gladiator in private sessions outside of the Colosseum.

These were friendly matches in which carefully selected associates would practice with him. Rather than duels to the death, the rounds would typically end with his opponent indicating defeat by removing their shield and lifting their index finger into the air. This would signal that Commodus had won the match, and he would stop engaging his opponent. Not everything always worked out as planned, however, and it is said that Commodus actually killed one of his training partners by accident on at least one occasion. He also apparently injured a few others. Some accounts report that he accidentally chopped off a nose in one instance and an ear in another.

Along with these instances of one-on-one combat, Commodus also practiced hunting animals on his own personal training grounds. The activity that probably took up the most of his time, however, was his practice runs on the track, racing chariots.

For this, he spared no expense, buying himself the best equipment, uniform, and horses for the enterprise. In addition to using his own private estate as his training grounds, Commodus is said to have even practiced at the official gladiator training school, located just outside of the Colosseum. Soon enough, however, Commodus himself would be performing in the arena as a gladiator. This horrified much of the Roman elite since it was considered scandalous for a noble Roman—let alone an emperor—to participate in the Roman games.

Nevertheless, Commodus took center stage in the Colosseum on wild beast hunts and in gladiatorial matches. It was the latter of which that would be the most shocking since Commodus had a penchant of wanting to be paired with disabled veterans or disadvantaged Roman citizens who were missing a leg so they couldn't walk. He also sought out those missing an arm or two, as they couldn't properly defend themselves. He would easily run through these poor, hapless souls with his sword.

Considering how much Commodus sought to be a heroic figure (he often likened himself to a reincarnated Hercules), it's appalling how cowardly his exploits in the arena truly were. Rome's economy began to suffer in the meantime due to the extravagance that Commodus routinely made use of during his cameos at the Roman games. Things became so bad, in fact, that the Roman currency became devalued.

Finally, in 190, Commodus, having grown weary of having to govern his empire (it took too much time away from training to be a gladiator), decided to hand over all daily governance to his top advisor, a former slave by the name of Cleander. Shortly after Cleander took over, the Roman Empire was rocked by famine.

Commodus was then conveniently able to blame the whole fiasco on Cleander, insisting that he was in charge of such matters. As the rancor against Cleander built among the populace, Commodus attended a series of Roman games during which he readily listened while an angry public clamored against Cleander.

The games were indeed an allowed space for the public to lodge their grievances to the emperor. It has been theorized, however, that much of this displeasure was organized behind the scenes in a highly orchestrated attempt to malign Cleander since he would have been officiating the games. The Roman historian Herodian seemed to capture this sentiment at work. He noted at the time how the public had "organized themselves in the theatres and shouted insults at him [Cleander] all together."

At any rate, the theatrics worked, and Commodus stepped up to answer the public's outcry against his top manager of affairs. Shortly after, he had Cleander summarily executed and his head placed on the tip of a spear for all to see in order to satiate the displeasure of the Roman public.

It has been said that Rome's people cried out for "bread and circuses" during this period. The wily Commodus, realizing a grain shortage would lead to a bread shortage, must have been hoping that the populace would be happy with at least one circus if they couldn't have the other. And in the year 192, in pursuit of providing the latter, Commodus hosted his famous Plebeian Games.

Here, Commodus not only hosted extravagant Roman games for the masses but also took center stage. Every morning at the start of the games, he would galivant around for a grand animal hunt in which he killed countless wild beasts by way of his spear and bow and arrows. There was more to come, however. By late December, it had been announced that the emperor himself would kick off the year 193 by hosting Roman games in which he would personally perform as a gladiator.

He would not live to see the day, though, since the immediate backlash that such talk sparked led to renewed conspiratorial intrigue against Commodus. All this conspiratorial talk would lead to Commodus's death on December 31st, 192. First, his mistress tried to poison him, but when this attempt failed, a trained wrestler was called in to finish Commodus off. It must have seemed ironically fitting that his life was ended in a form of martial combat straight out of the Roman games that Commodus so loved.

Chapter 8 – Chariot Races: The Roman Indy 500

"For at first there were only two colors: white and red. White was sacred to Winter because of the whiteness of its snow; red, to Summer because of the redness of the sun. But afterwards, when both love of pleasure and superstition had grown apace, some dedicated the red to Mars, others the white to the Zephyrs, the green to Mother Earth or Spring, the blue to Sky and Sea or Autumn."

-Christian writer, Tertullian

In the United States, the start of summer isn't complete without a running of the famous Indianapolis 500. For those who aren't aware of this American tradition, it consists of a four-hour-long race around a circular track by Formula One race cars hurling about at terrific speeds. Fans flock to Indianapolis, Indiana, from all over to see the so-called "Greatest Spectacle in Racing."

Along with the thrill of the speed, some (even though they might not admit it) are no doubt excited to see some of the inevitable car crashes as well. And it was very much the same in the days of Rome when folks would gather around a track to see not cars but horse-drawn chariots rushing around a race track. Romans would pick the chariot drivers they wished to win and root for their heroes. They would also stand and gape at the many dangerous and deadly wrecks that occurred.

But unlike the Indy 500, the Roman chariot racers didn't just crash on accident; sometimes, they would intentionally force each other off the road. It was quite common for these violent chariot races to end in both fatalities and severe injuries. Chariot racers employed fast yet flimsy chariots that were not at all well protected. The strategy was to be fast and not get hit by your opponent, but one wrong turn or a swipe from an adversary could easily lead to a charioteer's doom.

Interestingly enough, chariot races were one of the first to employ specific teams. These teams were designated by four specific colors, such as blue, green, red, and white. Fans would root for their team from the stands, and they would do so quite vigorously. On some occasions, fans would even spar with each other, and riots would erupt between fans of one team and another. During one chariot race, these riotous fans were so darned obnoxious that a Roman emperor in attendance—Emperor Vitellius—actually had them killed on the spot simply because they kept heckling the team he liked.

The race itself consisted of some seven laps around the track. There were seven egg-shaped, wooden objects placed around the track, and every time a lap was finished, one would be taken down to mark its completion. The races lasted for about fifteen minutes in total, and as many as twenty-four races could take place in one sitting. The location of chariot races was typically in a circus, and the famous Circus Maximus was a fan favorite. The term "Circus Maximus" basically translates as "biggest circus." This was the prime venue for racing chariots around a huge, circular track.

For the Romans, chariot racing was often the main event of their games. And according to writer and historian Roland Auguet, the Roman people actually believed that their very first chariot race dated all the way back to Rome's mythic founder, Romulus.

For those who are not aware of the legends behind Rome's founding, it is said that Romulus and his twin brother Remus were children of a woman named Rhea Silvia and the god of Mars. There's a lot to unpack in this Roman myth, but for the sake of simplicity, let's just say that somewhere in the twisting tides of fate, Romulus and Remus ended up being abandoned and raised by a "she-wolf." Yes, according to Roman legend, the mythic founders of Rome were literally thrown to the wolves. So, the story goes, it was actually the miraculous intervention of this she-wolf that saved these abandoned demigods' lives.

A conflict later erupted between Romulus, and he killed his brother. According to legend, a whole lot of drama ensued, but eventually, it's said that Romulus founded Rome. And when he did so, he was sure to host a few Roman games along the way. Writer and Roman researcher Roland Auguet is of the opinion that the original races were not chariot races as much as they were simple contests on horseback or even muleback.

By the time of Emperor Nero, however, an elaborate track for chariot races at the Circus Maximus was well established. It was established, but perhaps vulnerable would be a better description. The structures around the track were largely made of wood, and these would go up in flames during the Great Fire of Rome, which occurred in 64 CE, during Emperor Nero's reign.

As mentioned earlier in this book, it still remains somewhat unclear as to what may have caused this fire. Nero infamously blamed the Christians, but there is no evidence of any Christian saboteur. Others, in the meantime, would soon turn on Nero himself, theorizing that the ruler had purposely set fires as a form of ad-hoc demolition in order to remodel the Circus Maximus. The razed structures did indeed allow Nero to greatly modify and enhance the track when he built upon the ashes.

But there's no more evidence of Nero being an arsonist than there is that the Christians were. Nevertheless, Nero, who would commit suicide just a few years later, would go down in history as the one who "fiddled while Rome burned." Nero, despite his faults, was indeed a champion of the Roman games, chariot races in particular.

Nero, as mentioned, expanded the track at the Circus Maximus, and he also increased the number of games at the track, going from the standard twelve to a full twenty-four. Each of these matches was initiated by a game of chance or the so-called "drawing of lots." A charioteer standing in for each of the four teams (red, blue, green, and white) would cast lots to determine the starting positions. Once in place, these chariot racers would wait for their cue to take off, which was typically a piece of white fabric being thrown onto the track.

The chariots would then take off in a furious storm of pounding hoofbeats and grinding chariot wheels. These sounds were accompanied by the screaming spectators shouting out encouragement to their team of choice. The Roman Christian chronicler Tertullian described the experience, saying, "The praetor is too slow for [the fans]; all the time their eyes are rolling as though in rhythm with the lots he shakes up in his urn. Then they await the signal with bated breath; one outcry voices the common madness. Recognize the madness from their foolish behavior. 'He has thrown it!' they shout; everyone tells everybody else what all of them seen just that moment."

Tertullian seems to be annoyed at fans shouting their play-by-plays after the fact. But it's not any different than football fans at the Superbowl today, screaming that a team has made a touchdown when all the fans, as well as every TV in America, had already borne witness to it. Fans state the obvious not so much to inform but rather to punctuate the moment. Ancient spectators of the chariot races with their outbursts were no doubt doing much the same thing.

But spectators of the Roman games would take things to a whole other level through a little something called "curse tablets." Fans would literally try to invoke curses on the charioteers of the rival team. Writer and historian Alison Futrell has made note of one of these curse tablets found at a race track. The words of the curse tablet invoke an underworld deity and are glaringly blunt in purpose.

The tablet reads, "Most holy Lord Charakteres, tie up, bind the feet, the hands, the nerves, the eyes, the knees, the courage, the leaps, the whip, the victory and the crowning of Porphyras and Hapsicrates, who are in the middle-left, as well as his co-drivers of the Blue-colors in the stable of Eugenius. At the moment when they are about to compete may they not squeeze over, may they not collide, may they not extend, may they not force [us] out, may they not overtake, may they not break off [in a new direction] for the entire day when they are about to race. May they be broken, may they be draffed, may they be destroyed."

"May they be destroyed?" Really? Fans putting curses on rival players is more than a bit fanatical, to say the least. But that's just how seriously Romans took their games. It's interesting to note that in the later Roman Empire, after Christianity became the official religion of the state, such things were forbidden. But even so, fans would continue to try and hex their rivals in secret.

This was indicated in 364 CE when the son of Hilarinus, a charioteer, was accused of casting spells against his father's opponents. Alison Futrell quotes one Ammianus Marcellinus, who charged that Hilarinus had his son "instructed in certain secret practices forbidden by law, in order to use his help at home without other witnesses he was condemned to death."

The most dramatic part of the race was always the final lap. Here, the chariot racers were often neck and neck, and when one was desperately trying to edge out another, they would often attempt to literally run their opponents off the road. This was the moment in which these Roman games turned ugly, with chariot racers trying to grind their chariot wheels into the wheels of their opponents, all in an effort to break the wheel's axle, sending their adversary crashing to the side.

These crashes not only knocked the chariot racer out of the race, but on occasion, they also turned lethal. There are indeed many instances of charioteers falling from an out-of-control chariot and getting trampled by horses. Crashed chariots were called *naufragia*, which literally translates as "shipwrecks." Fans loved this drama and sat in rapt attention.

According to writer and researcher Roland Auguet, along with enjoying the show on the track, these spectators also enjoyed each other. The comradery was great among fans, especially among male and female fans. The audiences at the race track, you see, were not segregated by sex as the Colosseum would later be. And the track actually became known as a great place for lovers to hook up. According to some accounts, many of these spectators even consummated their love in the stands.

Roman poet Ovid humorously captures this experience at the Roman games in his whimsical piece called *The Art of Love*. Here, Ovid humorously instructs his readers, "Furthermore, don't overlook the meetings when horses are running; in the crowds at the track opportunity waits. There is no need for a code of finger-signals or nodding. Sit as close as you like; no one will stop you at all. In fact, you will have to sit close—that's one of the rules, at a race track. Whether she likes it or not, contact is part of the game."

After these remarks, Ovid then advises his readers, "Try to find something in common, to open the conversation; don't care too much what you say, just so that everyone hears. Ask her, 'Whose colors are those?'—that's good for an opening gambit. Put your own bet down fast, on whatever she plays. Then, when the gods come along in procession, ivory golden, outcheer every young man, shouting for Venus, the queen. Often it happens that dust may fall on the cloak of the lady. If such dust should fall, carefully brush it away. Even if there's no dust, brush off whatever there isn't. Any excuse will do: why do you think you have hands? If her cloak hangs low, and the ground is getting it dirty, gather it up with care, lift it a little, so! Maybe by the way of reward, and not without her indulgence, you'll be able to see ankle or possible knee. Then look around and glare at the fellow who's sitting behind you, don't let him crowd his knees into her delicate spine. Girls, as everyone knows, adore these little attentions: getting the cushion just right, that's in itself quite an art; yes, and it takes a technique in making a fan of your program or in fixing a stool under the feet of a girl."

Yes, more than a few Roman men were no doubt eager to see a little "ankle or possible knee" from female Roman fans. Ovid is obviously being humorous here, but such things certainly weren't without precedent. And romance at the games had worked quite well for none other than the Roman dictator Sulla during the days of the Roman Republic, for it was under similar circumstances in the stands of the Roman games that he met his future wife.

As the Roman historian Plutarch tells us, "There happened to be sitting near Sulla a very beautiful woman of a most distinguished family. Her name was Valeria. As she passed behind Sulla, she rested her hand on him, pulled off a little piece of wool from his toga and then went on to her seat. When Sulla looked round at her in surprise, she said, 'There's no reason to be surprised, Dictator. I only want to have a little bit of your good luck for myself.'"

Plutarch then goes on to say, "Sulla was far from displeased. After this they kept glancing at each other constantly turning their heads to look, and exchanging smiles. And in the end negotiations began for marriage." It seems that Sulla and his admirer were caught on the Roman equivalent of the "kiss cam" on the jumbotron. Everyone within radius now knew that Sulla and his admirer were quite smitten.

Besides the spectacle of racing and the spectacle of love-making, there were also additional acts on display, such as acrobatic circus-styled horse riding. It was a must-see event. And at this Roman version of the Indy 500, Romans were pleased with the spectacle on the track just as much as they were with the spectacle of each other.

Chapter 9 – The Gladiatrix: Female Gladiators in the Arena

"Illustrious Fame used to sing of the lion laid low in Nemea's spacious vale, Hercules' work. Let ancient testimony be silent, for after your shows, Caesar, we have now seen such things done by women's valor."

-Roman poet, Marcus Valerius Martialis

Although Rome, like much of the rest of the world at the time, was definitely a patriarchal society, strangely enough, there was some level of equality in the arena, as women were also allowed to fight. Female gladiators were always a good draw for spectators. Roman Emperor Nero, who reigned in the latter half of the 1ˢᵗ century CE, was among those who enjoyed the exploits of women warriors. Nero loved all things theatrical, and the extra flourish of female fighters appealed to his flair for the dramatic.

But not all Romans approved. Since gladiators were considered a lower class, it was considered dishonorable for women to participate. Laws were even enacted in an attempt to dissuade some of these more daring women from doing so. In fact, in 11 CE, the Roman Senate issued a *Senatus Consultum* or "Decree of the Senate," which stipulated age restrictions on women participating in the Roman games. These efforts were apparently made to keep youthful girls from being lured into the games.

One of the harshest critics of female participation in the Roman games was Roman historian Suetonius, who felt it dishonorable both to watch and for women to participate. Yet, the participation and spectating of these gladiatrices (feminine plural of gladiatrix) were fairly widespread. Roman Emperor Domitian, for one, seemed to enjoy female participation in the Roman games a great deal. Domitian, in fact, was known to host gladiatorial battles in which female warriors fought what in those days were termed "dwarves."

Yes, there wasn't much room for political correctness or even just plain correctness in the days of the Roman colosseums. The Roman citizens enjoyed such sideshows as well, and the arena was always packed for these events. It wasn't until the rule of Roman Emperor Septimius Severus in the third century CE that female participation in the Roman games was scaled back. Septimius Severus did not think it fitting for women to fight and eventually banned the practice outright.

There are plenty of records to indicate that female gladiators were a known quantity prior to the imperial ban. Emperor Domitian was the first emperor to preside over the fully-functioning Roman Colosseum, and the Roman poet Statius noted that Domitian sanctioned the participation of female fighters, who were associated with the legendary Amazons of Greek mythology.

Another Roman poet by the name of Marcus Valerius Martialis (better known simply as Martial) also alluded to Domitian's penchant for equality of the sexes in the arena when he wrote, "It is not enough that warrior Mars serves you in unconquered arms, Caesar. Venus herself serves you too."

Roman writer Juvenal held a pretty dismal view of all this as well. And in one of his epic written remarks on the subject, he stated, "What modesty can you expect in a woman who wears a helmet, abjures her own sex, and delights in feats of strength? Yet she would not choose to be a man, knowing the superior joys of womanhood. What a fine thing for a husband, at an auction of his wife's effects, to see her belt and armlets and plumes put up for sale, with a gaiter that covers half the left leg; or if she fights another sort of battle, how charmed you will be to see your young wife disposing of her greaves!"

Juvenal then goes on to declare, "Yet these are the women who find the thinnest of thin robes too hot for them; whose delicate flesh is chafed by the finest of silk tissue. See how she pants as she goes through her prescribed exercises; how she bends under the weight of her helmet; how big and coarse are the bandages which enclose her haunches; and then laugh when she lays down her arms and shows herself to be a woman!"

Juvenal and other Romans obviously held the practice of female gladiators in contempt and ridiculed the very notion of women participating in the Roman games. But, nevertheless, women were also fans of the Roman games, and in some circumstances, they did indeed actively participate. It seems the Romans were largely inspired by Greek tales of female warriors, and even the Greek pantheon of gods that made their way to Rome was most likely an inspiration for strong, robust, fighting women.

Pre-Christian Romans, after all, were known to have widely venerated the Greek goddesses of Athena and Minerva, who are both depicted as warriors who wielded weapons and engaged in battle. The Romans also looked toward recently conquered Britain, where female fighters were a very real part of the conflict. The Celtic Queen Boudica infamously led the Celts against the Romans around the year 60 CE. Although Boudica was ultimately defeated, being killed in the conflict, the conflict left scores of Roman soldiers, as well as civilians, in a bloody heap, buried in the rubble of what were once mighty Roman settlements, such as London.

London would be rebuilt, however, and in the restored city, new arenas would be forged in which Roman games would be played for the Roman settlers. And in these arenas, it wasn't long before a few women emerged to represent the mighty Celtic women who had fallen during Boudica's rebellion. The Romans were apparently both frightened and fascinated by the spectacle of these fierce female fighters.

Women who were either forced into the life of a gladiator or even those who chose it of their own volition would have been part of what was termed the *familia gladiatorum*. This was a special troupe of gladiators, which was controlled by a head honcho who managed the gladiatorial games in which this particular group of gladiators took part. Some troupe managers were harsh and brutal, but others could be somewhat kind and even protective of the gladiators who participated in the games under their watch. There are stories of these managers being particularly protective of female fighters under their care. But this, of course, was more likely the exception than the rule.

Much of the time, the handlers of the gladiatrix were about as callous and uncaring as they could be for those under their charge. This was demonstrated in 66 CE when, during the reign of Emperor Nero, Ethiopian female gladiators, as well as their own children, were made to do battle during a Roman game staged for the pleasure of the visiting Armenian Potentate, King Tridates I.

These Ethiopian gladiatrices apparently engaged in wild beast hunts, as well as combat with each other. It seems that while many Roman men did not take the idea of female fighters seriously, there were more than enough who were entertained by the sheer novelty of having women compete in the Roman games. And in many cases, the exotic nature of female combatants was reduced to an entirely absurd sideshow.

Under Domitian, for example, the gladiatrices often fought what the Romans called "dwarfs." Just imagine tall, muscular women locked in mortal combat with knife-wielding men of hereditarily short stature. Roman poet Publius Papinius Statius (better known as Statius) captures the absurdity of the moment. Statius chronicled the event, writing, "Women untrained to the rudis [a wooden sword given as an award to the victor] take their stand, daring, how recklessly, virile battles! You would think Termodon's bands were furiously fighting by Tanais or barbarous Phasis. Then comes a bold array of dwarves, whose term of growth abruptly ended has bound them once and for all into a knotted lump. They give and suffer wounds and threaten death—with fists how tiny! Father Mars and Bloody Virtus laugh, and cranes, waiting to swoop on scattered booty, marvel at the fiercer pugilists."

It's a little unclear what exactly Statius means by "knotted lump," but the contempt he has for the whole affair is pretty clear. But one of the most famous accounts of gladiatorial women in combat occurred in the 2nd century when it is said that two women referred to as "Achillia" and "Amazon" participated in the Roman games. The combatants seem to be what is known as *provactrices*.

Rather than being in one of the set categories of gladiators with specific gear that contrasted with their opponents' category, such as a Thraex and a Retiarii, the provactrices were participants who wore identical weapons and armor. Both female fighters are depicted with the same "leather-bound manicae" on their arms and the same type of "pleated and belted loincloths." They also had the same type of offensive weapons, with each participant wielding a "short sword." Their helmets, in the meantime, were cast to the side, displaying their similar tightly plaited hair wrapped around their heads. The climactic battle between these two is said to have ended in a draw, in which both women's lives were spared.

This strange age of female fighters would come to an end when Roman Emperor Septimius Severus banned the practice altogether in 200 CE.

Chapter 10 – Rome's Animal-Based Games

"Who does not reckon among the things of greatest interest the contests of gladiators and wild beasts, especially those which are given to you? But we, deeming that to see a man put to death is much the same as killing him, have abjured such spectacles."

-Christian writer, Athenagoras

This book has already covered, to some degree, the notion of wild animals being made part of the Roman games. The Romans used wild beasts to kill captives and even had gladiators battle them. Even Roman Emperor Commodus famously engaged wild beasts in the arena. But now, let's take a closer look at these animal-oriented games as a whole. Initially, the Romans held their main hunting games early in the day. This was the time the more respectable Romans were busy attending to their vocation. Thus, the fans present were most likely those without work or fresh-faced visitors to the city of Rome.

In many ways, the morning animal hunts were a warm-up for the later events that would be attended by the majority of the citizens later in the evening. Nevertheless, Roman authorities always made sure that the hunting games were elaborate and entertaining all the same. According to writer and historian Roland Auguet, the hunting games themselves took on a greater life of their own as the Roman Empire progressed. Soon the games were being held later in the afternoon with a larger crowd of Romans in attendance.

Auguet also cites archaeological inscriptions that have been uncovered that seem to suggest that some of these animal hunts not only lasted until the afternoon but actually went on for several days at a time. The animal hunting games seemed to really come into their own by the time of the Roman Colosseum, as the high ramparts of the building provided a protective structure for spectators.

Before the Colosseum, the animals were much less secure. Temporary structures were created, and in some cases, deep ditches were dug to create a barrier between fans and animals, but the risk of something going wrong was much greater. The Colosseum, on the other hand, finally provided an entirely safe atmosphere in which spectators could watch wild beasts running around the arena without any fear of them being able to charge the stands.

Later, even further measures were taken to provide security, such as huge nets being put in place to prevent even the slightest possibility of a lion leaping or climbing over barriers and attacking fans. Before the Colosseum, animals were showcased in outside circuses such as Nero's Circus Maximus. For many of these events of the early Roman Empire, the main draw was simply seeing wild exotic animals from foreign lands, as they were not native to Rome. In true circus form, some of these animals were event taught to do a trick or two by their trainers.

Going even further back, to the last days of the Roman Republic, Roman General Pompey held lavish animal-based games in 79 BCE in which elephants, recently imported from Africa, were put on display to the delight of Roman citizens. However, Pompey did more than just show his elephants off; he also had skilled hunters bring the beasts down. Men skilled in hurling javelins threw their weapons right into the elephants' heads when they were in mid-charge. This stopped many of the elephants in their tracks, but for others, the spears missed, and they kept running. These then had spears hurled at their feet, thereby immobilizing them. Still, a few hobbled around on their knees before finally giving up and huddling in the center of the arena, reduced to nothing more than a pathetic wreck. As the dying elephants wailed to the heavens, many Romans were stricken with guilt at the sight and pitied the poor animals. It was a rare showing of remorse, an emotional feeling that was usually not felt while watching the Roman games.

Roman historian Dio Cassius captured this rare moment, recalling, "The elephants had withdrawn from the combat covered with wounds and walked about with their trunks raised towards heaven, lamenting so bitterly as to give rise to the report that they did not do so by mere chance but were crying out against the oaths in which they had trusted when they crossed over from Libya and calling upon heaven to avenge them! It was recalled that they had refused to board the ships before they received a pledge under oath from their drivers that no harm should come to them."

It remains unclear where the Romans got the notion that the elephants were "given oaths" by their handlers that if they left their native Libya for Rome that they would be well cared for. But the superstitious spectators seemed to believe that the wailing of the dying and betrayed beasts was more than merely their last gasp of life but rather an omen of Rome's coming doom. It is true that the Roman Republic would soon be on the verge of collapse, giving way to the Roman Empire, but to say that Rome's problems were due to the vengeance of a group of mistreated circus elephants is a bit of a stretch.

Despite Pompey's brutal takedown of the elephants, simply seeing a lion, tiger, or elephant, especially during the initial Roman games, was a real novelty. The novelty soon wore off, though, and seeing these wild beasts was not enough. It was then that the animals were actively hunted, made to attack prisoners, or even made to attack each other. It was quite common for a half-starved lion and half-starved bear to be poked and prodded into the arena and sent crashing into each other.

The thrill of seeing these two super predators, both from different far-flung parts of the Roman Empire, doing battle was usually a crowd favorite. In the first variation, the animal hunt had adequately armed men pursuing and hunting down animals. This game had its dangers, and even though they were well provisioned, it wouldn't be uncommon for a hunter to be killed or maimed for life. These hunters were at least armed and stood a chance.

However, the condemned prisoners that were thrown to the lions most certainly did not. Condemned prisoners were executed by the beasts by either being thrown without arms into the arena to be mauled to death or even by being tied up so that there was zero chance of them putting up any kind of resistance. The aforementioned beast matches, where wild animals fight one another, were truly a spectacle.

According to writer Roland Auguet, the most impressive of these specimens was the rhino. Auguet relates how, despite the rhino's power, it was a challenging animal to provoke. Roman handlers in the ring had to poke and prod the beast to get it to charge, and much of the time, it would rather just stand back and stare off into space than actually engage its adversaries. But once it did, the charge of the rhino was something to behold.

Auguet tells us that "neither the bulls it eviscerated like straw dummies nor the bears it threw into the air like puppies" could stand up to the wild charge of a fully engaged rhino. The most frequent pairing, however, was that of a lion facing off against a bull. The bull was important in Greek and Roman mythology, and to see this epic creature so easily dispatched by a lion was stunning to Roman audiences.

Some other more unusual pairings have also been documented. For example, there were instances when crocodiles were pitted against lions, a match that must have been rather intense. Some depictions recovered also suggest seals were sicced on bears, which seems a little unusual, to say the least. If animals were not being pitted together, one other variant of beast matches was having predatory animals, such as lions or even a pack of wild dogs, being sicced upon a group of prey animals, such as deer. Such things clearly show the decadent indulgence of the Romans. These slaughtered deer could have fed an army, but after allowing wild lions or dogs to mow them down, the animals perished simply for the blood lust of watching spectators.

The beasts procured by the Romans did not always cooperate with their handlers, however, and on some occasions, they could not even be brought into the ring. During the reign of Nero, one such game was memorable because of this very fact. A group of obstinate lions absolutely refused to be forced into the arena and put up such a resistance that they had to be slaughtered on the spot. It's unclear what substitute act was given for the waiting fans, but the promised games involving lions obviously were not available that day.

Along with violence perpetrated against animals, there were occasions in which more lighthearted and even comedic acts were introduced. Rome's animal circuses, in fact, had their own acrobatic routines in which animal trainers cavorted around and displayed feats of great gymnastic skill before hungry beasts. There are accounts of animal trainers being protectively encased in baskets and buffeted about by bewildered bears, which were completely unable to render harm to those stuffed inside, to the amusement of the crowd.

Some animal handlers were also skilled in pole vaulting and were daring enough to stand in the middle of the arena as they faced down a charging bear or lion only to pole vault over the enraged animal's head at the very last minute. Only after the confused beast swiped at thin air did it realize that the animal trainer had vaulted safely out of reach. Writer and historian Roland Auguet has also pointed out that there were plenty of brilliant non-violent acts in which circus animals were taught benign amusements, such as animal trainers being able to get up close and personal with docile big cats, even giving them a kiss or two, without the beast getting hostile in the process.

Elephants were also taught to "dance" and cavort about in an amusing manner. If legends and folktales are to be believed, there are also some amusing instances that occurred seemingly of their own accord. The tale of Androcles and the lion is one of them. This tale alleges that a lion befriended a condemned man in the arena rather than eating him. Although most today would say the story is a complete myth, in ancient Rome, it was related as if it might have actually occurred. In fact, Roman writer Apion (he was originally from Egypt but carried out his later work in Rome) insisted that he witnessed this event himself.

At any rate, according to legend, the condemned man Androcles had previously made nice to a lion when he was hiding out in the wilderness. Androcles was hiding in a cave when a lion popped up and displayed a wounded paw. Androcles took the bloody paw and pulled a giant thorn out of it. The lion was supposedly grateful and began to do Androcles's bidding, bringing meat back to the cave to sustain the man.

Androcles was captured shortly thereafter, however, and he was brought to the arena. The audience was supposedly shocked to see the lion who was ordered to attack the prisoner instead lick the prisoner's feet. A leopard was dispatched shortly thereafter, but the lion came bounding up and killed the leopard, fiercely protecting Androcles.

This is all well and good for myths and legends, but what do we know for sure about the animal-based games? For one thing, it's certain that a whole lot of animals were killed. It's documented in Roman records that on the opening day of the Roman Colosseum alone, some nine thousand animals were slaughtered. Even if this figure has been somehow inflated or exaggerated, it suggests that even if the real amount was less than nine thousand, it must have been at least in the thousands. And even if it were only one thousand slain animals, that number of dead beasts on the arena floor is hard to fathom.

Chapter 11 – Roman Theater in the Roman Games

"Likewise, we renounce your public shows just as we do their origins which we know were begotten of superstition, while we are completely aloof from those matters with which they are concerned. Our tongues, our eyes, our ears have nothing to do with the madness of the circus, the shamefulness of the theater, the brutality of the arena, the vanity of the gymnasium. How, then, do we offend you? If we prefer different pleasures, if we do not want to be amused, that is our loss—if loss there be—not yours."

-Christian writer, Tertullian

Romans loved theater. They had inherited the tradition from the Greeks and made it their own. But once they were made part of the Roman games, the length that the Romans would go to in their dramatic arts was startling. Oftentimes, the Romans would reenact famous plays in the arena with prisoners playing the part of condemned characters. Amy Zoll, in her book *Gladiatrix: The True Story of History's Unknown Woman Warrior*, rightfully described these reenactments as being the Roman equivalent of snuff films.

For even though the Romans did not have the technology to film these grotesque events, just like their modern counterpart, they were narratives in which a captive is forced to act out a part that ultimately leads to their demise. One favorite was reenactments of the myth of Orpheus, who supposedly could "soothe the savage beast." Promoters of the games would allow for reenactments that would put a condemned individual into the role of Orpheus, who was then forced to play the lyre in front of authentically savage beasts. Yet, when the condemned were made to play for lions, tigers, and bears in the arena, to the absolute delight of jeering spectators, rather than soothe the beasts' fury, they were rather predictably mauled to death. It must have been a pure streak of sadism that brought pleasure to see a man attempt to play a soothing musical instrument only to be struck down by a wild animal.

Having a condemned man play Hercules was rather popular too. At first glance, it might have seemed nice for a prisoner to be able to play a Greek hero like Hercules, but the end for Hercules was not very pretty. According to Greek myth, Hercules ended his own life by setting himself on fire. The grand finale of a portrayal of Hercules by the condemned would end in such a manner.

The prisoner would have been given a tunic covered in a highly flammable material called pitch and would then have been set ablaze for the final act. It was a jolly good show for the Roman spectators to watch as the burning man ran around the arena. These spectators were uncaring and completely oblivious to the pain and suffering the condemned must have felt in those last few moments of life.

Another fan favorite was to have a condemned woman play the part of Rome's version of the evil stepmother Dirce from the Greek play *Antiope*, who ends up perishing after being tied to the horns of a bull. This feat was reenacted live in the arena, with terrible results.

Another reenactment that shows the Romans' strange fascination with bulls is the mythological story of Pasiphae. Pasiphae is a character who is said to have had sex with a bull. It was this union that supposedly gave rise to the half-man/half-bull minotaurs of Greek mythology. In the Roman games, these scenes were disturbingly reenacted by having a condemned female prisoner stuffed inside a "wooden bull" while a real one was coerced into having its way with her. Needless to say, the victim of this bizarre stunt did not survive the bull's efforts. The Roman poet Martial made mention of this sorry event in his famous *Book of Spectacles*.

In reference to the event, Martial had declared, "Believe that Pasiphae was mated to the Cretan bull: we have seen it, the old-time myth is now believed! And let not Caesar, marvel at itself: the arena makes real for you whatever Fame sings of." Martial was basically saying that the Roman emperor (also known as a Caesar) was able to bring ancient myths and legends to life. Not only that, but he was also able to alter them since the mythic Pasiphae survived her mating with a bull to give birth to a minotaur. The unfortunate victim of this Roman orchestrated "game," however, most certainly did not survive.

Another grotesque rendition of this macabre theater was a theatrical presentation of the mythical Addis who, after being driven mad, famously castrated himself. It's unclear how a condemned prisoner might have been forced to castrate himself in front of thousands of screaming spectators in the arena, but the Romans were no doubt crafty enough to find a way. These shocking shows were typically held at midday—effectively the half-time of the Roman games—and were called *ludi meridian.*

As outrageous as these acts sound, many were clearly documented by Roman historians. One that was described in great detail was the execution of a condemned man by the name of Selurus, who was made to act out a part in one of these infamous Roman-styled snuff films.

According to Roman writer and historian Strabo, "And recently in my own time, a certain Selurus, called the 'son of Aetna' was sent up to Rome because he had put himself at the head of an army and for a long time had overrun the regions round about Aetna with frequent raids; I saw him torn to pieces by wild beasts at an appointed combat of gladiators in the Forum; for he was placed on a lofty scaffold, as though on Aetna, and the scaffold was made suddenly to break up and collapse, and he himself was carried down with it into cages of wild-beasts—fragile cages that had been prepared beneath the scaffold for that purpose."

This Selurus was apparently a thief who, after being condemned to death, had been made the star of an elaborate theatrical production. He was placed on a mock Mount Etna, complete with fake shrubbery and rock outcroppings. On top of this artificial mountain, Selurus was tied up and made to play the role of Prometheus. One familiar with mythology might recall that Prometheus was said to have given fire to man. For giving humanity that spark of knowledge, the gods punished Prometheus by chaining him up and allowing a bird to peck at his liver.

According to the legend, the bird would eat Prometheus's liver every single day, and every single night, it would grow back so that his agony would continue. As it pertains to this condemned thief, however, he wasn't assaulted by a bird but rather a bear that was suddenly released from a cage.

However, not everyone was so excited about these atrocities, as indicated by the famed Christian apologist Tertullian. In one of his epic "apologies," Tertullian railed against this form of entertainment.

He declared, "Of course, you are more devout in the seats of the amphitheater where, over human blood and the filth resulting from the tortures inflicted, your gods do their dancing and provide plots and stories for the guilty—except that the guilty, too, often assume the roles of your gods. We once saw Attis, that god from Pessinus, castrated, and a man who was being burned alive played the role of Hercules. Then, too, at the gladiators' midday performance, in the midst of the cruelties of the entertainment, we laughed at Mercury testing the dead with his red-hot iron. We watched Jupiter's brother too, hammer in hand, dragging away the corpses of the gladiators."

He then further stated, "When the face of one of your gods sits on a disreputable and infamous head [the head of a condemned prisoner], when an impure body of someone and up for the art in all effeminacy represents a Minerva or a Hercules, is not the majesty of your gods insulted and their deity dishonored? Yet you not merely look on, but applaud."

These remarks by this early Christian writer provide some rather fascinating insight into Roman culture. Tertullian was obviously not a fan of the Roman gods, yet even he was amazed that the Romans would be so depraved that they would seemingly mock their own gods by having condemned criminals play them in the arena. Not only that but Tertullian was also perplexed at the Roman practice of taking gods sacred to the Roman pantheon and having them murdered live before an audience.

Early Christians would indeed have recognized the irony of Romans committing deicide (homicide of a deity) since, from their viewpoint, it was the Romans who had crucified Christ. This, of course, is an awful lot to unpack from the reading of the remarks of one ancient Christian apologist, but it is indeed a rather stunning thing to contemplate.

For some reason, the Romans were more than happy to see heroes such as Hercules burnt to a crisp or Dirce gored by a bull. On occasion, they would even watch as the wings of the mythical Daedalus fail him so that he could be mauled by a bear. It is rather strange for a society to wish to take depictions of their most revered figures and have them ripped limb from limb.

Conclusion: The Roman Games Come to an End

The Roman Empire was the first of its kind, an empire that spanned continents and held far-flung regions together with both its might and its rule of law. In fact, the Romans were obsessed with the law. Before the Roman Empire was forged, there was the Roman Republic, which had fashioned a Senate full of lawmakers. In the centuries of the Roman Republic and even the Roman Empire as well, countless legislation was adopted in efforts to create rules and regulations for how society should be maintained.

For such a legalistic society, it is indeed rather shocking to learn of all the abuses that took place in the famed arenas. Many have pointed out how the games had their roots in funeral practices, in which gladiators fought for the honor of the recently deceased. Later detractors of the games would speculate that these actions stemmed from even older funerary rituals that involved nothing short of human sacrifice for the supposed restless spirits of the dead. It has been argued that the evolution of having men fight to the death was, therefore, just a smokescreen for the urge to spill human blood over the graves of the dearly departed.

At any rate, gladiator matches, along with chariot races, wild beast hunts, and all the rest, soon became standard fare in Rome. So much so that it was said that as long as the Roman public had "bread and circuses" on hand, they would be just fine. The games became more and more elaborate as time passed, both to keep the public entertained and to display Roman power to the masses. Even in the frontier cities of the empire, arenas were established so that frontier peoples could be shown Rome's military might.

In the end, however, the Roman games became increasingly depraved. It was common for Rome to throw criminals and others rejected by society to the lions, but the ways in which the condemned were killed became more devious as the years rolled by. So much so, in fact, that elaborate theatrical acts were created in which the condemned were given a starring role as great figures of Roman myths and legends only to be executed in the final scene.

Strangely, Rome became famous for not only public executions but also for having those they executed play the role of their greatest figures. Was Rome killing their undesirables, or were they killing their own greatness? Hercules, Jupiter, and Attis could all be desecrated and dispatched at any moment, sent to their deaths, and then hauled off by a mime dressed as deathly Charon.

It was only when Christianity became the dominant force in Rome that Roman intellectuals began to seriously question the Roman games. They began to wonder why the spilling of all this blood was necessary. And once such things were honestly considered, the games were no more.

Part 3: Pompeii

A Captivating Guide to the City in Ancient Rome That Was Buried Because of the Eruption of Mount Vesuvius during the Rule of the Roman Empire

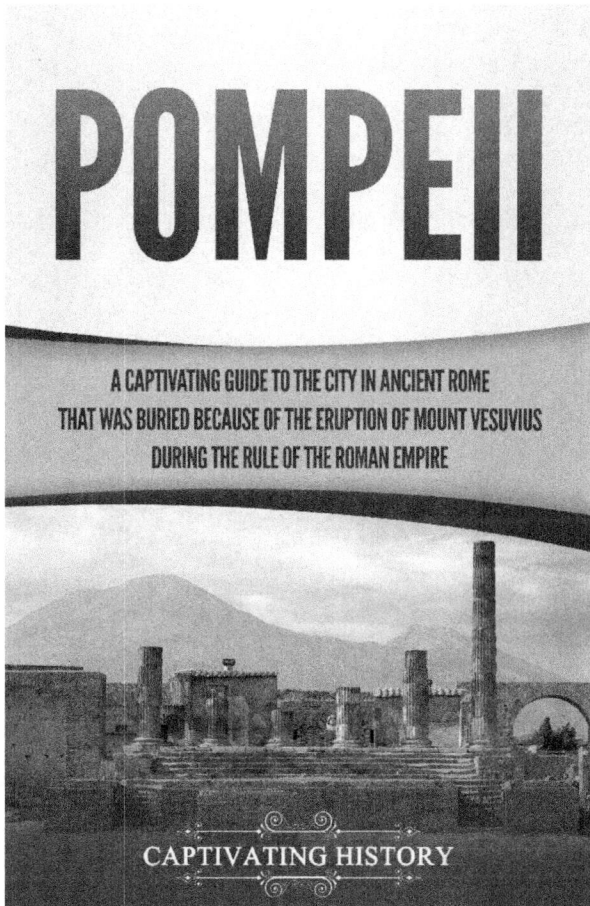

Introduction

The city of Pompeii, preserved under volcanic ash and pumice in the area of Campania, lies on an elevated plateau near the coast of the Bay of Naples and is overseen by Mount Vesuvius. Vesuvius gave Pompeii a chance for a thriving life and civilization, thanks to earlier eruptions that resulted in fertile soil, but it essentially took its life-giving ways back eight centuries later. Pompeii is now one of the most popular historical attractions and one of the most important archaeological sites in the world; today, it is protected by UNESCO (the United Nations Educational, Scientific and Cultural Organization). The first major excavations started in the mid-1700s and are still ongoing today; it is believed only a part of Pompeii's buried ancient treasure has been revealed so far. Archaeologists have uncovered hundreds of artifacts, meticulous documents and records, wall graffiti with forgotten Vulgar Latin, art pieces, sculptures, and magnificent villas. All of this evidence reveals the lives of those people who lost their lives on that fateful day of the eruption.

Every excavation and every uncovered artifact reveal the history of Pompeii, from the day of its founding to the day of its demise. Over time, a rich history of the people who called the city home has been unveiled, and by retracing the multitude of cultures that helped shape Pompeii, we can see why it was one of the wealthiest and most influential cities in Campania. Fertile lands, magnificent villas, vibrant social classes, and devastating wars all played a role in the evolution of Pompeii. The Oscans, Etruscans, Samnites, Greeks, and Romans all had a hand in shaping the formation of this great city.

Sail off across the Mediterranean shores and visit the ancient Italian Peninsula as we unveil some of the mysteries of the buried city of Pompeii.

Chapter 1 – The First Mentions of Pompeii in History: The Founding of Pompeii

The city of Pompeii, along with the neighboring cities of Herculaneum and Stabiae, all found life and death in Mount Vesuvius. The soil in the surrounding area was fertile due to the presence of volcanic ash, so the Osci, also known as the Oscans, created an agricultural society in the Sarno Valley sometime between the 6th century and the 7th century BCE, although there is archaeological evidence of earlier settlements dating from the Iron Age, between the 8th century and the 9th century BCE. However, the earliest written evidence of the existence of Pompeii dates from the 6th century.

Pompeii was one of the rare settlements in this area that were not founded and inhabited by Greek colonists but were strongly influenced by Hellenic (Greek) culture. Aside from forming the village of Pompeii in the Sarno Valley to take advantage of the fertile soil, the Osci chose this area due to the naturally formed volcanic terraces that acted as a defense against potential intrusions and attacks from neighboring cities and villages. Not far from Pompeii, the Osci could extract water from the River Sarno, which contributed to the agricultural and societal development of the Osci and their settlements. Historians cannot say with certainty where the Oscans came from, but they do know the Osci belong to the Italic people and were an ethnic Indo-European group that spoke one of the Italic languages, specifically, the Oscan language.

The natural terraces formed by volcanic activity before the settlement of the Osci could not isolate the Oscans from Greek influence. Since Pompeii was surrounded by Greek colonies, it soon assimilated with the culture of ancient Greece, and it also gave in to Etruscan influence. The Doric Temple, which was erected in the Triangular Forum in Pompeii, stands as a physical witness to this cultural assimilation. It is also known that the Oscans and the Greek colony of Cumae in Campania established a commercial exchange.

At the time, Pompeii received the status of an important trade center, which was how the Osci settlement became subject to Etruscan intrusions and expansion politics. The Etruscans penetrated the region of Campania and, with it, Pompeii. Pompeii was managed by the Osci at the time and had already been heavily influenced by the Hellenic culture through trade and the Greek colonization of the surrounding area. The Etruscans arrived around 650 BCE, coming from the north of Rome, and they became the leading force in the area, one that would last for more than fifty years. In the meantime, as the Etruscans spread their influence in Campania, the Greeks also extended their outreach in Campania, using Pompeii as a trading outpost rather than a colony since Pompeii was still a primitive settlement. Greek influence and colonies continued to expand across the Sarno Valley, affecting the native peoples in the area.

At the time, Greek colonies occupied the coastline and Campania as a whole, and as the Hellenic influence grew stronger with the power of the Greek colonies, the Greeks decided to drive the Etruscans out of Campania and Pompeii. In 474 BCE, the Etruscans suffered a defeat in the Battle of Cumae against the Greek colonies of Syracuse and Cumae. Cumae was the first Greek settlement in the mainland of Italy, and it was formed and colonized around the 8th century BCE. By 474 BCE, Cumae had become one of the strongest if not the strongest Greek colony in Italy.

Back in 504 BCE, before the Battle of Cumae, the Etruscans had tried to war against Cumae but failed. Even though they were weakened, the Etruscans managed to recollect their naval forces to launch a direct attack on Cumae, as they wanted to expand their territories to southern Italy.

The people of Cumae called for military assistance from Hieron I of Syracuse to drive the Etruscans out of the Bay of Naples. During the reign of Hieron I, who is known as the tyrant of Syracuse, the power of

Syracuse was increased greatly, which was why Syracuse was a worthy opponent to the Etruscans.

After the great defeat of the Etruscan forces, Hieron ended the battle as a hero, later dedicating a bronze helmet from the battlefield at Olympus to commemorate the event that saved the Greek colonies from the Etruscans' expanding influence. After the battle, the Etruscans not only lost their political influence but also their positions on the sea. Their territories were soon taken by the arriving Samnites, Romans, and Gauls.

In 440 BCE, the territories that had once belonged to the Etruscans were slowly occupied by the Samnites. The Samnites were an Italic people. They were related to the Osci and even spoke a similar language, although they never identified with the Oscans. The Samnites arrived from the harsh Apennine Mountains located in central Italy and occupied Pompeii. Both Pompeii and Herculaneum became a part of the Samnite territories in the 5th century BCE as the power shifted from the Etruscans to the Greeks to finally the Samnites before the Roman occupation took place.

The Samnites had a plan to commercialize the area and use it for trading, and they established dominance over the Mediterranean to control the lowlands and the Tyrrhenian Sea. After taking Pompeii, the Samnites built a thriving city with homes, ritual buildings, and a two-mile city wall to protect Pompeii from potential attacks and intrusions. The Samnites also buried their dead within the strongholds of Pompeii. The oldest grave excavated in Pompeii so far belonged to a thirty-five-year-old to a forty-year-old Samnite woman of unknown origins and social class. Pompeii slowly became the jewel in the Samnites' crown of Campania and the surrounding area, as the city thrived during the rule of this Italic civilization.

Nearly a hundred years after the Samnites occupied Pompeii and Campania, the Romans arrived. In 343 BCE, armed conflicts commenced between the Samnites, Romans, and Greeks. The great melting pot that was created by these multiple power shifts eventually reached its boiling point.

The First Samnite War and the Arrival of the Romans at Pompeii

The Roman Republic (510–27 BCE) was already taking an interest in the area of Campania as a part of the republic's expansionist and diplomatic politics. When the Romans arrived at Pompeii, the Samnites represented the dominant force in the region, as they were still expanding across Campania and attacking the surrounding cities. One such city was Capua, which was located in southern Italy and was a part of the Campania region. The Romans' arrival to Campania was most likely the result of the Campanians and the cities that were suffering attacks from the Samnites pleading for outside assistance. At the time, the Roman Republic had not expressed much of an interest in expanding to the region of Campania.

In 343 BCE, the series of battles known to history as the Samnite Wars commenced. The first armed encounter between the Romans and the Samnites is known as the Battle of Mount Gaurus (Mount Gaurus is also known as Mount Barbaro). Titus Livius, better known as simply Livy, the famous Roman historian, described the battle in the History of Rome, which was written in Latin between 27 BCE and 9 BCE. Modern historians argue that many events regarding the Battle of Mount Gaurus were mostly invented either by Livy's sources or the historian himself.

At the time of the First Samnite War, the Roman Republic was led by two elected Roman consuls: Marcus Valerius Corvus and Aulus Cornelius Cossus.

Marcus Valerius Corvus was elected as a consul six times. He was first elected at the age of twenty-three, and he was only twenty-seven when he led his army, which joined with Aulus Cornelius Cossus's army, against the Samnites. Corvus was also appointed as dictator two times and was an important military commander and politician in the Roman Republic. Corvus was a member of the gens Valeria. The gens Valeria was a prominent patrician (ruling class) family of ancient Rome, and they were influential from the beginning of the Roman Republic to the end of the Roman Empire.

The other consul, Aulus Cornelius Cossus, who also led his army into the Battle of Mount Gaurus, was a member of the gens Cornelia. The gens Cornelia was one of the oldest patrician families in ancient Rome, and it was famous for producing at least seventy-five consuls. For seven hundred years, the house from which Aulus Cornelius Cossus originated produced more generals and statesmen than any other patrician family in all of Rome.

What the Samnites could not predict upon attacking the northern tribe of Campania known as the Sidicini was that the Romans would meddle with their plans of invasion and break the treaty. At the time, the Roman Republic had a treaty with the Samnites, although the exact terms weren't listed by any of the relevant historians of the era. A condition that was known, however, was that the Liris River represented a border that shouldn't be crossed by either the Romans on its north banks or the Samnites in the south. However, the republic ignored the treaty once they were summoned to aid the Campanians. Before pleading for the Romans to come help against the invading Samnites, the city-state of Capua tried to defend the Sidicini but was beaten in battle. The republic then declared war against the Samnites, and Valerius arrived at Mount Gaurus, where he set up his military camp.

The Samnites moved to Campania with all their might and force, and Valerius utilized his position to test the enemy's strength with light infantry and light cavalry, known as skirmishers. Neither side could gain the upper hand, so Valerius decided to send the Roman cavalry in full charge to try and break the Samnite lines.

The cavalry had to retreat when the Samnites attacked with a greater force. With this failed counterattack behind him, Valerius decided to lead the infantry in person in another attempt to break the Samnite forces. Livy states this second attempt also failed, but Valerius did not give up, charging forward with another attack. The Samnites chose to retreat, and the Romans fully took their camp by the next morning.

Even though the Romans won the battle against the Samnites, the war was yet to be won. The second battle of the First Samnite War was the Battle of Saticula. This time around, the Roman military forces were led by Consul Aulus Cornelius Cossus. Saticula was one of the Samnite cities at the time, and it was located near the frontier of Campania. As described by Livy, Cossus and his men were attacked by Samnite forces in a mountain pass after marching from the city of Saticula. Livy writes that one of the Roman military tribunes, Publius Decius Mus, led a group of men to the top of the hill to distract the enemy forces so that the consul could flee with the army.

However, as with the other Samnite battles, modern historians doubt the events Livy describes in the History of Rome; unfortunately, Livy's book is the only source that details the battles in any depth. Another reason historians doubt Livy's version of the Battle of Saticula is the fact that there is a strong similarity to the resolution of another battle in the First Punic War, where the Roman army was also saved by a distraction made by a military tribune.

The third and last battle of the First Samnite War was led by Corvus and is known as the Battle of Suessula. Suessula was an ancient city located in southern Campania, and it was also the place where the Samnites gathered their military forces ahead of the last battle. Corvus responded to the gathering by marching his forces to Suessula to seize the opportunity and attack the enemy. Livy is once again the only source that describes the battle and claims that the Roman army launched an attack on the Samnite camp once a part of their army went foraging for food. Both Corvus and Cossus were rewarded with a triumph (a victory parade) once they got back to Rome, the "Eternal City."

In 341 BCE, the Roman Senate responded to the Samnites' appeal to reflect on the former treaty it had with Rome and agreed to peace.

The Second and Third Samnite Wars

The Second Samnite War commenced in 326 BCE after the Roman Republic declared war against the Samnites after the Samnites were unable to prevent their subjects from attacking and raiding the city of Fregellae, a city located in Latium where the Roman Republic had a colony. The war lasted until 304 BCE, ending with a victory for Rome.

In 310 BCE, the city of Pompeii is first mentioned in Roman records. During the Second Samnite War, the Roman fleet arrived to one of the ports in Pompeii, known as Sarno. The fleet had intentions to launch an attack on the neighboring city of Nuceria, which turned out to be futile for the Romans. The Roman fleet pillaged the city of Nuceria, but they found it difficult to subdue it, despite its great strategic position from the port of Pompeii.

In 300 BCE, each city of Campania arranged an individual treaty with Rome, forming a confederation and granting the cities the status of allies with complete rights to have an independent government. The Samnite culture, however, was still dominant in the area, which included Pompeii.

Only a year later, in 299 BCE, the Etruscans prepared to wage war against Rome. It is presumed that the reason behind this was the fact that Rome had set up a colony near Umbria in Narnia (Narni). These plans were intercepted by the Gauls when they invaded Etruscan territory. The Etruscans offered them an alliance in which they would pay for their support, and the Gauls agreed. The Etruscans counted on their alliance with the Gauls to help them win the war against Rome. However, the Gauls disagreed with fighting a war against Rome, stating that the agreement only referred to not claiming or devastating Etruscan territory. As a result, the Etruscans dismissed the Gauls, paying and releasing them from their agreement.

At the same time, the Samnites were also preparing for war, of which the Romans were warned by their new allies, the Picentes, the people who lived in today's territory of modern-day Marche on the Adriatic coast.

Rome sent an army to Etruria in 299 BCE, with consul Titus Manlius Torquatus at its head. He was fatally injured in a riding accident on his way to Etruria. The Etruscans believed that this event was an omen when it came to waging war against Rome. Rome soon sent a replacement for the deceased consul: Marcus Valerius Corvus, who was the consul during the First Samnite War. Despite the Etruscans' beliefs, the Roman army ravaged Etruria; however, the Etruscans refused to leave their fortifications.

In the meantime, in 298 BCE, a Lucanian delegation traveled to Rome to ask the Romans to protect them against the Samnites, who had invaded their territory and threatened their safety. The Romans agreed and formed yet another alliance. Lucania was the land of the Lucanians, who were an Oscan-speaking people living in the area from the Tyrrhenian Sea to the Gulf of Taranto. An order was sent to the Samnites to leave the Lucanian territory at once. However, the Samnites refused and once again threatened the safety of the Lucanians. Due to the treaty it had made with the Lucanians, Rome intervened, openly declaring war on the Samnites. Some historians suggest that it was in the best interests of Rome to start another war with Samnium (the region of southern Italy inhabited by the Samnites), which was why they deliberately formed alliances with the Samnites' enemies. At the same time, Rome probably feared that the Samnites would only grow stronger if they managed to subdue the Lucanians.

The Romans defeated the Etruscans in a battle near Volterra in 298 BCE. The only source of the battle is once again Livy; however, it seems there are few inconsistencies, even though there are no parallel sources to which to compare Livy's records.

The elections for the next pair of consuls took place in 297 BCE, around the time rumors were spreading that the Samnites and Etruscans were gathering huge armies against Rome and were planning to come as far as the Eternal City. Wanting to prepare for the rumored conflict, the Romans sought to elect Quintus Fabius Maximus Rullianus.

Rullianus was certainly the most experienced military commander in Rome; however, he refused to become a consul unless Publius Decius Mus became his colleague consul. The two had also been elected as consuls together in 308 BCE. Rome obliged, and the pair were sent off to war.

In the meantime, the news of Etruria suing for peace arrived in Rome, which meant that Rullianus and Decius Mus could march their armies to Samnium. In 297 BCE, the Battle of Tifernum took place in the valley near Tifernum. The Samnites were prepared to launch an attack against Rome, but Publius Decius Mus intercepted their plans by setting up his military camp at Maleventum, a city in Campania where an Apulian army was supposed to join the Samnites in their attack against Rome. Rome ended the battle in victory.

In 296 BCE, Appius Claudius Caecus and Lucius Volumnius Flamma Violens were elected as consuls, although the previous consuls had their consulship extended for six more months. They served as proconsuls, which allowed them to carry out the war against the Samnites. Decius Mus went on to attack the Samnite territories, mostly ravaging the surrounding villages to intimidate the Samnites.

In the meantime, the Samnites asked the Etruscans for an alliance or, at the very least, aid. The Samnites emphasized that they were not able to defeat Rome by themselves and that by combining the riches of one of the wealthiest nations in Italy with the power of the Samnite armies, they could drive the Romans out of Campania.

The Etruscan cities voted in favor of war while the Samnites gathered a massive army. Publius Decius Mus was, by this point, attacking the Samnite cities; however, there were no recorded triumphs for the consuls of Rome at the time, prolonging the conflict for yet another year.

Before the decisive Battle of Sentinum took place, the Samnites raided the cities of Roman allies across Campania, which urged Rome to take further action. In the meantime, the Etruscans were gathering their forces, joining their armies with the Gauls, Umbrians, and Samnites. This was the first time that Rome faced an enemy alliance of four different nations.

To prepare against one of the biggest battles Rome had ever seen, Publius Decius Mus and Quintus Fabius Maximus Rullianus were elected as consuls once again for their exceptional military command. The command of Lucius Volumnius Flamma Violens was also extended for another year—Rome needed to win so it could remain influential in Campania. Rullianus and Decius Mus combined their armies with the allied forces from Campania, which would be led to Etruria. Violens was sent to Samnium with two legions.

Even though the Samnites created a powerful coalition with the Gauls, Umbrians, and Etruscans, Rome won the Battle of Sentinum, thus winning the Samnite Wars and allowing them to establish their dominance in central Italy. It appears that the coalition was not ready for Rome. Although the Romans lost eight thousand soldiers in the battle, the allied Samnite forces lost twenty thousand men. The consuls returned to Rome victorious and were celebrated in a triumph.

The Aftermath of the Roman-Samnite Conflicts

These battles and frequent shifts of power created a unique and versatile cultural history that impacted the city of Pompeii. However, before Roman power was firmly established in Pompeii, Rome would face more challenges. For although Rome won the Battle of Sentinum, the Samnites were not ready to give up on Campania just yet.

The Samnites raided three Roman armies in 294 BCE, one of which was supposed to return to Etruria, the second to defend the borders, and the third to raid Campania. The Samnites attacked the Romans in the fog, killing many men and several officers. The Romans managed to repel the Samnites, but they were unable to pursue them due to the fog.

In 293 BCE, Spurius Carvilius Maximus was elected as one of the consuls, and he took experienced troops to take over Amiternum, which was located in Samnium. The other elected consul was Lucius Papirius Cursor, whose father had led Roman troops in the Second Samnite War. Lucius Papirius Cursor led his troops in an attack on Duronia, taking the Samnite city by storm. These types of conflicts would remain until 290

BCE, when the last Samnite stands of resistance would be overtaken by the Roman armies.

Pompeii would remain heavily influenced by the Greeks and the Oscans until after the Social Wars in 89 BCE, when the Oscan language was replaced with Latin and heavily transformed by Roman culture. As a punishment for participating in the Social Wars, Pompeii was first turned into a Roman colony of war veterans, serving as a military garrison before becoming known as one of the wealthiest cities in Campania.

Chapter 2 – Cultural Heritage That Formed Pompeii and Survived the Influence of Rome

When talking about the history of Pompeii, there is a great emphasis on the culture and heritage of Rome since Pompeii was under Roman rule at the time of the famous eruption that "froze" the ancient world and its inhabitants in time until excavations commenced in 1738, over 1,500 years after the eruption of Vesuvius.

When observing the name of the city, "Pompeii," we can see how the Latin language shaped the form of the word (Pompeii, -orum). However, the origin of the word is found in the Oscan language, pompe, which means five in Oscan. It is believed the city consisted of five hamlets (smaller settlements or villages).

By studying language morphology and the origins of the city's name, historians can determine that the Oscan people once inhabited Pompeii and that the Oscan heritage remained in the very foundation of the city even after the arrival of the Romans. The Samnites were also one of the first people to inhabit Pompeii, and their cultural heritage also survived the tooth of time.

At the very beginning of the city's history, fertile lands and rain contributed to the development of early agricultural settlements. Still, archaeologists are finding new evidence of the first civilizations that lived in the city, and the image they previously had about the life and culture of the Samnites is changing with new discoveries. But let us start with the first civilization to influence Pompeii: the Oscans.

The Oscans (Osci)

It is believed the Oscans founded five smaller villages on the location of Pompeii in the 8th century BCE, and it is presumed that they were the first people to inhabit the city and utilize its natural riches. The city was built 40 meters (around 131 feet) above sea level on a coastal plateau created by earlier eruptions of Mount Vesuvius. The plateau declined into the sea to the west with a steep fall to the south. Pompeii once bordered the coastline but is now seven hundred meters away from the coast.

Sadly, the remains of the Oscan culture could not defy time and decay. The only remains of the Oscan heritage in Pompeii are found in literary references, place names, and a small number of Roman scriptures. Historians and archaeologists cannot know with certainty how the Oscans lived or what their buildings looked like. It is presumed that the first settlements were primitive, given the time the city of Pompeii was founded. However, the cultural legacy of the Osci remains in the name of Pompeii, as it is thought they built the five hamlets that once made the foundation of the city.

As a civilization, the Oscans were just not strong enough and lacked the military power and riches needed to repel invaders, namely the Romans. They managed to maintain their independence for many years, mostly by finding ways to play one state against another; for instance, the Oscans did this to the Samnites and Romans during the Samnite Wars.

After the Second Samnite War, the Oscans lost their independence against the Romans and quickly assimilated with their culture when Rome decided to secure the tribes that thrived on the border. What might have made the assimilation of the Oscans with Roman culture easier was the fact that the Oscan language was closely related to Latin. Still, the Oscan language evolved after the Romans arrived in Campania, and it was used by several sovereign tribal states, such as the Samnites, Sidicini, and Aurunci. The Sidicini and Aurunci were often referred to as the "Osci."

Oscan graffiti has been found on the walls of Pompeii, which indicates that the language was still spoken in the city into the 1st century BCE, beyond the Samnite Wars. One of the oldest pieces of evidence written in Oscan dates back to the 5th century BCE. This is the Tabula Bantina, which translated from Latin means "Tablet from Bantia." The Tabula

Bantina is one of the major sources of the ancient Oscan language, with text on both sides of the bronze tablet. The inscription on one side is written in Latin, while the other side is written in Oscan. The tablet dates somewhere between 150 BCE and 100 BCE.

The Samnites

The Samnites also spoke the Oscan language; however, the Samnites never identified themselves as Oscans, nor were the Oscans known as Samnites. The Samnites lived in a region of southern Italy, which was known among the Romans as Samnium. The Samnites also formed a confederation with other tribes in the region: the Pentri, Caraceni, Caudini, and Hirpini.

The Samnites and Romans were not always enemies, as they formed an alliance against the Gauls in 354 BCE. However, the Samnites later became enemies of Rome, and the two forces clashed in a series of wars known as the Samnite Wars. After Rome ended the wars in victory, the Samnites helped the enemies of Rome, including a Greek king named Pyrrhus, who waged war against the Roman Republic between 280 BCE and 275 BCE. Some Samnites even joined forces with Hannibal Barca in the Second Punic War, which lasted from 218 BCE to 201 BCE.

The Samnites fought Rome once again with other Italic tribes in the Social Wars in 91 BCE. At the time, many of these cities and tribes were allies of Rome, and the reason for waging war against the Roman Republic was the fact that they wanted to have Roman citizenship. Rome did not want to grant Roman citizenship to the various Italic tribes, and as a punishment, the Republic declared war. The Social Wars ended in 87 BCE, and the Romans began their efforts to bring all of Italy under their thumb. (The Social Wars will be discussed in more depth in a later chapter.)

Before the Samnites were completely Latinized and had assimilated with Roman culture, Pontius Telesinus, a Samnite military leader, made one last attempt to lead his people into battle against Roman domination. He was one of the rebel military commanders who fought in the Social Wars, and he also intervened in the Roman civil wars in the hopes of gaining a better position. However, in his attempt to do so, he was killed in a battle against Sulla, a Roman general, in 82 BCE. After Telesinus died, the Samnites scattered. (As an interesting side note, some historians claim that Pontius Telesinus might have been an ancestor of Pontius

Pilatus, the Roman governor of Judea who ordered the execution of Jesus Christ.)

After the Samnite defeat, Sulla ordered that anyone who played a role in the rebellion should be hunted, severely punished, and killed. Due to this order, many Samnite cities were turned into small villages, and some were destroyed and/or deserted. With this turn of events, the Samnites lost their political importance, and they completely submitted to the Romans.

On the cultural front, a team of European archaeologists discovered a pre-Roman temple in 2005 during an excavation, which revealed a new image of the Samnite people. The Samnites were mostly described in history, at least in the surviving sources, as mountain folk and warriors that thrived thanks to their pact with Rome before the start of the Samnite Wars. A strong militaristic nature was what characterized the Samnites in history until the 2005 discovery of a temple in Pompeii dedicated to the Samnite goddess Mephitis (Mefitis).

The temple was built sometime around the 3rd century BCE and was dedicated to the goddess of swamps, although she was also celebrated as the goddess of underground water sources and springs. The fact that many of these underground sources were sulfurous led the people to associate Mephitis with volcanic vapor and poisonous gases, so it is no wonder that Mephitis was worshiped in Pompeii, a city with a view of Mount Vesuvius. The Romans embraced the temple and adopted it after colonizing the city in 80 BCE. Temples dedicated to Mephitis were also found in Samnium, Cremona, and Esquiline Hill in Rome.

The Etruscans

The earliest evidence of Etruscans dates back to 900 BCE, the period of the Iron Age in central and northern Italy, known as the Villanovan culture. With the ending of the Villanovan phase, the Etruscans fell under the influence of the ancient Greeks around 750 BCE.

The Etruscans were known as Tyrrhenians to the Greeks, while the Romans referred to the Etruscans as Tusci, which, translated from Latin, means "people who build towers." This name fits the Etruscans well, as they often built their towns on cliffs and surrounded them with tall walls.

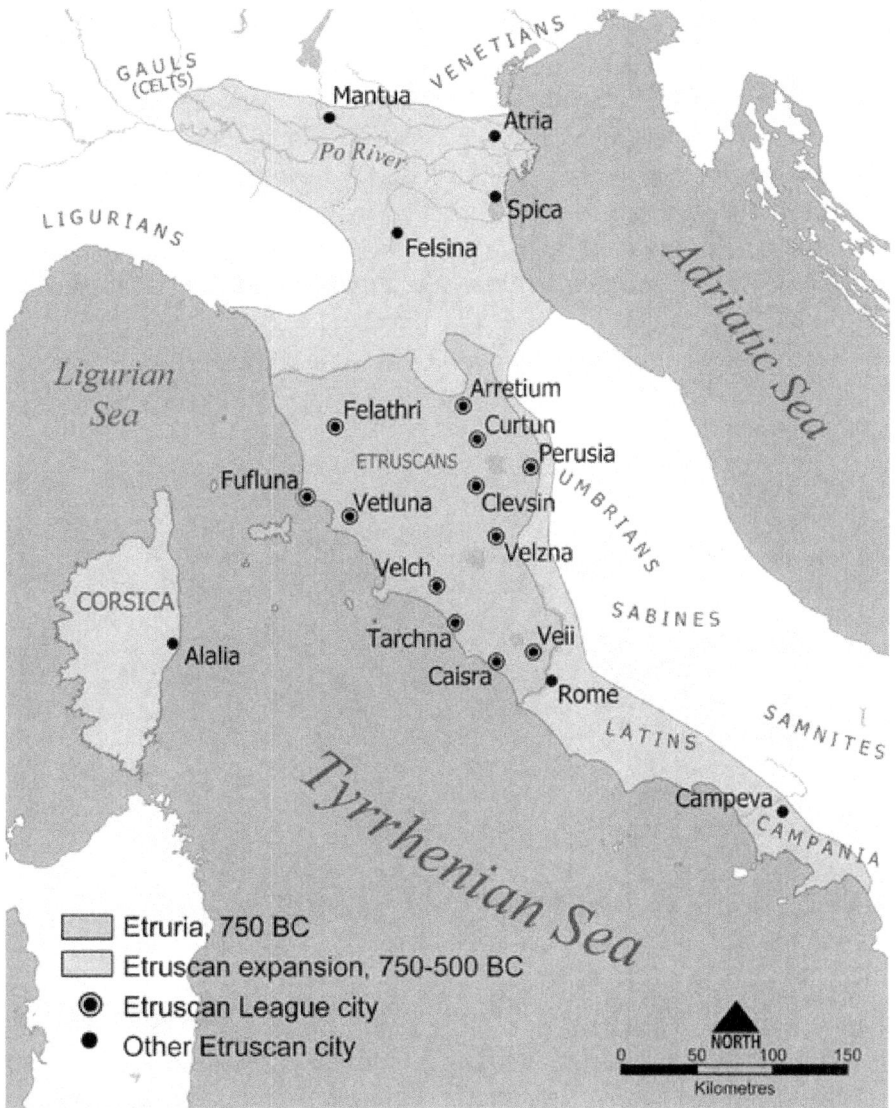

Etruscan civilization and the league of twelve Etruscan cities (900 BCE to 750 BCE).[1]

Around 500 BCE, with the arrival of the Romans, any political balance of power that the Etruscans might have held shifted to the Roman Republic. Before the Romans arrived, every city in Etruria had an independent government, with noble families most likely posing as the city's rulers. The Etruscan families earned their riches through trading with the Celtic people and the Greeks, which gave them more than enough capital for their luxurious tombs, which were filled with all kinds of goods, valuables, and artwork.

The connection between the Romans and Etruscans goes back to the very founding of Rome and the first supposed king of Rome: Romulus. It is hard to sort fact from fiction when it comes to Romulus, but this book will assume that he ruled from 753 BCE to 716 BCE. According to legend, sometime in the 8th century BCE, during Romulus's reign, the Fidenates, an Etruscan people who lived in Fidenae, an ancient town of Latium located only eight kilometers (five miles) north of Rome, wanted to remove the menace that Rome was threatening to become. So, they decided to lay waste to the land. Romulus responded to that provocation by marching with his army to Latium. Romulus set up an ambush and waited for the Fidenates to leave the city. Once that happened, Romulus took the town by surprise.

Former Etruscan town of Bagnoregio, Latium, Italy. Jonathan Fors.[2]

The Roman-Etruscan conflicts continued in the Roman-Etruscan Wars, which took place under both the Kingdom of Rome and the Roman Republic. The last resistance of the Etruscan people was crushed in 264 BCE, and Etruria was finally under the influence of Rome. However, the Etruscans managed to leave an imprint on the culture of Rome. To testify to the influence of the Etruscans, the common word "person," which exists in many cultures in the same or similar form, might be derived from an Etruscan word, *phersu*. *Phersu* means either "mask" or "masked man." Some scholars believe it could possibly mean "actor" since Etruscan actors wore masks.

More reminders of Etruscan civilization survived Roman colonization and assimilation, such as architecture, statues, sarcophagi, tombs, and art. The Etruscan concept of large villas with spacious gardens, as well as arched gates and large temples, was adopted by other cities and states in Italy. However, there is no substantial evidence of any Etruscan architectural remains in Pompeii, suggesting that many of the Etruscan buildings were completely removed and demolished to make space for those built by the Romans.

The center of the Etruscan society was the married couple, and monogamy was enforced. Thus, tombs were seldom made as individual resting places; couples were often buried together in the same sarcophagus, with the idea that monogamous pairings in the afterlife would be celebrated and cherished.

Unlike in Greece and Rome at the time, respectable women of Etruria could freely socialize with men, although this freedom might have been confused with vulgar availability in the eyes of Greeks and Romans, whose respectable women spent their time inside their homes. The fact that both the names of the mother and the father was written on Etruscan tombs emphasizes the importance of female figures, especially mothers, in Etruscan culture.

The Etruscan Sarcophagus of the Spouses; the Louvre, Paris, France.[3]

The Greeks

Hellenic influence in Pompeii and Campania started with Greek colonization, which took place between the 8th and 6th centuries BCE. According to the numerous findings over the years, the Greeks had established their culture in Pompeii by the 8th century BCE, at the very beginning of their colonization. At the time, Greeks were expanding to the Black Sea and the Mediterranean Sea, as well as southern Italy.

During the 8th century BCE, the Greeks occupied the coastal area of southern Italy, inhabiting not only Campania, where the city of Pompeii was located, but also the regions of Calabria, Basilicata, Apulia, and Sicily. Many native civilizations in these regions were Hellenized during the period of colonization and adopted Greek culture. The Greeks, for the most part, organized colonies in southern Italy due to the need for new ports and outposts that would improve trading, aid in finding new resources and raw materials, and make the colonization process smoother.

In part, colonization was necessary for the Greeks at the beginning, as many moved to Italy to escape famine and overcrowding. Greek colonization was also driven by the civil wars that affected many Greek city-states on the mainland. These civil wars were known as stasis. Staseis happened throughout all of Greece, with political opposition against the ruling party rising up to decry economic or social problems. When Greek colonization first started, tyrannical authorities were taking power in mainland Greece; as a result, many early Greek colonists were political exiles.

Due to colonization, the Greeks exported their culture to southern Italy. However, the Hellenic culture developed further from that point, interacting with the many Italic civilizations and their cultural characteristics.

In Rome, the regions that were inhabited by Greek colonists were known as Magna Graecia, which means "Greater Greece," as southern Italy was densely populated by the Greeks. Greek colonists created city-states that became very rich and powerful over time, some of which still stand to testify to the glory of the ancient Greeks who colonized the Italian Peninsula.

The Greek colonists adapted to their new environment and successfully influenced the Italic civilizations that were native to the region. In addition, the Greek colonies contributed to the development and growth of the metropolises by strategically directing colonists to new areas that should be colonized. Establishing new colonies was something that was carefully planned to provide secure and beneficial conditions for future and current colonists. The area of a future colony would be carefully analyzed, and if it passed the inspection, which looked at the area's usefulness and advantages, colonists would arrive to build in the region. One of the leading criteria for choosing future colonies was safety from raiders and attackers.

The Greeks did not establish a colony directly in Pompeii, although the city of Pompeii was near one of the biggest Greek colonies in Italy, Naples, also known as Neapolis ("New City") in the ancient world. As you can imagine, Hellenic influence must have been strong in Pompeii due to its proximity to Naples, which is about 25.5 kilometers (about sixteen miles) from Pompeii. At the same time, since the Greeks did not directly colonize the city of Pompeii, it was somewhat independent in the cultural and political sense.

Ancient Greece was one of the greatest early opponents of Rome. However, despite political conflicts and later wars and battles between Greek colonies and Rome, the Romans did not hide their fascination with Hellenic culture, and they did not seem to mind the influential culture and religion of the ancient Greeks. After the Roman Kingdom was overthrown, the Roman Republic started to take over Greek city-states and colonies, with Neapolis being the first to be taken by Rome in 327 BCE. Rome then conquered other Greek colonies, continuing their expansion during the Samnite Wars and the Pyrrhic War (the war waged by the aforementioned King Pyrrhus). The last colony to fall under Roman rule was Taras (today's Taranto) in 272 BCE. Syracuse was the only Greek colony to remain independent during the bulk of Roman expansion, thanks to the friendly political relations between Rome and the king of Syracuse, Hiero II (r. 270-215 BCE). Syracuse lost its independence in 212 BCE due to its king, Hieronymus (the grandson of Hiero II), granting an alliance to one of Rome's enemies, the famous Carthaginian general Hannibal.

It is amazing to think about how Pompeii was touched and influenced by so many civilizations. When one civilization left, another swooped in to take its place, melding their culture with what had once been there.

The excavations of Pompeii have revealed a rich cultural history, and we will now look at that history, with a larger emphasis being placed on the Greek culture, which was adopted and preserved by the Romans long after the Greek colonies were conquered.

Chapter 3 – The Greeks in Pompeii: Culture, Architecture, Art, Religion, Literature, and Drama

Pompeii was founded by the Oscan people and was later shaped and developed over the years by numerous cultures that were drawn to the region of Campania and southern Italy, mostly because of trading opportunities and agricultural riches. While traces of all these cultures can still be found in Pompeii under layers of volcanic sediment that buried the entire city in 79 CE, the Hellenic culture is still the most dominant in Pompeii, with numerous testimonies of Roman appreciation for Greek culture, which included their opulent architecture, art, religion, literature, and drama. The Romans valued the Greek culture so much that they made sure to adopt and preserve it.

The Legacy of Greek Culture in Pompeii

The influence of Greek culture can be seen in the architectural composition of Pompeii. While most of the preserved buildings were built by the Romans after their conquest of southern Italy, they were heavily influenced by the Hellenic and Hellenistic architectural styles. To make the difference between the two clear for readers, Hellenic refers to the people of ancient Greece before Alexander the Great's death in 323

BCE, while Hellenistic refers to the period after Alexander the Great's death and the rise of the Roman Empire. The Hellenistic style incorporates influences from the East, namely west and central Asia, with Greek culture.

The Basilica in Pompeii might be one of the most splendid buildings in the Forum that was uncovered during the excavations. In the time of the Roman Republic and later the Roman Empire, the Basilica was used for the administration of justice and city business. The Basilica also features an imposing decorated suggestum, which was a platform where the judges would be seated while managing judicial affairs. The Basilica was most likely built between 130 BCE and 120 BCE, and it shows clear Greek influence through the use of its Ionic and Corinthian columns, which was characteristic of Greek architecture. In the center of the Basilica's interior was a statue of a horse rider, complimented with surrounding walls decorated with stucco, which was often used for decorating walls in ancient Greece and Rome.

The influence of Greek culture on architecture in Pompeii is also seen in the Palestra (or Palaetra), which was built by the Romans in the eastern part of the city. Palestras, which means "gyms," were often used by the Romans for exercise and training; these structures originate from the Greeks, who called them gymnasions ("gymnasium" is the Latinized version of the word). The Palestra in Pompeii was probably built between 40 BCE and 20 CE, sometime during the Augustan Age.

The streets of Pompeii were also inspired by the Greeks. The Pompeiians used insulae to divide the city into blocks. Insulae is a city block that can also refer to a house similar to an apartment building. The streets were built in a way so that all the city districts were seamlessly connected through the use of insulae, and it allowed several main streets to be inventively interconnected with a great number of smaller streets.

The affinity the rich and powerful inhabitants of Pompeii had for Greek culture is witnessed in the use of peristyles, which were inspired by the Greeks. The peristyle is a columned walkway that surrounds either a courtyard or a part of a building, typically around an enclosed garden. Many villas and private homes that were unveiled hundreds of years after the eruption of Mount Vesuvius had peristyles surrounding gardens.

The House of the Faun, featuring two different kinds of peristyles built during different periods of time, Pompeii, Carol Raddato.'

The House of the Faun

The House of the Faun, one of the most elaborate villas that have been uncovered in Pompeii, uses two peristyle systems; the peristyles were built during different timeframes during the 2nd century BCE. The House of the Faun is a rather important piece of archaeological evidence, as it provides us with a glimpse of life in Pompeii during the time the Roman Republic established itself as a predominant force in the region. Historians and archaeologists claim that the House of the Faun stands as the perfect testament of life in the Roman Republic. Since the House of the Faun was buried in the residue of volcanic ash from the eruption that destroyed the city, artwork, such as the House of the Faun's famed mosaics, and other artifacts were left, for the most part, intact. German archaeologists began the initial excavations of the House of the Faun in 1830, and the treasures they unearthed were priceless to scholars.

The House of the Faun got its name after an archaeological excavation revealed a statue of a dancing faun made from bronze. It was found at the front of the impluvium, which is a part of the house intended for collecting rainwater. The fact that the Romans would choose a faun, the protector of forests and untamed life of the woodlands, also testifies to the influence of Greek culture, as the Romans often connected fauns to Greek satyrs (fauns are typically depicted as half-human, half-goat, while satyrs are usually depicted as men with horse-like features).

Archeologists also discovered insignia bearing the name of Saturninus, indicating that an important and old Roman *gens*, the Satria, lived in this lavish house. They also found a ring bearing the name of the gens Cassius. Cassius was a Roman family name during great antiquity. This evidence suggests that someone from gens Cassius married someone from the Satria family and that they made the House of the Faun their home.

A copy of the dancing faun statue found in the House of the Faun.[5]

Although the House of the Faun is an exceptional piece of Greek-inspired Roman aristocratic housing, the house was originally built during the period the Samnites inhabited the city. The house was not used for a while after the Samnites left the area, but it was later renovated to house the family of Satria. The size of the house also speaks on behalf of aristocratic life in Pompeii during the Roman Republic, as the house takes up over three thousand square feet and covers an entire city block, also known as insulae.

Another important work of art found in the hidden riches of the House of the Faun was the *Alexander Mosaic*. The mosaic depicts the Battle of Issus (also known as the Battle of Issos), which took place in 333 BCE. This battle involved the forces of Alexander the Great and those of Darius III of Persia. The battle is notable for being one of Alexander the Great's earliest victories in his campaign to conquer Asia, and it was the first time he met Darius III in pitched battle. The *Alexander Mosaic* once decorated the floor of the House of the Faun; it was one of many floor mosaics that have been discovered in the estate. The work contains several different artistic influences, such as Hellenistic and Roman. Archaeologists believe that the mosaic was either copied from or inspired by the original painting of the battle, which was possibly painted by an Eritrean painter named Philoxenus sometime in the 4th century BCE. The mosaic is notable for its depiction of fifty men (which was no small feat back then, considering the amount of work it took to arrange the tesserae, the colored tiles that make up a mosaic) and its attention to detail, especially considering it found its home in a private residence. Today, the original *Alexander Mosaic* is displayed at the Museo Archeologico Nazionale di Napoli (the National Archaeological Museum of Naples), although you can view a recreated copy at the House of the Faun, which is open to the public.

The original Alexander Mosaic from the House of the Faun, photographed in the National Archaeological Museum of Naples, 2008.[6]

If you get the chance to visit the House of the Faun, you will notice that at the entrance to the three-thousand-square-foot house, there is a sign that says "HAVE," which was a variation of the Latin word *ave*, which was used as a salutation. When translated, *ave* is an imperative form of the verb *avēre*, which means "be well," and it was used as a greeting and to say goodbye to parting guests.

The "HAVE" inscription at the entrance of the House of the Faun.[7]

Among the preserved art pieces was an erotic mosaic of a satyr and a nymph, as well as one of a fish. A mosaic depicting theater masks, accompanied by fruit and flowers, was also discovered. The surviving art excavated from the volcanic residue reveals only a glimpse into the luxurious lifestyle the aristocratic Roman families in Pompeii enjoyed.

A Quick Look at How the Romans Incorporated Greek Culture

As you can see from the above examples, the Romans were fascinated by Greek culture, whether it be their art, philosophy, or even religion and religious motifs. By taking a look at the *Alexander Mosaic* found in the House of the Faun, we can find out more about the Romans' inclination toward Greek art and motifs simply by examining the location and the position of the mosaic in the House of the Faun. The mosaic was located in the center of the visual axis between two peristyles, hinting that this art piece was a central decoration in the house. In fact, it would have been the first thing a visitor noticed when stepping into the room. By placing the artwork in such a noticeable spot, scholars presume that the Romans living there wanted to make sure their guests understood the kind of power their hosts wanted to emulate. So, even though Alexander the Great was Macedonian (the Macedonians were related to the Greeks, although there were some notable differences), the Romans chose him over a prominent Roman figure. The mosaic also features some classic Greek elements, with an emphasis being placed on the emotional expression of the fighters.

Another significant find reflecting the influence of Greek art on Roman culture is *The Three Graces*, a fresco that was discovered in the house of Titus Dentatus Panthera. The Graces were a part of Greek religion as minor goddesses, and they represented charm, beauty, goodwill, fertility, and human creativity. The fresco depicts the Three Graces naked, dancing in a circle and carrying myrtle while wearing wreaths. Although three was the typical number for the Graces in Greek myths, there could be more.

The Three Graces, found in the house of Titus Dentatus Panthera, created sometime in the 1ˢᵗ century CE. A fresco located in the National Archaeological Museum of Naples (the Museo Archeologico Nazionale di Napoli).[8]

One of the most popular art pieces that were inspired by Greek art that has been found in Pompeii was the *Doryphoros*.

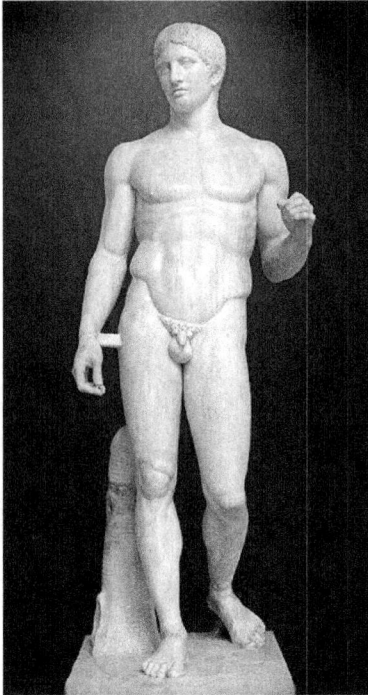

A preserved copy of the Roman Doryphoros. It is made of marble and stands almost seven feet high. Located today in the National Archaeological Museum of Naples.[9]

The *Doryphoros* ("Spear-Bearer) was sculpted by Polykleitos, and it depicts a muscular warrior with a strong build. The statue originally had a spear that balanced on the soldier's left shoulder, hence the name of this art piece. The original statue, which was made of bronze, was lost sometime around 440 BCE (in fact, none of Polykleitos's works survived to the modern era). However, it inspired numerous marble copies, which were mostly made by the Romans.

The influence of this statue might lie in the fact that the *Doryphoros* was supposed to represent the perfectly balanced proportions of a young man, as Polykleitos designed it with the intention of showing what one can accomplish in the sculpted form. He created the sculpture so he could depict what he wrote in his "Canon," translated as "measure." Polykleitos's "Canon" was his vision of a man's perfect proportions.

The notable Greek doctor and writer Galen wrote about the *Doryphoros* sometime in the 2nd century CE:

"Chrysippos [a Greek philosopher] holds beauty to consist not in the commensurability or 'symmetria' [i.e., proportions] of the constituent elements [of the body], but in the commensurability of the parts, such as that of finger to finger, and of all the fingers to the palm and wrist, and of those to the forearm, and of the forearm to the upper arm, and in fact, of everything to everything else, just as it is written in the Canon of Polyclitus. For having taught us in that work all the proportions of the body, Polyclitus supported his treatise with a work: he made a statue according to the tenets of his treatise, and called the statue, like the work, the 'Canon.'"

Unfortunately for scholars, Polykleitos's "Canon" has been lost in the sands of time. The marble copy that was found in Pompeii dates to sometime between 120 BCE to 50 BCE, and it stands at a whopping six feet eleven inches.

The House of the Tragic Poet

Greek writers greatly influenced Roman culture. The Romans were fascinated by Greek mythology, tragedies, stories, and legends. Greek literature had an impact on Roman writing, and many of the classics of ancient Greece were translated from Greek to Latin. Modern scholars can thank the Romans for preserving many classics that were written by the ancient Greeks.

Greek literature was likewise depicted on murals and walls of wealthy homes in Pompeii. Perhaps the most valuable evidence of Pompeiians embracing Greek literature through art can be found in the House of the Tragic Poet, also known as the Homeric House or the Iliadic House.

This home was most likely built around the 2nd century BCE, like most of the surviving Pompeiian buildings. The house is famous for its detailed murals and mosaics, which depict scenes from Greek literature and Greek mythology. The house was discovered during the excavations that took place during the 1800s, and to the surprise of the archaeologists working on the site, the house revealed works of an artist who must have been a meticulous master of their time. They were, of course, inspired by Greek culture.

The size of the house does not imply that it belonged to a wealthy family; however, the number of discovered murals and mosaics and the quality of the work make scholars believe that this house indeed belonged to a noble family. As with many things of the ancient world, nothing is entirely for certain, and certainly nothing is known about the family or individual who lived in what we now refer to as the House of the Tragic Poet. It is likely the house belonged to someone who was wealthier, as archaeologists have confirmed that the house once had a second story.

The House of the Tragic Poet was originally the home to more than twenty painted mosaics and murals, many of which contained scenes from Homer's *Iliad* and *Odyssey*. The building also housed numerous scenes from Greek mythology, including a mural depicting Zeus, the god Hypnos (the god of sleep), and the goddess Hera on Mount Ida, also known as the Mountain of the Goddess, which is mentioned in the *Iliad*.

The Wedding of Zeus and Hera on Mount Ida, found in the House of the Tragic Poet, located today in the Museo Archaeological Nazionale di Napoli (the National Archaeology Museum of Naples).[10]

The mural, now known as *The Wedding of Zeus and Hera on Mount Ida*, depicts Hypnos presenting Hera to Zeus, who is seated on a throne. At the bottom of the throne, the artist painted three male figures that might depict Dactyls. Dactyls are mythical creatures in Greek mythology that represent male spirits and are associated with the cult of the Great Mother (either Cybele or Rhea, as both are seen as mother goddesses).

Another mural found in the House of the Tragic Poet that most likely referenced both the *Iliad* and Greek mythology depicts Aphrodite. The mural was almost completely destroyed when it was discovered, but it has been suggested that the part of the painting that is missing showed a seated man, most likely Paris. Aphrodite was painted as a smaller figure compared to other murals, so it is entirely possible there was more to the painting. Thus, scholars suggest that the mural depicted the Judgment of Paris, which is a scene from the *Iliad* that brought about the Trojan War due to Paris having to judge who was the most beautiful of the goddesses who claimed the golden apple.

Another scene from the *Iliad* found in the House of the Tragic Poet depicts Achilles as he gives up Briseis, who was given to Achilles as a prize of war. Achilles was furious that he had to give his prize up, and he refused to join the battle, although he did so once Patroclus was killed. The scene shows Achilles seated as he reluctantly gives up Briseis. Patroclus, who was most likely Achilles's lover and who was later avenged by Achilles on the battlefield, leads Briseis, holding her by the wrist and taking her to Agamemnon's messenger.

Achilles surrendering Briseis to Agamemnon, a fresco found in Pompeii and now located in the National Archaeological Museum of Naples, photographed by Sailko.[11]

Yet another exceptional illustration of Greek literature and mythology can be found in the House of the Tragic Poet, that of Helen of Troy boarding the ship to sail back to her homeland. Although the mural was not entirely preserved, it is suggested that Paris was depicted, most likely already seated on the ship while waiting for Helen.

These examples are just a handful of what was found in the House of the Tragic Poet, as almost the entire home was decorated in marvelous, breathtaking paintings of scenes from Greek literature, showing the extent of the influence of Greek culture on Romans and their lifestyle.

Greek Theater

Greek drama was born with the Greek tragedy, and it soon became a popular form of art and entertainment across the Mediterranean and Rome. Ancient Greek theater dates back to the 6th century BCE and draws its roots from Athens, the cradle of Greek civilization. Greek theater was very much alive and popular in Pompeii as well, and the most valuable proof for that is found in the House of the Faun. The excavations of the House of the Faun revealed not only a private theater but also a mosaic with theatrical masks surrounded by flowers, fruit, and garlands.

Theatrical mask, mosaic found in the House of the Faun, Pompeii, author Marie-Lan Nguyen, 2011.[12]

However, the vast majority of the people of Pompeii enjoyed theater out in the open. In fact, Pompeii was home to two stone theaters before the first permanent theater was even opened in Rome. The largest theater in Pompeii was built sometime in the 2nd century BCE, and it could hold around five thousand people. It is believed that the theaters of Pompeii mostly held gladiator games, although dramas and concerts would have also taken place. The Amphitheatre of Pompeii has undergone many renovations over the years, and a restoration effort has taken place in recent years so it can once again be used for its original purpose: entertaining the masses.

Greek Religion

Greek religion also found its way to Pompeii and into the hearts of the Romans. One of the most important religious cults in Pompeii (and the Roman territories in general) was the cult of Apollo, who is the Greek god of archery, prophecy, music, dance, and poetry. The location of Pompeii's Temple of Apollo reveals its importance in the religious life of the people, as it was built in the center of the city in the Forum. The temple was built by the Romans to honor this ancient cult, which could be found across all of Magna Graecia (present-day Campania, Apulia, and Sicily, among other southern Italian regions), revealing the popularity of Apollo, who was one of the main deities in Rome.

The excavations of the Temple of Apollo have revealed that it was originally built in the 6th century BCE, making it one of the oldest religious buildings in Pompeii. However, it was rebuilt as the years passed. Sometime in the 2nd century BCE, the temple had been rebuilt (whether it was due to a natural disaster or not is unknown). The temple was once again updated after the massive earthquake that took place in 62 CE (it is believed this earthquake was a warning for what was to come later on in 79 CE). The temple was not entirely reconstructed by the time of the fateful eruption of Mount Vesuvius, though.

The Temple of Apollo, Pompeii.[13]

Temples were the center of religious life for the Pompeiians. However, the people of Pompeii did not solely practice their faith by visiting temples. Mystery cults and festivals were also some of the ways they expressed gratitude to the gods, whether they were Greek, Roman, or foreign.

Another popular cult was that of Dionysus, the god of wine and fertility. The Romans worshiped Dionysus under a different name, though. They referred to him as Bacchus, which again shows signs of the Latinization of foreign cultures and religions. The Romans would keep spiritual motifs from other religions but would often name the gods differently compared to the source religion. Some well-known examples are Jupiter (the Greek Zeus) and Neptune (the Greek Poseidon).

Until 186 BCE, festivities were organized by the cult of Bacchus to celebrate the god of wine and fertility. These festivities were known as Bacchanalia, and according to the Roman historian Livy, these festivals included sexual promiscuity and endless rivers of alcohol, which, predictably, caused aggressive behavior and festive chaos in the streets of Rome and Roman provinces. Most likely because the cult negatively affected public and political life across the Roman territories, the festivities were outlawed along with the cult in 186 BCE by the Roman Senate. However, while Bacchanalias became a thing of the past in Rome, these festivities were still celebrated in Pompeii and Campania, and its people kept the cult of Dionysus very much alive.

The Villa of the Mysteries

If one wants to understand the importance and the popularity of the mystery cults, one needs to look no further than the well-preserved suburban villa known as the Villa of the Mysteries. The Villa of the Mysteries is home to some of the most beautiful frescos found so far in the excavations of Pompeii. A single room in the Villa of the Mysteries contained a whole series of frescos that are thought to depict the initiation of a woman into a mystery cult. The frescos were discovered in 1909, but they were badly damaged due to poor protection from the elements and an earthquake that rocked the area a few months after the villa was discovered.

One of the frescos, depicting the reading of rituals for a mystery cult found in the Villa of the Mysteries, Pompeii, The Yorck Project, 2002.[14]

The series of frescos was most likely created between 70 BCE and 60 BCE, and many historians believe that the series depicts a woman being initiated into the cult of Dionysus, although the subject of the series is still being debated today. One of the main clues that indicate the painting was about the cult of Dionysius (or the cult of Bacchus) is what appears to be the depiction of maenads, the female followers of Dionysius.

For those unfamiliar with mystery cults, they were characterized by the use of secrecy. It is believed the cult worshipers were carefully selected. Once chosen, they would partake in an initiation ritual and be sworn to keep the cult's secrets, which included their practices; thus, historians have to rely on other sources to learn more about the mystery cults, sources that may be biased against them. For instance, Justin Martyr, a Christian writer, referred to mystery cults as "demonic imitations."

The fifth fresco, depicting a rite in honor of Bacchus, the Villa of the Mysteries, Pompeii, The Yorck Project, 2002.[15]

The House of the Garden of Hercules and the House of the Vettii

The Romans also worshiped Heracles, the son of Zeus, only under a different name, Hercules. The Romans regarded the Greek demigod as the ultimate hero, as he was renowned for his strength and might. According to the Romans and the Latinized myth of Heracles, Hercules was the son of Jupiter, the Roman equivalent of Zeus, who was famous and worshiped for his many adventures. The House of the Garden of Hercules and the House of the Vettii have survived as testaments of the importance and significance of the cult of Hercules in Pompeii.

In the House of the Garden of Hercules, a statue of Hercules was found along with a shrine and an altar dedicated to the cult. (The home was also known for its garden; pollen analyses indicate that roses, lilies, and violets were once grown there.)

More evidence of the cult of Hercules was revealed in the reception room in the House of the Vettii, which was one of the largest homes in Pompeii. Many frescos were discovered in the home, including a mural depicting a mythological scene in which baby Hercules strangles the snake that Hera sent to kill him after she found out about Zeus's affair with Alcmene (also known as Alcmena), Hercules's mother.

Hercules as an infant, strangling a snake, the House of the Vettii, Pompeii.[16]

Remains of Egyptian Culture in Pompeii

Pompeii was influenced by Egyptian culture to some extent since Rome and Egypt shared political interests during the early 2nd century BCE. However, Rome was not truly influenced by Egypt until the conflicts between Octavian Augustus and Mark Antony and Cleopatra ensued. As a result of being subdued by the Romans in 30 BCE, Egypt started to send new riches and materials to Rome, such as papyrus, glass, and various ores. Due to these new goods coming from Egypt, the Romans became fascinated by the Egyptian culture, which resulted in the Romans embracing Egyptian art, architecture, and even religion. This influence was present in Pompeii as well.

The remarkable House of the Faun testifies to this fascination with Egyptian art and culture, as archaeologists have discovered a table stand in the form of a sphinx, as well as a magnificent mosaic depicting the Nile River and its fascinating flora and fauna, including crocodiles, ibis, and hippopotamus. The Sphinx was a decorative motif that the Pompeiians embraced, as it was discovered in various public and private establishments around the city, providing a glimpse into the widespread acceptance of the Egyptian culture and mythology among the people of Pompeii.

The House of Julia Felix

The House of Julia Felix, a large property in Pompeii, was home to an impressive peristyle thought to represent a branch of the Nile Delta. The garden also has a series of connected water channels and marble walkaways, and it is decorated with tall, elegant columns and statues.

The House of Julia Felix was named after its owner, a woman who is said to have owned the building and the property surrounding it. Although Julia Felix was a public figure in Pompeii, it is likely she was an illegitimate daughter, as an inscription states she was the "low-born, illegitimate daughter of Spurius," meaning she was born out of wedlock. However, not all historians agree, as other scholars believe that Julia descended from freedmen.

It is not known for certain how Julia Felix got her hands on the house, but it is known that she rented it out as apartments or some kind of living unit after the 62 CE earthquake. Owning land as a woman was somewhat disputable during Julia's lifetime (it is not known when she lived, but she was alive in 62 CE, which means she might have been alive when Mount Vesuvius erupted in 79 CE). During that time, women were not allowed to legally own property without a male guardian of some kind, whether that be a father or a husband, unless she wanted to jump through many hoops (however, if a woman was of noble birth, she would not have faced as many challenges as those of lower stations did). Some women were allowed to own property if they were independent of their male guardian, which appears to have been the case with Julia Felix.

The Temple of Isis

Egyptian culture can be traced to religious cults in Pompeii as well. Aside from worshiping Graeco-Roman gods and goddesses, the people of Pompeii seem to have grown fond of Egyptian deities, as they celebrated Anubis (god of the afterlife), Bes (god of childbirth and fertility), and Isis (goddess of the rain, although she held many other roles).

The cult of Isis was one of the many mystery cults that sprang up in the area, and it was important to the city judging by the Temple of Isis, which was erected in the same district where the theater and gymnasium were built. Historians think the cult first made an appearance in Pompeii around 100 BCE, with it most likely being introduced by the Greeks due to their acceptance and admiration of Egyptian culture, and it gained traction due to its popularity with slaves, freedmen, and women. The cult later found a following with noblemen. It is thought the cult of Isis was so attractive to such a wide audience due to the people's belief that Isis could grant immortality. According to Egyptian mythology, Isis raised her own husband, Osiris (god of the dead), from the dead after he was killed by his brother Set (god of disorder and violence).

The Temple of Isis, Pompeii, author Juliana Bastos Marques.[17]

The temple was destroyed in an earthquake in 62 CE. However, the temple was soon rebuilt, which shows how popular the cult of Isis was in Pompeii. In fact, it was the only temple that was completely rebuilt after being damaged by the earthquake before the eruption of Mount Vesuvius in 79 CE.

At the Temple of Isis, priests would engage in daily rituals. Twice a day, priests would hold ceremonies, with the first ceremony starting before sunrise, which symbolically celebrated the re-birth of Osiris, Isis's husband. During the second ceremony, which took place in the afternoon, the priests would bless water that had been taken from the Nile to acknowledge their gratitude to Isis.

The paintings found in the Temple of Isis were done in the Hellenistic style, which was likely done to ensure the people accepted her into Roman culture. One fresco depicts a priest wearing the mask of Anubis, a god who was often shown having the head of a black jackal.

Anubis is believed to be one of the oldest gods among Egyptian deities since he was the god of the dead. Anubis is related to the afterlife and mummification in Egyptian religion, but he was accepted as a god and worshiped by the Romans in Pompeii. More evidence of the worship of Anubis was found in the House of the Golden Cupids (named for the Cupids found on the portico, a roofed structure that attaches the porch to the building). The House of the Golden Cupids is an amazing look into how much the Pompeiians revered Egyptian deities, as the house contains a shrine dedicated solely to them; it is possible that the owner was a priest in the cult of Isis due to the many objects in the house that pertained to her.

Anubis is depicted in the shrine as a man with a canine hand, which is typical for his portrayal in paintings, but there is also a detail that is not seen in Egyptian artwork, at least before the Greeks began to influence them. In the shrine, Anubis is seen holding a caduceus, which is a staff characteristic for the Greek god Hermes (or the Roman god Mercury, which would have been the case in Pompeii). This combination of the two gods resulted in a god with the name of Hermanubis, and he signified the Egyptian priesthood.

Portrayals of Bes, the god of sexuality, music, humor, and childbirth, to name a few attributes, were also present in Pompeii. Bes was often depicted as a dwarf with monstrous features, such as large eyes, oversized ears, bowlegs, and exaggerated genitals. In the Temple of Isis, a portrayal of Bes is found in the Sacrarium, which is a small shrine that could be located in either a public or private sanctuary.

As an interesting side note, the Temple of Isis influenced the art world almost a full century later when thirteen-year-old Wolfgang Amadeus Mozart visited the temple. His visit later gave him the inspiration to write *The Magic Flute*, a well-received opera that premiered shortly before his death.

Chapter 4 – The Romans in Pompeii: Life in Pompeii under Rome

Rome's influence on Pompeii began during the Samnite period. As mentioned above, the Romans finally subdued the Samnites in 290 BCE, and with the Samnites' submission came their territories, which included Pompeii. Although Pompeii was certainly in the Roman sphere of influence, it was, for the most part, left to its own devices. That changed about two hundred years after the Samnites were subdued, as the Pompeiians wanted more out of their arrangement with Rome.

The Social Wars, which lasted from 91 BCE to 87 BCE, was briefly touched on in a previous chapter, but it had significant ramifications for Pompeii and other cities in Campania, so it is essential we take a closer look at them. During these conflicts, the Roman Republic once again had to reinstate its dominance in Italy, for Italian cities, which had been a part of the Roman territory for centuries, started to rebel against Rome. The match that ignited the flames of the Social Wars was a request for Roman citizenship. Although these Italic tribes and cities were allies of Rome and technically a part of the Roman Republic, they did not have the same rights as those who lived in Rome. The people of these Italian cities wanted to have all the privileges and rights that came with Roman citizenship, namely the right to vote. By having the right to vote, the people could have a say in who represented them in the Senate. They could choose people who had their best interests at heart, someone who could help fight against the land and wealth inequality that the people had been facing for many years. The people of these Italian cities knew they aided Rome by sending soldiers, yet they did not see any benefits to this, as most of the land remained in Roman hands while their men faced the chance of dying in war. As the Greek historian Appian put it, the "Italic people [were] declining little by little into pauperism and paucity of numbers without any hope of remedy." The people of these cities also knew that Roman citizenship and the right to vote would grant them more influence, both within their city and in Rome itself, allowing them to further increase their status.

Since these cities had been a part of the Roman Republic for over two hundred years, they felt Roman citizenship was the least Rome could offer them for staying so loyal. While these cities were independent, at least in terms of governance, they could still owe tribute to Rome, and they did send Rome many soldiers; it is estimated that between one-half and two-thirds of the soldiers in the Roman army came from these Italian cities. The people just wanted Rome to treat them equally as "children of the Republic," but Rome did not want to hear about it. What Rome did not know was that another war was about to break out.

In 91 BCE, Marcus Livius Drusus championed the cause of the Italian cities. However, he was assassinated before making any real headway, inflaming the people's passions and leading them to believe they had no other choice but war. The Social Wars involved many Italic tribes, such as the Marsi and the Samnites, but other people groups, such as the Latins and the Etruscans, refused to get involved, with the Latins actively remaining loyal to the Romans while the Etruscans just remained neutral (they were later granted Roman citizenship to keep them from entering the war). It is possible they stayed out of the war because they feared what would happen to them in case the rebels' efforts were thwarted by the mighty Roman Republic. The Pompeiians were some of those who battled against Roman rule, and they remained in the fight for two years.

The rebels sought not only to separate from Rome but also to create their own confederation, which would, hopefully in time, rival that of Rome. Of course, this never came to fruition. The rebels certainly put up a good fight, though, especially in the first year of the conflict. By 89 BCE, the tides had turned. Lucius Cornelius Sulla, better known simply as Sulla, was a gifted general, and he, along with Gaius Marius, another brilliant commander, led the charge. Sulla overtook the city of Pompeii, causing the people to finally wave the white flag, but they were not alone. Since most of the rebel leaders had been killed, the war was essentially over (except for the Samnites in the south), although the resistance carried on in small pockets of Italy.

Though the Samnites were still a fairly large threat to the Romans, Rome began granting Roman citizenship to those Italian cities who had rebelled but surrendered under a new law called the *Lex Plautia Papiria de Civitate Sociis Danda*. It was a smart move on Rome's part; it gave the people what they had wanted, ensuring that more cities would surrender. Although the formation of a confederation would be off the table, the people could now vote or run for public office. The Samnites held out until the bitter end, and when the Social Wars began to morph into a different civil war, that of Sulla's civil war, the Samnites continued their fight against the general. Sulla won that war as well, and the Greek historian Strabo stated that some of the Samnites' cities "dwindled into villages, some indeed being entirely deserted."

The end of the Social Wars, as well as the end of Sulla's civil war, resulted in the complete Romanization of the Italian cities, which began to fully embrace the Roman way of life. As a result, they were slowly stripped of their cultural and linguistic identities through natural and political assimilation. Rome had finally established its complete hegemony over the Italian Peninsula, which included the city of Pompeii.

After the Social Wars ended, Pompeii became a Roman colony named Colonia Cornelia Veneria Pompeianorum. Although much of the land in Pompeii went to Sulla's veterans and although those who had supported the Social Wars had their property stripped from them, the Pompeiians quickly adapted to Roman citizenship, even adopting Latin as their main language. And the city rapidly became a jewel in the crown of Rome, thanks to its favorable geographic position, fertile lands, and great potential for economic growth.

Pompeii had always been a leading city in Campania when it came to maritime and trading activities, and its riches had helped merchants and entrepreneurs establish themselves in the city and reap the many benefits that Roman citizenship offered them. Merchants become so rich that they even competed with noble families in building the grandest villa! This new "middle class" probably bothered the nobility somewhat, as the nobles had a standard to keep when it came to splendor. Traditionally, this power and influence had always belonged to the nobility, and the newly rich middle class enjoyed outdoing the nobles by building marvelous villas and gardens with flower beds, fountains, pools, and statues. The middle class showed off their wealth through ornaments and jewelry as well, which had also been only characteristic of the aristocracy.

Although Pompeii had been one of the wealthiest cities in Campania for hundreds of years, the Romans wanted to place an even larger emphasis on its riches and its desirability, which caused people to flock there in droves. And who could blame them? Wealth, riches, and prosperity call to everyone. Scenic views, rich farmland, and the thought of accumulating more wealth were enough to make the noblemen of Rome move to Pompeii and call it their home, erecting astonishing villas and commissioning artists to create masterpieces of antiquity, some of which managed to stay preserved under the volcanic ash.

In general, the standard of living significantly improved across all social classes. One sign of the burgeoning wealth in Pompeii was the Via dell'Abbondanza, one of the main streets in Pompeii. The Via dell'Abbondanza was actually the longest street in Pompeii, sitting at around nine hundred meters (almost three thousand feet). It had an intersection with the Forum, which was the center of daily life. At the intersection with the Forum sat two major public buildings: the Eumachia building (it is unknown what the purpose of this building was; it is possible it was a marketplace or used as a guild's headquarters) and the Comitum (the polling place). Near the Forum, Romans could pay tribute to some of the main deities they shared with the Hellenic culture, as they could visit the temple of Apollo, Venus (known to the Greeks as Aphrodite), or Jupiter (the Greek god Zeus).

The Via dell'Abbondanza translates to the "Street of Abundance," and it is easy to see why. As one of the main streets of Pompeii, it was naturally one of the most crowded streets, packed to the brim with shops, workshops, bars, bakeries, and restaurants. It was a busy, colorful street that perhaps demonstrates the life and wealth of the city. The street also had a large public bath, and its crossroads led to many important establishments, such as the theaters.

Like other Roman cities, Pompeii had an aqueduct system that supplied the city with water, which was used for public baths and fountains. Wealthy Pompeiians even had running water in the comfort of their splendid villas. Instead of a modern-day toilet, they used a wooden seat that was built over a pit. After disposing of their waste, they would flush it away with a bucket of water, which then drained into either a cesspool beneath the street or close to the house. Although much of Pompeii was preserved, the aqueduct was one of the features that were not.

The view on the coast was breathtaking, which was perhaps one of the many reasons aristocrats from Rome were drawn to Pompeii. Summer homes adorned Pompeii's coastline, which overlooked the nearby Bay of Naples. Since the city was built 40 meters above sea level (around 131 feet) on a plateau created by previous eruptions of Mount Vesuvius, the view of the landscape was perhaps unparalleled to any other city in Campania except nearby Herculaneum, to some extent. One such summer villa was Oplontis, which is believed to have been owned by Poppaea Sabina the Younger, Emperor Nero's second wife, although scholars are still unsure if it truly belonged to her.

The front garden of the Villa Poppaea, photo by Miguel Hermoso Cuesta.[18]

Although many wealthy Romans and noble families were able to take advantage of summer homes by the water on those hot sunny days, not everyone could. Like other major cities, Pompeii was home to plenty of poor people. Antonio Varone, who was once the director of the excavations at Pompeii, said, "There was an extraordinarily well-off class that really enjoyed itself. From the excavations we have seen that there was a huge part of the population that lived in poverty, that struggled with daily life." It is believed around ten thousand to twenty thousand people lived in Pompeii, while some estimations suggest that fifteen thousand inhabitants is a somewhat more accurate number.

The people of Pompeii enjoyed their entertainment, which went hand in hand with the splendor and wealth of the city. They could visit a massive amphitheater that had the capacity to seat perhaps up to twenty thousand people, although it is more likely that the amphitheater sat closer to twelve thousand people. There, the people could watch gladiator games, which was a tradition derived from Roman culture. These were free to watch, and Varone hypothesizes that "the masses were helped in this way, [as] the powerful wanted them to remain tranquil."

Aside from the large amphitheater, there were several public and private theaters that hosted musical concerts, plays, and religious festivities. The theater area in Pompeii, with the large amphitheater as the centerpiece, also had the Odeon and Quadriporticum. The Odeon was a smaller theater; it is believed it could have seated around 1,500 people. The other major structure in the theater area, the Quadriporticum, was a covered walkway behind the theater, which allowed the people to travel to their destination without getting rained on. During the Roman Empire, these theaters were almost completely repurposed for gladiator games.

Inside of the Amphitheatre of Pompeii, Buckeye~commonswiki assumed (based on copyright claims).[19]

The Amphitheatre of Pompeii was built around 70 BCE, and, as mentioned above, it is the oldest preserved Roman amphitheater made of stone, preceding the Colosseum in Rome by an entire century (it should be noted that stone theaters were built in Rome before the establishment of the Colosseum, but the one in Pompeii still predates those). Previously, the Romans built their amphitheaters from wood. The term *amphitheatrum*, from which we derive our modern-day term of "amphitheater," was not in use when the Amphitheatre of Pompeii was built. Instead, Romans called it the *spectacula*. The amphitheater was so modern for its time that it even had a washroom in a nearby palestra, which also housed a gymnasium where wrestlers and boxers could practice.

The Amphitheatre of Pompeii was also the site where a major confrontation occurred between the people of Pompeii and the Nucerians (a city near Naples) in 59 CE, a little over a half-century after the Social Wars broke out in the Italian Peninsula. The Roman historian Tacitus wrote the following passage about the brawl:

"About this time [59 CE] there was a serious fight between the inhabitants of two Roman settlements, Nuceria and Pompeii. It arose out of a trifling incident at a gladiatorial show...During an exchange of taunts—characteristic of these disorderly country towns—abuse led to stone-throwing, and then swords were drawn. The people of Pompeii, where the show was held, came off best. Many wounded and mutilated Nucerians were taken to the capital. Many bereavements, too, were suffered by parents and children. The emperor [Nero] instructed the senate to investigate the affair. The senate passed it to the consuls. When they reported back, the senate debarred Pompeii from holding any similar gathering for ten years. Illegal associations in the town were dissolved; and the sponsor of the show and his fellow-instigators of the disorders were exiled."

The Amphitheatre of Pompeii, detail from a larger fresco, National Archaeological Museum of Naples, U.D.F., Paris - Robert Etienne: Pompeii, die eingeäscherte Stadt, Ravensburg 1991.[20]

The games most likely did not incite the violent confrontation that day. Back during the Social Wars, Nuceria was one of the cities that did not rebel against the Roman Republic. It is likely they held a grudge against the Pompeiians, who received the same benefits as they did even though they rebelled against Rome. This dormant hostility was awoken around two years before the riot took place when Emperor Nero placed a group of veterans in Nuceria. It is even possible that the Pompeiians believed those lands belonged to them, which would make tensions more hostile between the two.

While Emperor Nero and the Roman Senate concluded that the Amphitheatre of Pompeii should not host gladiatorial games for ten years, it is quite probable the ban was not fully enforced. Evidence found during the excavations suggests that the amphitheater was still serving its purpose during the ten-year ban, most likely because of Nero's second wife, Poppaea Sabina the Younger, who was born in Pompeii. She might have intervened with this decision as her mother's family still lived in Pompeii (it is also possible Poppaea herself had a summer home there). At the very least, beast hunts and athletic competitions still took place during the ban.

In 62 CE, only a couple of years after the incident, a major earthquake devastated the city of Pompeii and Herculaneum, and the Amphitheatre of Pompeii was damaged along with many other buildings. Even buildings in Naples and Nuceria suffered damage, although not nearly to the extent in Pompeii. The earthquake was, in reality, a warning to what was about to happen to the entire city of Pompeii seventeen years later. Another minor earthquake was felt two years later, in 64 CE. Although some of the city was rebuilt by the time of the eruption, a good chunk of it was still damaged. The Amphitheatre of Pompeii was one of the buildings that were repaired before the volcano erupted, and as a way to placate the people who had suffered so much, it was quickly reopened to the public.

The Roman Republic ruled a large portion of the Mediterranean and had established its dominance in other territories as well, such as Africa and western Asia. The Roman Republic was essentially an empire before it officially became one. During the years of wars and battles, the Romans enjoyed art, played games, and even practiced the modern-day concept of "summer vacation." And Pompeii might be the perfect example of the splendor and wealth that now characterizes Rome.

In 27 BCE, the Roman Republic officially became the Roman Empire, with Rome as its only capital. Long before the Roman Empire would come to an end in 476 CE, which coincides with the beginning of the Middle Ages and the massive adoption of Christianity, Pompeii would have already found its demise in the ashes of Mount Vesuvius.

Chapter 5 – Daily Life of the People of Pompeii

Daily life in Pompeii can be traced back many hundreds of years, for the eruption that took the lives of all the citizens essentially froze the city in time, preserving evidence that can provide a clearer insight into how the people of Pompeii went about their daily lives and routines.

Although wars and conflicts were a constant occurrence ever since Pompeii was founded by the Oscans to the day it was colonized by the Roman Republic, the Pompeiians' daily life, for the most part, was far from stressful and mostly consisted of simple and mundane activities that created nearly carefree routines. It might be hard to imagine a time when street lights and electricity were not around, as they are such a constant part of our lives today. However, we have to go back to a time where people would rise early in the morning with the first signs of the sun.

In the period between four and six in the morning, which was known as hora prima diurna ("hour before daytime"), people would rise to go to work. The first thing they would do was fetch water from the public fountains, which were accessible to everyone in the city. Only the richest and the wealthiest had running water in their homes. Over time, the Romans placed great emphasis on their hygiene. Water was important, as the Romans used it for bathing, washing, and drinking.

Initially, the Romans were a fairly dirty bunch, especially by today's standards. Thanks to the Gauls, the Romans discovered a milder form of soap. The Gauls, however, used this soap to dye their hair, and men actually used it more often than the women. As time passed, the Romans began placing a greater emphasis on hygiene, utilizing the soap they had discovered from the Gauls. Bathing was extremely important in self-care. Unlike in many parts of the world today, bathing was often a public affair, so citizens would visit public baths to rinse the grime from their bodies. Of course, as we know today, this practice is incredibly unhygienic. Unless one replenishes the water in the public baths with fresh water, bacteria is sure to grow. But even though the Romans did not understand the concept of bacteria, they knew that bad water could cause one to have poor health. Archaeologists have even discovered several tombstones that state, "Baths, wine, and sex corrupt our bodies, but baths, wine, and sex make life worth living." Of course, those lucky enough to be rich could enjoy the comfort of private baths, meaning they did not have to fear the spreading of disease like others.

Just as it is today, breakfast was an important part of the morning. For breakfast, Pompeiians would typically eat cheese and bread, although they would sometimes have fruit or vegetables on the side. One of the earliest shops to open were barbershops, which usually opened at sunrise. At barbershops, the people would get their hair trimmed; barbers would also remove stray hairs and warts and clean nails, which included cutting the corns from people's feet. In ancient Rome, barbershops were more than just a place to ensure one looked good. People would flock to these establishments to relax and chat with others. Barbershops were a good place for getting the latest news and gossip, so these places were often packed with people.

Hora secunda ("second hour") lasted from six to seven in the morning. During this time, everyone would go about their work, whether they were slaves or merchants. All the shops were open by this point, not just the barbershops. Markets were also open for business, ready for those early visitors, and farmers were out in the field, going about their business before it got too hot.

At *Hora quarta* ("fourth hour"), which would be around eight to ten in the morning, there were more people out and about. They could be visiting shops and markets, or perhaps they were taking a stroll in the Forum, which would have certainly been teeming with life by this hour. At the Forum, people gathered to discuss problems, whether they be personal or related to the city itself, as well as chat with others about mundane and private things. By going to the Forum, one was able to connect with other citizens and find out if there might be any novelties in town or even gossip about a neighbor, a nobleman, or a politician.

Hora septima ("seventh hour") was the time of the day between noon and one in the afternoon. This time was reserved for relaxing and taking a break; it was essentially a siesta, as the weather can be very hot in Italy, and taking a break allowed the people to avoid working during the hottest part of the day. If Pompeiians decided to use their break to eat, and if they could afford it, they would often snack on fish, cake, bread, and fruit (the topic of food will be discussed in more detail below). At times, the aristocracy of the city would organize gladiator games, in which case people would head to the Amphitheatre of Pompeii. It may be hard for us to imagine that someone would enjoy a cruel fight between gladiators, considering the violence and gore that took place, but for the people of antiquity, gladiator games were entertaining. Spectators would have their favorites, and they would cheer for their champion and even quarrel with other spectators when they hooted for their champion's opponent, similar to the way people enjoy watching football games and have their favorite teams, the extreme blood and gore excluded.

During *Hora Octava* ("eighth hour"), which lasted from about one to two in the afternoon, the Romans used thermal baths. Although the baths could be dirty, people still flocked there, not just to bathe but also to socialize. Even slaves who were third-class citizens with few rights could enjoy the public thermal baths. In fact, there were three entrances to the baths—women, men, and slaves. Eventually, mixed bathing became the norm.

There were at least five public thermal bath complexes in the city of Pompeii, where citizens could exercise, sweat, and then take a dip afterward. One could also purchase food or perfume, stop by the library to read a book, and even enjoy a musical performance. Not all of this would be located in the bathhouse itself (sometimes, it would be located adjacent to the building), and not every bathhouse contained such extravagant amenities. Thermal baths were also places where business and politics were talked about, where gossip was shared and the latest scandals revealed. As you can see, bathing was not just a mundane activity for the Romans; it was a well-ingrained routine and a way to practice a well-known maxim, *mens sana in corpore sano*, which translated from Latin means "a healthy mind in a healthy body," a phrase that refers to both bathing and physical exercise.

Speaking of health, it is thought the Romans had an average lifespan of twenty-five to thirty-five years. However, infant mortality was high back then, which considerably drops the average life expectancy. It is thought that around half of the Roman populace did not live past the age of five. So, if one was to factor the high infant mortality rate out, the average Roman would live to around fifty, maybe even late fifties.

At around two in the afternoon, the Romans would partake of their largest meal of the day (*cena*). As with many other aspects of Roman culture, the *cena* evolved as time passed. For instance, the Romans initially ate both the *cena* and the *vesperna*, a lighter meal at night. However, in time, the *cena* grew to become such an important and social affair that it replaced the *vesperna* entirely. The poor typically ate porridge and had vegetables or fruit on the side when possible. The wealthy, of course, ate much finer fare. They would dine on eggs, cheese, and sometimes even some kind of meat.

At *Hora Decima* ("tenth hour"), which would be around the time between four and five p.m., the people of Pompeii would have already been active for twelve hours of the day, and as the sun was slowly setting, citizens would leave their workplaces, markets, and shops and head home. Nighttime was a dangerous time of the day in Rome, so it is believed the same would have been true of Pompeii. After all, there were no street lights, and the only good source of light would have been the moon if the weather allowed for it. The thousands of oil lamps discovered in the excavations could hardly mitigate the darkness of gloomy nights. On top of this, alleys and streets were narrow and twisting. And there was also the chance of having someone throw their waste upon you since the darkness would have obscured your form. The Roman poet Decimus Junius Juvenalis, better known simply as Juvenal, touched upon this:

"And now think of the different and diverse perils of the night. See what a height it is to that towering roof from which a pot comes crack upon my head every time that some broken or leaky vessel is pitched out of the window! See with what a smash it strikes and dints the pavement! There's death in every open window as you pass along at night; you may well be deemed a fool, improvident of sudden accident, if you go out to dinner without having made your will...Yet however reckless the fellow may be, however hot with wine and young blood, he gives a wide berth to one whose scarlet cloak and long retinue of attendants, with torches and brass lamps in their hands, bid him keep his distance. But to me, who am wont to be escorted home by the moon, or by the scant light of a candle he pays no respect."

A popular nighttime activity for those who dared to stay out on the streets of Pompeii was writing graffiti on the walls of the city. One of the many wall inscriptions discovered in the city was signed by "the late drinkers," which testifies that life in Pompeii still went on during the evening and nighttime hours.

Over eleven thousand instances of graffiti were found in Pompeii alone. Graffiti was used for many purposes, such as advertisements for gladiator shows, businesses, warnings, and even personal messages. A good number of the preserved wall graffiti talks about inappropriate and bawdy subjects. For instance, outside the gladiators' barracks, archaeologists found graffiti that read, "Celadus the Thracian makes the girls moan!" (And that is a tamer example, believe it or not!) Some graffiti testify unrequited love, like the one that reads, "Successus the weaver's in love with Iris and she doesn't give a toss," painting both a colorful and mundane picture of life in the city.

Before going to bed, people would have their dinner, which, if one was poorer, usually consisted of olives and chicken eggs. Those who could afford it would possibly add meat, fish, or cake to their supper, going to bed with full stomachs.

The Romans were a busy people, and they did not always have time to go home and prepare a meal. Instead, and it might sound crazy to some of us today, they relied on fast food to get them through the day. Of course, their concept of fast food is different than ours, but there are similarities. It is believed the city of Pompeii had at least two hundred dining establishments, which would equate to one café for every sixty citizens. At these cafés, people would buy cheap hot food that was sold in jars. These cafés also sold wine, which the owners stacked behind the counter, which was typically long and stretched along the street to catch the eye of passersby. Oftentimes there was a room with tables and chairs in a room behind the counter, where people could sit while they grabbed a quick bite to eat and giving them yet another chance to socialize with their neighbors. The rich and wealthy would usually eat at home, where they had slaves and servants to accommodate them at their dining table in the privacy of their magnificent homes and villas. The poor lived in tiny rooms and often had no other option but to eat out since they did not have the facilities or time to prepare their food.

Although it sounds like the average Pompeiian did not have much food available to them, most Pompeiians had a rather healthy diet, even when buying cheap café food. This is known due to the seven hundred bags of waste that were collected from the sewers in the nearby city of Herculaneum. By examining the remains, scientists have discovered that these people ate fish and chicken, food normally reserved for the wealthy. Even the bodies of the poorer citizens that have been discovered show no signs of malnutrition, meaning the food they ate was most likely somewhat similar to what the nobles ate.

Since the region was perfect for farming, many different fruit and vegetables were cultivated. One of the most praised was cabbage. Cato the Elder (234–149 BCE) wrote about his love for cabbage and its beneficial impact on digestion. He also interestingly believed that if a person was sick, they should eat a lot of cabbage and then bathe in their urine so the sickness could leave their body faster. To give some credit to Cato, cabbage is incredibly healthy, as it is packed with vitamins and antioxidants. And although there are groups of people today who bathe in urine, no scientific evidence thus far has pointed out any positive benefits of doing so. The Romans also ate other vegetables, namely peas, rutabaga, artichokes, and brussels sprouts. However, these are not the same versions as we know them today; the modern-day versions of these veggies only began to be cultivated during the late Middle Ages.

Meat from a butcher's shop was incredibly rare, although the most popular meat was pork. Everyone but the extremely poor could afford pork as it was cheap, and since it was salted, it could last long without spoiling while traveling from the farms to the city. Beef was practically nonexistent, although the Greeks dined upon it. The Pompeiians would have also eaten wild game, mainly ducks and geese. However, fish was more likely to be on the table for meals, along with cheese. Slaves even ate seafood, although what they ate was mollusks (the people from Naples referred to mollusks as the mussels of the slaves). The rich people of Pompeii loved buying extravagant meat to show off their wealth. There have been reports of Romans eating flamingos and even giraffes! Of course, this was still incredibly rare. Another interesting delicacy that the wealthy ate was dormice. At dinner parties, they would even bring out the dead dormice to weigh in front of their guests to flaunt their wealth even more.

The most common fruit eaten in Pompeii were apples, pears, pomegranates, figs, blackberries, dates, and grapes. Fruit was often eaten as an appetizer or dessert. Figs and dates were perhaps the most popular fruit among the wealthy. For instance, the dates could be stuffed with walnuts, pine nuts, and pepper, after which they were salted and then fried in honey. Olives and nuts were also an important part of the Pompeiians' diet, and wine would typically accompany a meal.

But without a doubt, bread was the most important staple in Pompeii. Both rich and poor alike ate bread, and the bread they ate did not really differ based on wealth. It was one of the few food items that crossed the social divide. Eighty-one carbonized loaves of bread have been found throughout the thirty-four bakeries that have so far been discovered.

The food the Pompeiians ate was not plain at all. According to archaeologists, the people of Pompeii had access to homegrown as well as exotic herbs and spices, which allowed them to enjoy both traditional and spicy dishes. Most families that had more than one room would also have a homegrown garden where they would cultivate, on a small scale, fresh herbs, spices, and some vegetables and fruit for personal use. Over time, these gardens transformed into massive gardens that displayed their wealth.

There was rarely a dish in Pompeii, as well as Rome, that did not use fish oil or the fermented fish sauce known as garum. There was also at least one shop in Pompeii that made and sold this smelly and, at least perhaps to us, repulsing concoction that consisted of rotten fish. One of the richest families in Pompeii actually made their fortune through solely trading garum. This is known due to their house, as their entrance hall was decorated with garum jars. Garum merchants knew how to expand their business, for they even produced kosher garum that contained no shellfish so they could sell garum to a local community of Jews that lived in Pompeii.

Most of the people from Pompeii were not wealthy from selling garum. Instead, most of the wealth and power the rich were able to hold came from owning real estate. Almost every palatial house had a property a little outside the city where farmers and slaves could cultivate grapes or olives or raise sheep. These properties have not all been discovered, as it is hard to know where they might be located. However, one of these preserved estates has been found a few miles away from the city, and it most likely belonged to the family of Nero's wife, Poppaea Sabina the

Younger.

As you can tell, the Romans were very into their food, as even the rich made sure they had their own private stock of it. It can be said that the Romans were also fascinated with their dining habits, as they wrote many of their recipes down, one of which even included bears. It is not known whether the Pompeiians themselves also favored these extravagant menus, but excavations have recovered traces of fish bones, peppercorn, and mint leaves that perfectly fit into a recipe from a Roman cookbook published in the 4th century CE, which was translated from Latin in the Middle Ages.

The recipe stars a rather extravagant dish with the use of herbs and spices: "Ostrich meat, fish sauce, celery seed, roasted cumin, pepper, mint, dates, honey, vinegar, raising vine, and a little olive oil. Place all the ingredients in a pan and bring to a boil. Pour over ostrich meat and serve with sprinkled pepper."

Kitchens, even in the richest homes of Pompeii, could hardly have been equipped and roomy enough to prepare an entire banquet to accommodate guests. For the most part, kitchens mostly occupied small, cramped rooms. There was not much light and featured only basic kitchen equipment, like cauldrons and industrial-size sieves. It is known the rich held lavish banquets, so preparations would have most likely extended to the rest of the house. For example, a slave would prepare food and clean vegetables and fruit on the front steps or in the garden, while the meat would be prepared in front of the guests on portable braziers that would be brought forward for that occasion. Some kitchens were large; for instance, at the Villa of the Mysteries, a kitchen was found that covered a nine-by-twelve-meter area.

The kitchen would have been located on the first floor of a house or villa. Villas had upper floors, but many of these floors were destroyed after the eruption. However, some remained intact, such as Fullonica di Stephanus, which is three stories tall. There, the Romans would have washed their clothes, which was done with a mixture of clay and urine. And while the people waited for their clothes to be washed, they could partake in a snack. Today, you can visit the site to see a recreated kitchen. Historians believe it looks almost exactly as it did almost two thousand years ago.

Going to the dark side of life in Pompeii, it is known that violence and xenophobia took place in the city. While the Roman Empire was brought up with a fusion of multiple cultures, including Egyptian and Greek, not all citizens of Pompeii tolerated foreigners in the city, and some could even be classified as xenophobes. A painting in Pompeii stands as a testimony to the xenophobia present within the walls of the city, despite foreign traders and interactions with foreigners. This painting depicts a made-up scenario involving pygmies (a group of people native to Central Africa) on the Nile. The imagery includes non-flattering scenes, which include group sex and cannibalism, which means someone or several people in Pompeii saw this demographic as savage and primitive, although, in reality, that was not the case at all.

Violent behavior could also be noted through the presence of hooligans invested in the gladiator games and those who engaged in binge drinking in public. One example would be the aforementioned 59 CE incident in the Amphitheatre of Pompeii between the Pompeiians and Nucerians, which Tacitus, a Roman historian, described as a clash of "illegal gangs."

If one ventured to the dark alleys and located an establishment on the corner that looked rather drab, they would have arrived at the ancient brothel of Pompeii. The brothel was decorated with a series of erotic paintings, and it hosted a single lavatory along with five cubicles, where paying customers were satisfied. Hundreds of graffiti samples have been found on the walls of the brothel as a testament to satisfied customers who were more than likely to return. However, the brothel on the corner was not the only place where Pompeiians could pay for sex, for sex workers earned their bread in all kinds of places around the city, which included cramped lodgings and even cafés that sold wine and food. The rich and wealthy, instead of wandering on the city streets, used their slaves for sex services in the comfort of their homes.

It is not known how many slaves lived in Pompeii, but archaeologists and historians suggest that rich and wealthy households had between five to seven slaves, while more impressive households had many more. Slaves would perform various tasks for their masters, from fetching water from the public fountains to cooking, cleaning, shopping, and running other errands. They also fulfilled sexual desires and carried the rich above the mobs in the streets in litters. Slaves lived in cramped lodgings and service rooms in rich households. They would never enter through the main door since that was reserved for the family and their guests;

rather, they would go through the side door.

Businesses also employed slaves. For example, fulleries (a shop where clothes were cleaned) depended on slave labor. As mentioned above, Pompeiians used urine as a cleaning agent due to its high concentration of ammonia. Urine would be collected in jars, then taken to the shops. The slaves would spend their time cleaning clothes by standing in small tubs that were filled with a mixture of urine and water, stomping on the clothes to clean them.

Speaking of clothing, slaves could not be immediately recognized by their clothing alone, as they were not distinctive in any way. Actually, slaves wore tunics like their masters, even though Roman citizens could wear togas (they were the only group that could wear them). However, togas could easily get dirty and were hard to clean, so even Roman citizens would stick with tunics.

Slaves were kind of invisible in regards to Roman society. Since slaves were seen as property, they play more of a role in documents and laws than in paintings and mosaics. One of Pompeii's laws states that if a slave was injured by someone's animal, a person, or a passing donkey cart, the slave would be considered "damaged" property, and the party responsible for that damage would need to provide retribution to the owner of said property. It might be hard for us to imagine someone owning another human being and treating them this way, but the practice of slavery was common throughout the world, not just in Rome.

Through the eyes of a slave, Pompeii was not a lavish, breathtaking place with colorful streets and an easygoing life. Some slaves either escaped or tried to escape. Many of those who attempted to break free of their chains were found, with some even being kept in literal chains as punishment. Since the slaves were unable to escape the eruption of Mount Vesuvius, a great number of them were found in prisons designated for slaves during the excavations hundreds of years later.

Slaves did have the potential to become freedmen, which was a status between a slave and a citizen of Rome, although it was possible to become a fully-fledged Roman citizen through formal manumission. A slave could become a freedman by purchasing themselves from their owners or by being freed by the will of their owner.

While slaves performed all kinds of odd jobs and daily tasks for their masters, numerous citizens sought out various professions in Pompeii. Professions like carpenters, painters, innkeepers, architects, perfume sellers, traders, laundrymen, and even pig keepers were, for the most part, considered to be low-income jobs, and former slaves and the poor of Pompeii would tend to be employed in those industries. But what would happen to a Pompeiian who did not have a job? In most cases, these people would work as unskilled laborers, jumping from job to job without any steady income. Romans considered these people to be on the same level as a slave, and for the most part, the comparison was apt, as these jobless people did not have any rights. If one could not work at all, they had to beg in the streets to earn money. Some Pompeiians likely were professional beggars, as some people made decent money from begging in the city of Rome.

One profession that seems to have been favored was that of an artist. Painters and sculptors were busy painting marvelous murals and masterpieces, many of which have been excavated and preserved. The Pompeiians, as well as the Romans in general, loved their art, and artists were painting until the very last day Pompeii breathed life, even seconds before the eruption. In one of the more recently excavated Pompeiian houses, archaeologists discovered an artist frozen in time as he fled from the coming eruption, leaving behind his latest work, the last painting of his four works. Fifty pints of paint, as well as ladders, paintbrushes, and tools of the trade, were discovered at the scene, along with the artist and his assistant, who tried to flee for their lives in the middle of the eruption.

Another prominent profession was in banking, which might be better described as lending. Romans did not have banks or checks, so money lenders were the closest profession to bankers. Lenders would profit on both sides by charging a commission from sellers and by taking a hefty provision from the buyers who borrowed the money.

Male Roman citizens were allowed to vote every year for four officials who would take care of their city's business. There would be two senior officials, who would be in charge of delivering justice, and two junior officials, who would oversee the markets, city property, and streets of Pompeii.

Women did not have that privilege and were not allowed to vote. In general, the women of Pompeii had a major role in domestic life and would take care of their families and households. However, what is known about Pompeiian women is that they had more rights than other women in the ancient world. They were allowed to own property, could have prominent religious roles, and could own a business. Still, most women worked in shops, on farms, as sex workers, or were slaves. Sex workers were mostly female, although there were male prostitutes as well, and they were required to register as prostitutes and pay taxes to the city based on their earnings. However, women's voices could be heard in Pompeii, at least through the wall graffiti. Around 15 percent of election graffiti that was used as political campaigns was written by women.

It was once believed that education was reserved only for those who could afford it and "deserved it," which was essentially the boys from wealthy families. However, partly due to the graffiti found in Pompeii, scholars have realized that most boys of Rome learned the basics of reading and writing, and they could either have gone to school or learned from their parents. Girls also learned how to read and write, but, for the most part, this was reserved for those in the upper classes.

Although working-class Roman boys would go to "school," there was no building built for the specific purpose of educating children. It was possible the boys might have had their parents instruct them, but it was probably more common that they attended an open classroom with other children since their parents were busy from dawn to dusk. These open classrooms had one teacher for reading, writing, and basic arithmetic, and it must have been somewhat distracting to learn in the one in Pompeii as it was located near the Forum, the busiest part of the city. Misbehaving students were disciplined with sticks and would be made an example to the other students to ensure they behaved and paid close attention to their lessons.

Wealthy children were commonly educated by private tutors, with rich families mostly hiring Greek tutors since the Romans respected their culture and saw it as a status symbol to have their children speak and write impeccable Greek.

You can probably already tell, but Romans did not have the same idea of childhood as most modern societies do today. For many today, childhood is a carefree period of our lives, full of fun and painted in innocence. In Pompeii, children were treated almost like adults as soon as they were able to work, and young girls could be married as early as the age of twelve.

When a baby was born to a Pompeiian family, the infant would be wrapped tightly in cloth strips to keep the baby safe. The baby would be placed at the feet of their father, who would be seated when seeing his child for the first time. If the father took the baby and put it on his knees, he was confirming that the baby was his own flesh and blood. If the father did not accept the baby as his, it is possible the disowned infant would be left to die outside the city walls—a cruel practice unimaginable and punishable in modern times.

Since the infant mortality rate was so high, parents would not name their baby for at least a week or two. Many babies would not survive the first two weeks of their short life, while many children would not even survive past childhood. Many diseases that we treat with ease were not treatable in ancient times, hence the high mortality rate among infants and children.

Some girls from lower social classes were taught how to read, write, and do administration work, but for the average Pompeiian family, their daughters would be married off at a young while their sons would become a part of the working class. Girls helped around the house and did chores as soon as they were around seven years old. Some were involved in chores at an even earlier age, pretty much as soon as they could receive instructions and learn from their parents. A girl was expected to take care of her family's home until she was able to have children and marry. While girls could marry at twelve years old, they usually married around the ages of fourteen and fifteen. Having a baby at that age is incredibly stressful on the body, so most girls would die after giving birth to their first child.

Rich families would not always give their daughter's hand as early as a plebian family would, so well-educated, upper-class girls who were unwed mostly spent their time weaving. Upper-class boys would be sent to learn rhetoric at a university, which, again, is not exactly the same as a modern-day university. The boys, who would typically be around the age of fifteen, would be sent abroad, often to Athens or Rhodes. There, they would learn how to become orators and climb the ladder of political success and influence.

You might be wondering if Roman children had any fun growing up. Few toys have been uncovered, but children certainly did not work all hours of the day, every day of the week. For entertainment, they would enjoy the same things their parents did: attend gladiator fights, watch chariot races, and play with dice, to name a few activities. In a way, this exposure at a young age to violent activities as an option for entertainment allowed the bloody practice of fights and races to continue.

Although the lack of a carefree childhood might sound cruel and even disturbing in modern times, family was indeed very important in Pompeii and to ancient Romans. Families lived together and cared for each other, in sickness and in health, while sharing chores, work, and other commitments.

Chapter 6 – The Famous People of Ancient Pompeii

It is not difficult to imagine that some citizens of Pompeii were more popular than others, more appreciated by the general public, or were just lucky enough not to be lost to history after the horrific eruption of Mount Vesuvius covered the city in ash and volcanic debris. With new excavations, some names and buried stories of prominent and famous Pompeiians have been uncovered, allowing us to take a glimpse into their lives and unveil at least some of the Pompeiian mysteries surrounding preserved villas, homes, and documents. These are the people of Pompeii, who may have come from different social classes, professions, and backgrounds but all suffered the same fate long ago.

Lucius Caecilius Iucundus

One of the most notable citizens of Pompeii was Lucius Caecilius Iucundus, who was born to a freedman named Felix. His popularity was not based on his character, of which we know very little, or even his influence, but rather on his notable profession. Lucius was an *argentarius*. Translated from Latin, *argentarius* means "money changer" or "money exchanger," which would be the equivalent to a modern-day moneylender or banker. Romans did not have banks, so citizens relied on professionals like Caecilius, who acted as a middleman in auctions.

Plaster cast of Lucius Caecilius Iucundus made of Roman bronze and marble, found in the House of Caecilius Iucundus, Pompeii, National Archaeological Museum of Naples.[21]

If someone needed to purchase something from a merchant or pay someone for a service, Caecilius would cover the payment then provide a timeframe for the borrower to return the loan. Caecilius would receive interest on the loans he provided, along with a commission for his services.

What is known about Caecilius's work has been taken from the meticulous records that he kept for all his loans. In these documents, he listed witnesses, names, loan amounts, and other details. By examining these records, historians can see that Caecilius provided his services to the rich people of Pompeii, as well as other social classes. Caecilius did not work exclusively with Pompeiians or with the rich and wealthy, for the documents found in his house show that he traveled to Nuceria as well, where he helped Publius Alfenus Varus resell a number of slaves that he had previously purchased. The Pompeiian elite seemed to have enjoyed doing business with Caecilius, as many names of rich, noble, and wealthy individuals appear in the documents he left behind. The ancient Romans did not use paper, which was a boon to historians, as paper fades and disintegrates if not kept in the proper conditions. Instead, Caecilius used wax tablets, although wealthy Romans also had access to parchment and papyrus.

Caecilius was a rather interesting figure since he got rich on his wits and became a part of the elite through his name, deeds, and profession, even though his father was once a slave. It is thought that Caecilius did not die in the eruption that swallowed the entire city of Pompeii, as his records stop a few days before the 62 CE earthquake, suggesting that he perished on that day. Caecilius would have been around forty-eight years old when he died.

Poppaea Sabina the Younger

Poppaea Sabina, better known as Poppaea Sabina the Younger to avoid confusing her with her mother of the same name, was born in 30 CE. She was perhaps one of the most influential and most powerful people born and raised in Pompeii. However, she did not spend her entire life in Pompeii or even witnessed the eruption of Vesuvius (she died before it took place).

Poppaea was born to a wealthy and influential family. Her mother, as mentioned above, was Poppaea Sabina the Elder, the daughter of a consul, and her father was Titus Ollius, who was a quaestor, a public official, during the rule of Emperor Tiberius. The family owned magnificent properties in Pompeii and near Herculaneum. Perhaps the family's most well-known villa was Oplontis, which was talked about in a previous chapter. The villa is now known as the Villa Poppaea. It is also thought that the family owned the House of Menander, which was one of the wealthiest homes in Pompeii. It was named for the well-preserved image of a playwright named Menander, which was found in the house, although some argue the picture does not show Menander but rather the owner of the house reading Menander's works. The house was (and still is) rather impressive, covering 1,800 square meters (19,000 square feet), and it was built to show off the owner's wealth and political influence. And who would be more influential than a family with a long line of influential politicians and members of the Roman elite? Graffiti found by the entrance and elsewhere in the house also point to Poppaea Sabina's family being the owner.

Private baths in the Villa Poppaea. The centerpiece motif painted on the wall shows Hercules in the gardens of Hesperides.[22]

Poppaea was first married to a noble, Rufrius Crispinus, in 44 CE when she was only fourteen years old. Rufrius Crispinus was the leader of the Praetorian Guard for the first ten years of Emperor Claudius's rule (Emperor Claudius was the father of the future emperor, Nero, Poppaea's future husband). A few years after Claudius married Agrippina the Younger, Nero's mother, and she removed Rufrius Crispinus from his position in 51 CE. In 66 CE, Nero, who came to power in 54 CE, had him executed. Poppaea had a son with Rufrius Crispinus, who was named after his deceased father. Nero also killed him, drowning him while they were on a fishing trip (it should be noted this was done much later in Nero's reign, after his mother died).

During Nero's rule, Poppaea married a good friend of the emperor, Otho, who would later become an emperor in 69 CE, ruling for three months as one of the four emperors who took power the year after Nero's death. It is said that Poppaea the Younger married Otho only to get closer to Nero, as she sought to become the empress of Rome. The ambitious Poppaea eventually succeeded in her mission, as she managed to make Nero fall in love with her and allowed her to become his mistress even though she was still married to his friend Otho. In either 58 or 59 CE, Otho and Poppaea were divorced, and Otho was sent to the Roman province of Lusitania to become its governor, allowing Poppaea to focus on her goal of becoming the empress and Nero's wife.

At the time, Nero was married to his stepsister, Claudia Octavia, the daughter of the late Emperor Claudius, Agrippina's husband. As the Roman historian Tacitus claims, Poppaea's next scheme involved pressuring Nero to kill his mother so she could marry him since Agrippina would have been a direct threat to Poppaea's influence on Nero. Modern historians, however, consider that Nero's motives to kill his mother were, in reality, enticed by Agrippina's plans to set her second cousin, Gaius Rubellius Plautus, on the throne. Plautus was Nero's greatest political opponent, and by helping him plot his way to the throne, Agrippina signed her death warrant, which would be served by her son in 59 CE.

Now that Agrippina was gone, Poppaea had a clear path to pressure Nero to divorce Claudia Octavia so he could marry her instead. However, Nero did not marry Poppaea until 62 CE. This marriage came about after Poppaea was with child, after which he divorced Claudia and married Poppaea twelve days later. He exiled Claudia and sent her to Campania near Pompeii, then sent her to the island of Pandateria (modern-day Ventotene). Pandateria was a common location for banished members of the royal family who had committed adultery. However, Nero never accused Claudia Octavia of adultery, instead claiming she was barren and unable to grant him children and an heir to the throne.

In 63 CE, Poppaea gave birth to a girl and named her Claudia Augusta. The baby died when she was only four months old. "Augusta" was an honorable title that Nero granted to his daughter and his second wife, Poppaea, as soon as the little girl was born.

Nero's rule was marked by debauchery, extravagance, and the persecution of Christians, and he was greatly influenced by Poppaea, which was why the two probably were not Rome's favorite couple. For instance, it is thought that Poppaea intervened in the case of prohibiting gladiator games for ten years in Pompeii after the incident between the Nucerians and Pompeiians, convincing Nero to allow games before the expiration of the decade-long prohibition. If this is true, then Poppaea had an immense influence on Nero even when she was nothing but his mistress. It seems that Poppaea had a talent for playing political games.

She was often described by contemporary historians as a beautiful woman who used schemes and intrigue to become the empress and get whatever she wanted.

Poppaea regularly resided in Rome with her husband, but she would frequently visit the villa today known as the Villa of Poppaea.

Statue of Poppaea, Archaeological Museum of Olympia, Greece.[23]

In 65 CE, Poppaea was awaiting the birth of her second child with Nero. This was also the year of Poppaea's sudden death. Many writers and historians of the time blamed Nero for Poppaea's death, claiming that he either poisoned his wife or kicked her in the stomach during a quarrel. Cassius Dio, a Roman historian, who was biased and formed a negative opinion about Nero based on his imperial rule, claimed that Nero leaped upon her belly, either unintentionally or on purpose, which caused her to die from pregnancy complications. Modern historians argue that Poppaea might have died during childbirth since she might have had a stillborn or miscarriage in the last weeks of her pregnancy.

If one was to judge whether Nero did it or not based on his mourning alone, one would conclude that he did not have anything to do with Poppaea's death. He went into a deep depression, and he gave her an extravagant state funeral. According to Tacitus, she was even embalmed, even though cremation was the custom at the time, with her body being filled with herbs and spices and buried in the Tomb of the Julii. However, Poppaea's body was not found there, so the place of her burial remains a mystery.

Aulus Vettius Restitutus and Aulus Vettius Conviva

The names of Aulus Vettius Restitutus and Aulus Vettius Conviva were uncovered with the excavations of the House of the Vettii hundreds of years after the deadly eruption. The House of the Vettii, which was mentioned in a previous chapter, is one of the most imposing and wealthiest properties discovered in Pompeii, which makes it somewhat strange that this villa belonged to two freedmen of the Vettii family who had been either lucky or smart enough to become wealthy after they were granted freedom. The House of the Vettii testifies that its owners were extremely wealthy. Although some of the paintings have been lost, twelve mythological scenes were preserved.

Restitutus and Conviva were related, but their relationship has not been clarified. They might have been brothers or cousins. Conviva belonged to the Brotherhood of Augustus, carrying the title of an Augustalis. The Brotherhood of Augustus was an order of priests originally appointed by the second Roman emperor, Tiberius, who ruled the empire from 14 CE to 37 CE. The order was supposed to maintain the cult of Julii, one of the oldest patrician families, and the cult of Augustus, the first emperor of the Roman Empire. Conviva's name even appears in receipts and documents found in the home of Lucius Caecilius Iucundus. Conviva donated a large sum to be used for public work projects, which hints that the Vettii did not build a splendid villa to display their riches but were genuinely wealthy and contributed to the city with their financial power.

The story of the Vettii is not entirely revealed to us, except for the fact that Conviva and Restitutus were related and were once slaves who managed to earn the status of freedmen and become wealthy merchants. Thus, their story (what is known of it, at least) is a perfect example of the mobility of social classes in Pompeii and Rome at the time. The theory is that the Vettii brothers became rich by selling wine, and in time, they were able to earn the status of being part of the wealthy middle class. Since Conviva was an Augustalis, he was most likely closer to the status of nobility than of the wealthy middle class.

Julia Felix

Julia Felix was the owner of a large property in Pompeii, which was named after her when archaeologists unveiled the house during the excavations that began in 1755. Julia Felix lived in a large house located on the Via dell'Abbondanza. It was originally her home until she converted some of the rooms to apartments, which she rented after the earthquake of 62 CE. The location itself and the size of the property speaks in favor of Julia's wealth. But who was Julia Felix? Was she a noblewoman, a wife of a prominent politician, or perhaps a daughter of a Pompeiian merchant?

Unfortunately, we do not know who Julia Felix actually was, but we do know that she was a savvy businesswoman and a prominent public figure. Some scholars suggest that Julia was a low-born daughter, possibly even born out of wedlock, while others think she might have been from the imperial elite and somehow inherited the wealth she later multiplied with her clever business tactics. Others suggest that Julia was a descendant of an imperial freedman, which would once again demonstrate the rise of the new middle class.

As you can see, little is known about Julia's past and early life. Still, the preserved home reveals that Julia became a public figure in Pompeii, who generated more wealth by renting apartments and installing gardens for public use, as well as building luxurious baths she most likely rented to elite Pompeiians. Renting the baths to the elite would have given her a great fortune at the time since most public baths were closed for repairs after the 62 CE earthquake.

In ancient Rome, women were not allowed to own property unless they had a legal male guardian in their life. Some noblewomen, however, could own houses and lands if they were independent of their husbands, fathers, or other legal guardian, which lends credence to the idea that Julia came from a noble family since she was the sole owner of the villa. However, there is strong evidence that suggests she came from a lower class. The inscription on the entrance of her estate reads, "To let, in the estate of Julia Felix, the daughter of Spurius: elegant baths for respectable people, shops with upper rooms, and apartments. From 13th August next to 13th August of the sixth year, for five continuous years. The lease will expire at the end of five years." Sprurius was not actually a person; rather, the phrase "daughter of Spurius" means she was born out of wedlock. In addition to this, Liisa Savunen, a scholar of Roman history, suggests the name Julia indicates that she or her father might have been a slave, as "most of the Julii in Pompeii were imperial freedmen and their descendants."

Eumachia

Eumachia was a priestess of the imperial cult in Pompeii. She was a prominent and rich woman who earned respect and admiration through her devotion to the city of Pompeii and its citizens. She also draws her origins from one of the oldest families in the city.

The statue of Eumachia, the British Museum, Life and Death in Pompeii and Herculaneum, exhibition of 2013; the statue was originally located in the National Archaeological Museum of Naples.[24]

Wealthy women from prominent families in ancient Rome could not become politicians, but they could still have important roles in religion and religious cults. Eumachia was the matron of Concordia Augustus, which was a cult that honored the deified Roman emperor Augustus. She was also the matron of the Fullers guild (a *fullo* was a Roman laundry worker). There were several fulleries, also known as *fullonica* in Latin, around the city of Pompeii, and the rich would build *fullonica* as a part of their estate, employing slaves as laundry workers.

By WolfgangRieger - Filippo Coarelli (ed.): Pompeji. Hirmer, München 2002, ISBN 3-7774-9530-1, p. 137, Public Domain. The man on the left is brushing a wool cloth, and the man on the right is whitening fabrics beneath a caged dome. On top of the cage is an owl, which represents Athena, who was the goddess protector of wool merchants.[25]

Eumachia was a prominent public figure, which went hand in hand with her status and her good deeds as a benefactor. In fact, Eumachia used part of her wealth to build the east side of the Forum in Pompeii, which may have been a building for the Fullers guild since the building contained a statue of her.

This building is also significant since it allows us to find out more about Eumachia's life through a dedicatory inscription. She was a daughter of Lucius and a priestess, and she also had a son named Marcus

Numistrius Fronto. The name of her son might have been mentioned to set up a fruitful terrain for him in case he ever decided to enter politics.

Eumachia is a perfect example of how a woman could get involved in social politics and the public life of Pompeii.

Chapter 7 – The Last Days in Pompeii before the Eruption

Seventeen years before the people of Pompeii would live their last days on Earth, a devastating earthquake turned half the city into rubble. If the people of ancient Pompeii knew that the earthquake was, in reality, announcing the eruption of Mount Vesuvius, they would have probably left before it was too late to save themselves. It would have been difficult for the rich and wealthy to leave everything they had behind, such as their luxurious villas, magnificent artwork, paintings, precious possessions, and even the beautiful city of Pompeii, the jewel in the crown of the Roman Empire, but at least they would leave with their lives. Unfortunately, nobody knew what the earthquake was foretelling.

The earthquake in 62 CE was strong and horrific, and it destroyed buildings in Pompeii as well as the neighboring city of Herculaneum. The aftershocks shook the ground for days after the main quake. Seneca the Younger, a Roman philosopher, statesman, and dramatist, wrote that a flock of six hundred sheep died due to the poisonous fumes that appeared due to the earthquake.

Seneca the Younger wrote about the effects of earthquakes in the sixth book of his *Naturales quaestiones*, attributing the devastating force of the earthquake, which happened on February 5th, 62 CE, to the movement of the air. It is hard to know for certain if Mount Vesuvius caused the earthquake or not, but it certainly was catastrophic. Most scholars believe that it registered at between 5 and 6.1 in magnitude, although some estimates go as high as 7.5. In his work, Seneca touched upon how terrifying an earthquake can be:

"What hiding-place will creatures find, where will they flee in their anxiety, if fear arises from below and is drawn from the depths of the earth? There is panic on the part of all when buildings creak and give signs of falling. Then everybody hurls himself headlong outside, abandons his household possessions, and trusts to his luck in the outdoors. What hiding-place do we look to, what help, if the earth itself is causing the ruin, if what protects us, upholds us, on which cities are built, which some speak of as a kind of foundation of the universe, separates and reels?"

After the ground had settled and the damage had been assessed, the citizens of Pompeii started to rebuild. Many of the wealthy citizens decided to leave, allowing the rich middle class to take their place at the top of the totem pole. Repairing the city was a slow and lengthy process. As might be expected, the most affected were the poor, whose homes were almost entirely destroyed. Businesses like the one conducted by Julia Felix would have boomed since people would have been looking for accommodations and a place to live until their homes could be rebuilt. It is less likely that the poor could afford to stay at the Felix villa, but the rich who remained in the city would have found comfort in the luxurious baths of the prominent house. Nero gave money to Rome to help with the repairs since his wife, Poppaea Sabina the Younger, had once called the city home.

Only two years later, in 64 CE, another earthquake shook the region, affecting Pompeii once again. However, it was nowhere near as devastating as the first one. The earthquake was recorded by Suetonius, a Roman historian, as well as by Tacitus, who also wrote about Emperor Nero's first performance in the grand theater of Naples. Suetonius wrote about Nero's performance as well, which took place during the earthquake itself, noting that Nero continued to sing on stage even though the ground had started to shake. The emperor would not leave the stage until he had finished the song, and as Tacitus and Suetonius both remarked, the theater collapsed moments after the emperor and the auditorium had been evacuated.

By the time of the eruption in 79 CE, the city was mostly rebuilt, although there was still plenty of buildings that remained damaged. It is not likely that the Pompeiians were aware of the far greater threat that was about to swallow the entire city and freeze it in time. Instead, life in the city went on with its usual routines, even though there was a series of earthquakes four days before the eruption in 79 CE.

As Pliny the Younger, a prominent magistrate and author, noted, the people of Campania were so accustomed to earthquakes that they considered it to be a normal thing, not even suspecting that Vesuvius was about to erupt. Pliny the Younger was in Pompeii before the eruption, although he was just a teenager, and his letters to Tacitus, which he wrote about twenty-five years after the event, would be perhaps the most fateful testimony to what the final days of Pompeii looked like.

Thus, the Pompeiians decided to dismiss the violent warnings that continued for four days before the eruption, perhaps even setting up a celebration for Vulcanalia. Vulcanalia was a festival that was celebrated every year on August 23rd. Ironically enough, it was dedicated to the god of fire and volcanos, Vulcan, meaning he would have been the god to protect the people of Pompeii from the destruction that was about to ensue. Vulcan, who is known as Hephaestus in Greek mythology, was also a skillful master of metalworking. To celebrate Vulcan, Pompeiians would set up large bonfires around the city and displayed shrines dedicated to the god. They held numerous games to celebrate the god of fire and volcanoes while offering sacrifices to please him. They also threw live fish and small animals into the fire during the festivities.

It is possible this festival took place either a day or two days before the eruption, and if that was the case, the volcano would have been showing some signs of life. There would have been small earthquakes and smoke, but because of the festival, the people would have seen these as good signs that Vulcan was busy working on his forge on Mount Vesuvius.

Statuette of Vulcan, the god of fire, volcanoes, and metalworking, created approximately around the 1st century CE, bronze. Photo credits: By Marie-Lan Nguyen, 2008-12-26, CC BY 2.5.[26]

However, it is hard to know exactly when the eruption happened. Pliny the Younger wrote letters to Tacitus around twenty-five years after the eruption, and in them, he states the eruption took place on August 24th. As time has passed, scholars believe the date was copied incorrectly and that it could have been a variety of different dates, such as October 30th or November 23rd. This variety in dates is due to the Romans' convention for calendar dates, which can be somewhat difficult to follow.

Beginning in the 18th century, scholars began to suggest that the eruption happened after August 24th, although this theory was not fully embraced until recently. In 2007, scientists concluded that the debris pattern of the eruption is more consistent with the winds in the fall than in the late summer. In 2018, archaeologists found an inscription that was dated October 17th. Since the inscription is thought to not have been older than 79 CE, that means October 18th, 79 CE, is the earliest possible date for the eruption of Mount Vesuvius, although historians think it took place later in the month or even in November.

Chapter 8 – The Eruption of Mount Vesuvius and the Demise of Pompeii

On the day of the eruption, the people of Pompeii rose with the sun to catch the first glimpses of daylight just as they would do any other day. They would have had breakfast, went to the market, visited shops, and went to work. Aside from the minor tremors they would have felt and were already accustomed to, it seemed like an ordinary day.

Pliny the Younger, who was born around 61 CE, was seventeen years old when the eruption took place. His uncle on his mother's side, who was called Pliny the Elder, was the commander of a Roman fleet stationed at Misenum, which was a part of the Italian province of Naples and one of the naval bases of the Roman Empire.

The letters that Pliny the Younger wrote to Tacitus describing the last day of Pompeii as Pliny knew it represent a rich source of information on how the most horrific volcanic eruption in Europe destroyed a strategically and economically important city of Campania.

The Last Day of Pompeii, oil on canvas, Karl Bryullov, created 1830–1833. Bryullov visited Pompeii in 1828 and made sketches depicting the eruption in 79 CE that destroyed Pompeii. He later painted this work, which is considered to be one of his greatest works of art. It later inspired Edward Bulwer-Lytton's book, The Last Days of Pompeii.[27]

Pliny the Younger notes in his letters to Tacitus that his mother had noticed a massive, unusual cloud appearing around Mount Vesuvius. As Pliny the Younger records, the cloud must have appeared around the seventh hour of the day, which would have been around noon. Ash carried by the winds soon appeared near Pompeii. It was not clear to Pliny's mother or Pliny's uncle, who, in addition to being a naval commander, was a naturalist (perhaps one of the greatest of ancient Rome), that the first phase of the eruption had already commenced. At this point, Vesuvius was ejecting hot gases high into the stratosphere while also ejecting volcanic debris.

Pliny the Younger describes the first hours of the eruption like so:

"On the 24th of August, about one in the afternoon, my mother desired him [Pliny the Elder] to observe a cloud which appeared of very unusual size and shape. He had just taken a turn in the sun, and, after bathing himself in cold water, and making a light luncheon, gone back to his books: he immediately arose and went out upon a rising ground from whence he might get a better sight of this very uncommon appearance. A cloud, from which mountain was uncertain, at this distance (but it was found afterward to come from Mount Vesuvius), was ascending, the appearance of which I cannot give you a more exact description of than by likening it to that of a pine-tree, for it shot up to a great height in the form of a very tall trunk, which spread itself out at the top into a sort of branches; occasioned, I imagine, either by a sudden gust of air that impelled it, the force of which decreased as it advanced upwards, or the cloud itself, being pressed back again by its weight, expanded in the manner I have mentioned; it appeared sometimes bright and sometimes dark and spotted, according to as it was either more or less impregnated with earth and cinders. This phenomenon seemed to a man of such learning and research as my uncle extraordinary and worth further looking into."

What may not be clear at first when reading one of the 247 surviving letters (it is thought many more were sent) that Pliny the Younger wrote to his friend and historian Tacitus is the phrase "He had just taken a turn in the sun." The phrase refers to the ancient Roman practice of walking and sunbathing naked in the sun while covering one's body in oils. This was considered to be healthy, and Roman men would practice this routine daily. The fact that Pliny the Elder would take a turn in the sun, bathe, and then have lunch tells us that he was not aware of the danger the city was facing at that moment.

Around one p.m., ash and pumice started to fall upon Pompeii. It is believed that the accumulations were between ten and fifteen centimeters (between four and six inches) per hour. By five p.m., there was a layer of pumice 280 centimeters (a little over nine feet) thick. A roof even collapsed under the weight of ash and pumice stone, and it was just the first of many. By this point, there was no natural light left. Dogs were howling and barking, people were screaming and fleeing, while some were killed by collapsing buildings and the volcanic stones falling upon the city.

Before the pumice and ash would start to cover the city entirely, Pliny the Elder was already heading with the galleys under his command to help the cities and people who were close to Vesuvius. The wife of Bassus, Rectina, who was mentioned in the letters, feared the imminent danger since she was stranded in Stabiae, which was about sixteen kilometers (nine miles) from Mount Vesuvius. As Pliny the Elder rushed to aid Rectina and others who were in danger, pieces of cinder and hot black stones fell on the ships' decks. Instead of docking at Herculaneum, which had seen little ash fall, Pliny the Elder steered to Stabiae. He could not dock to meet Rectina, though, and it is unknown if she made it out alive.

However, Pliny did make it to Stabiae, where he met his friend Pomponianus, a Roman senator who witnessed the eruption, assuring him that everything would be all right and that fortune favored the brave. According to Pliny the Younger's letters, Pliny the Elder was stuck at his friend's villa due to the winds. So, he decided to make the best of it. He bathed and had supper with Pomponianus. The sunlight was slowly leaving the sky as evening fell, and the night emphasized the brightness and clearness of the flames, which came out of several sides of Vesuvius.

Pliny the Younger could see the flames from Misenum, as well as the groups of people escaping and fleeing, some without any belongings. However, many Pompeiians remained in the city. It is known based on the excavations that took place centuries later that there were at least two thousand people in Pompeii who sought shelter in the cellars of various buildings, hoping they would be able to wait out the danger.

The eruption continued throughout the night. At around eleven p.m., the first surge hit Herculaneum and neighboring cities. At this point, the Pompeiians still had a chance to flee from the imminent danger, but many of those remaining in the city chose to stay.

John Martin, 1821, The Destruction of Pompeii and Herculaneum, the restored version.[28]

Fear among the people grew with the view of the night sky, which was almost swallowed by the fire coming from Vesuvius. Around midnight, the column above Vesuvius reached thirty-three kilometers (twenty miles) in the air. In the next seven hours, six pyroclastic surges would strike the vicinity. Pyroclastic surges are clouds of ash, rock, and volcanic gas that stick low to the ground and move with hurricane-like winds. The temperatures of these surges would hit several hundred degrees on both the Celsius and Fahrenheit scales. It is more likely that the heat killed the people rather than burning in lava, which never actually made its way to Pompeii, or from being covered by ash while still alive. A leading volcanologist named Giuseppe Mastrolorenzo states that "temperatures outdoors—and indoors—rose up to 300°C [570°F] and more, enough to kill hundreds of people in a fraction of a second...when the pyroclastic surge hit Pompeii, there was no time to suffocate...The contorted postures are not the effects of a long agony, but of the cadaveric spasm, a consequence of heat shock on corpses."

Around one a.m., Herculaneum was destroyed with the first pyroclastic surge. It is estimated that the surge measured between 400 and 450 degrees Celsius (752 and 842 degrees Fahrenheit). It was so hot that wood and leather were carbonized, and the flesh of those still alive burned right off.

Pompeii was the next major city to be hit. Around 6:30 a.m., a pyroclastic surge hit the city. This surge was not as hot as the one at Herculaneum. Instead of burning the bodies, a hard shell was formed around them, which allowed archaeologists to make the famous body casts of those who died in the eruption.

Pliny the Elder and his friend, Pomponianus, were still alive at this time. Sometime during the night or early morning (possibly even shortly after the people of Pompeii were wiped out), the house shook awake those inside (if they had even fallen asleep to begin with), and they had to make the fateful decision as to whether they should stay or make a run for

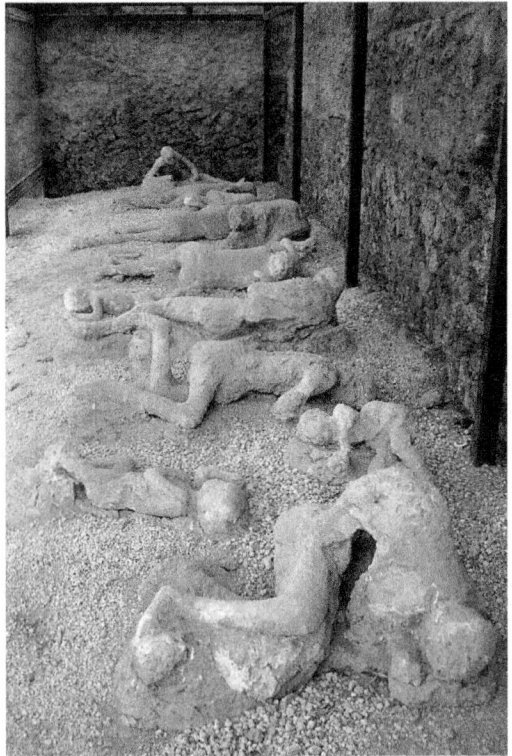

The casts of some victims in the so-called "Garden of the Fugitives," Pompeii. Author: Lancevortex.[29]

it. They decided to leave, strapping pillows on their head to try and somewhat protect themselves from the falling stones.

Pliny the Younger and his mother also fled from Misenum, and they were lucky enough to find safety. Pliny the Elder was not so lucky. The following is how Pliny the Younger believed events played out in regards to his uncle's death.

"It was now day everywhere else, but there deeper darkness prevailed than in the thickest night; which, however, was in some degree alleviated by torches and other lights of various kinds. They thought it proper to go farther down upon the shore to see if they might safely put out to sea, but found the waves still running extremely high, and boisterous. There my uncle, laying himself down upon sailcloth, which was spread for him, called twice for some cold water, which he drank, when immediately the flames, preceded by a strong whiff of sulfur, dispersed the rest of the party, and obliged him to rise. He raised himself up with the assistance of two of his servants and instantly fell dead; suffocated, as I conjecture, by some gross and noxious vapor, having always had a weak throat, which was often inflamed. As soon as it was light again, which was not till the third day after this melancholy accident, his body was found entire, and without any marks of violence upon it, in the dress in which he fell, and looking more like a man asleep than dead."

The Aftermath

Just as we are simultaneously fascinated and horrified by this horrendous event, the Romans were perhaps in an even greater state of shock. Judging by the large number of written documents that recorded the events in Pompeii and the effects that the eruption left on Campania and, with it, on the Roman Empire, this event left a strong and deeply emotional and physical imprint on Rome. The process of healing would be long and hard considering that entire cities were destroyed, along with agriculture and the economy of Campania. It would take a lot of time for the region to recover, and the wound left in the empire's collective memory was deep, and it slowly healed. As a testimony of that impact, many Roman authors and historians wrote about the event, among which are Pliny the Younger's letters.

The Roman statesman and historian Cassius Dio also wrote about the eruption, which is mostly veiled in superstition:

"Many huge men, greater than human size, as giants are depicted, made an appearance, now on the mountain, now in the surrounding countryside and the cities, wandering day and night on the earth and passing through the air. After this were terrible droughts and sudden violent earthquakes, so that the whole plain seethed and the summits leaped up, there were roars, some underground like thunder, some on the surface like the bellowing of oxen. The sea too roared and the sky re-echoed it. Then a sudden portentous crash was heard as if the mountains were collapsing, and first enormous stones were thrown up to reach the height of the mountain-tops themselves, then great quantity of fire and endless smoke so that the whole sky was shaded, the sun completely hidden as if eclipsed.

So day became night, light darkness. Some thought the giants were rising in revolt (for many of their forms could be seen through the smoke, and in addition a sound of trumpets was heard). Others thought that the whole universe was being consumed by chaos or fire. Therefore they fled, some from their houses into the streets, some from outside indoors; from the sea inland and from there to the sea, since in their confusion, they thought that wherever they were not was safer than where they were. At the same time, an unbelievable quantity of ash was blown out, covering land, sea, and all the sky. Not surprisingly, it did a great deal of damage to men, farms, and cattle. It destroyed all fish and birds and, in addition, it buried two whole cities, Herculaneum and Pompeii, while its population was sitting in the theatre. The whole cloud of dust was so great that some of it reached Africa, Syria, and Egypt; it also reached Rome, filling the sky above it and darkening the sun. It occasioned no little fear for several days since people did not know and could not imagine what had happened, but thought that everything was being turned upside down and that the sun was vanishing into the earth and the earth being lifted into the heavens. However, this ash did them no great damage, but later brought a terrible plague on them."

At the time of the eruption, Titus had been the emperor of the Roman Empire for a few months, and he was judged by the way he helped those affected by this horrific natural disaster. It was not an uncommon thing for Rome to aid its colonies and cities that suffered a disaster, and Titus's reign was tested by many disasters as Suetonius and Cassius Dio both describe:

"In his reign, several dreadful disasters occurred—an eruption of Mount Vesuvius in Campania, a fire at Rome that burned for three days and nights, and one of the worst ever outbreaks of the plague. In the face of all these disasters, he displayed not merely the concern of an emperor but also the deep love of a father, whether by offering messages of sympathy or by giving all the financial help he could. He selected by lot some senators of consular rank to regenerate Campania, and allocated the property of those who had died in the eruption and who had no surviving heirs to the renewal of the afflicted towns."

- Suetonius

"In the following year, a fire on the ground spread over a very large part of Rome while Titus was away following the disaster in Campania...Titus, therefore, sent two ex-consuls to Campania to refound the settlements and gave money and the possessions of those who had died without heirs. Titus himself took no money from individuals or cities or kings although many kept giving and promising him large sums, but restored all the damage from his resources."

- Cassius Dio

The excavations of Pompeii have uncovered 1,150 bodies, although it is estimated that 2,000 people died in the eruption. The excavations have demonstrated the power of nature and have also unveiled the once wealthy and beautiful city of Pompeii. Pompeii still holds unearthed secrets, so excavations continue to this day, revealing more mysteries of antiquity. Today, Pompeii stands as a powerful source of knowledge about the lives of the Roman people and those of other cultures who were subdued by the Roman Republic and, later, the Roman Empire.

Conclusion

In the centuries following the eruption, the name and location of Pompeii were lost. The first known year of someone stumbling onto Pompeii was 1592. Domenico Fontana, an architect, discovered paintings while digging an aqueduct. However, he kept the news to himself, so no one investigated the area to see what else could be uncovered. In 1738, men found Herculaneum while settling the foundations for a royal palace. This discovery led archaeologists to find other cities that had been affected by the eruption, even though they did not know the names of the places for which they were searching. In 1763, an inscription was found that identified the city as Pompeii.

Although the city had been forgotten, once it was rediscovered, people were fascinated by the site and the tragic fate that befell its people. And as the discoveries continued, people found more reasons to fall in love with the city. Its origins date as far back as the 8th century BCE, and it was home to wealthy individuals who essentially treated the city as their summer vacation spot.

Pompeii is now one of the most visited archaeological sites in the world, and it is listed as a UNESCO World Heritage Site. Pompeii is still revealing its secrets through its art, artifacts, architecture, and people, some of whose lives and names survived the tooth of time. The last series of excavations took place in 2018, and the archaeologists targeted locations around the city, and it resulted in new findings of historical importance.

Our fascination with Pompeii and the sympathy we have with those who lost their lives coincides with the terror we feel when trying to imagine how the fateful day of the eruption must have played out. Pompeii remains one of the most important archaeological sites, as it provides detailed examples of Roman life, culture, architecture, and history. The communities of the city were comprised of a multitude of different cultures, and it is certain that the excavations will continue to reward us with discoveries and a more complete understanding of antiquity and the people who lived during that time.

Part 4: The Colosseum

A Captivating Guide to an Icon of Ancient Rome Known for Hosting Roman Gladiator Battles and Public Spectacles

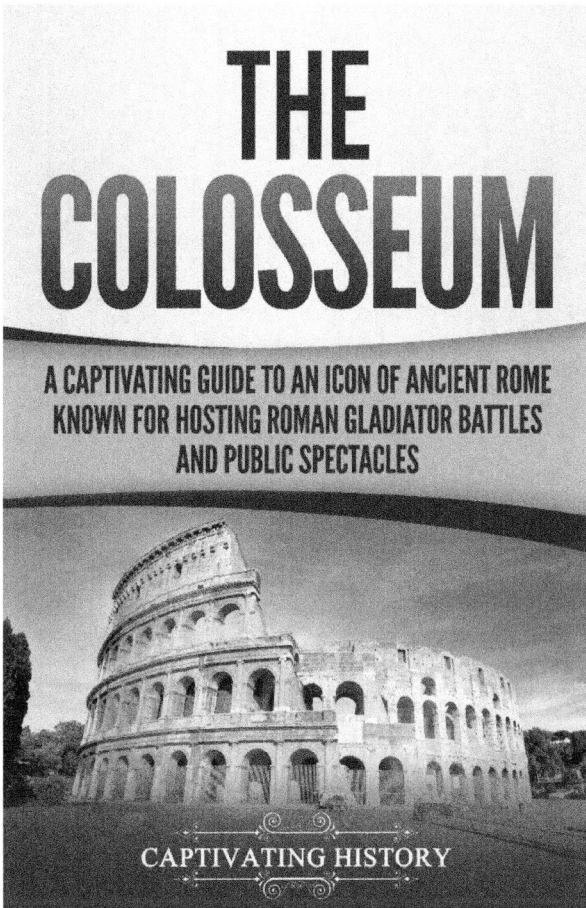

Introduction

The Colosseum is one of the most easily recognized structures from ancient times (along with the Great Wall, the Parthenon, and Stonehenge), but there is a lot more to the famous ruins than most people realize. While there are a lot of movies and media that cover gladiator tournaments, these were only a part of the Colosseum's history. So much happened within those iconic, round walls that are both entertaining and horrifying, especially as Rome played such a vital role in the history of an entire continent.

From its inception, the Colosseum has been a symbol, although the meaning of the structure has changed over the millennia. Emperor Vespasian had his own plans for the grand structure when he initiated its construction sometime between 70 and 72 CE. It took roughly a decade to complete the massive arena, and it was one of the tallest structures in Europe for centuries. Able to hold up to possibly eighty thousand people, the Colosseum became one of the best places to visit in Rome.

Emperor Titus had come to power by the time the Colosseum was completed, and he ensured that the newly constructed facility was something people would be discussing for a long time, though he likely had no idea that people would still be aware of it over two millennia later. Almost as soon as the structure was completed, it had a one-hundred-day celebration of gladiatorial games. When the throngs of celebrators arrived, they were greeted by an impressive, three-story structure that has withstood the ravages of time, wars, and disasters, representing Rome long after the empire fell. Even today, it remains an incredibly impressive structure, but it must have been a truly impressive structure when it was first built.

Over time, the Colosseum moved from being a place of entertainment to a place used by the emerging Roman Catholic Church. It was a fortress during medieval wars and became a dilapidated structure when the elements and the sands of time began to break away parts of the structure. Earthquakes and human warfare were far more damaging than vandalism, but pollution caused the worst damage to the structure, as it eroded the walls and lower levels.

As it lost its relevance as a place for entertainment and became too dangerous for casual use, people and communities in the surrounding areas began to pull out all of the valuable components, including marble and ivory, from the once magnificent structure. For roughly one thousand years, this symbol of a lost empire was seen as a quarry to be used to build up growing towns and cities around Italy.

The historical importance of the structure wasn't considered until the 1800s, and it was then that efforts were made to preserve it. While it had lost a lot of its opulent components, the Colosseum is still a spectacular ruin that shows just how capable the Romans were at creating buildings and other structures. It has become one of the biggest attractions; people from all over the world visit this historical marvel for themselves to experience a fraction of the splendor that Romans experienced over two thousand years ago.

Chapter 1 – Planning and Construction

Well over 1,500 years since Rome ceased to be an empire, we still use the expression "Rome was not built in a day," indicating just how impressive the empire once was. It actually took the Romans several hundred years to create the structures, government, and culture that lived on long after their civilization had collapsed.

Part of what helped to shape the empire was the way the Romans took inspiration from their neighbors, even though they fought those same neighbors. The ties that the Romans had with Greece were obvious in many aspects of their burgeoning culture, especially in their religion. The Romans had the same gods and goddesses as the Greeks but gave them different names and personalities. Over time, the traits of the Roman pantheon adapted to take on the values of the Romans. In the same way, Greek architecture influenced early Roman works, which is clear from the way the Colosseum appears, as it looks similar to Greek architecture. However, they weren't the only neighbors the Romans took ideas from. The Etruscans were another notable civilization that influenced Roman culture and architecture. Rome was one of the most dominant powers in North Africa and Europe for hundreds of years. However, the empire had its fair share of poor rulers. Emperor Nero was so awful that his name remains synonymous with horrible, callous rulers over two thousand years later. Emperor Nero lost the ruling family a lot of support from a large portion of the Romans who could actually force change.

Nero's inability to rule is unknown. Some historians have attributed his horrible methods of ruling to a range of issues, such as mental health and genetics. Other historians have attributed his failed tenure as emperor to the very things that people have been saying since Nero's death, saying he was selfish and that his actions were a reflection of more modern diagnoses, such as psychopathy and a lack of concern for the people under his care.

Emperor Vespasian, who was the emperor who ruled after the succession crisis after the death of the incompetent Nero, knew that it would be important to regain the people's trust. After all, there had been a string of rulers in quick succession. Rebellions and changing alliances were typical of this period, which was called the Year of the Four Emperors. It is thought that the Colosseum was a calculated move to gain the respect of the population who were turning against the rule of an individual. Emperors who understood the importance of winning over the people often started with a populist movement in the beginning. Vespasian hoped not only to show off how strong and capable the Romans were but also to rebuild trust and favor after several disastrous emperors. Vespasian wanted to show the people that he was the kind of ruler who would focus on improving the empire, offering the kinds of entertainment and pride that had once helped the people celebrate the strength of Rome. To do this, he needed to help them forget his predecessors. The Colosseum was a new kind of solution, as there wasn't anything quite like it.

Since Emperor Vespasian had been the one to emerge victorious after the succession crisis, there was still the question of whether his reign was legitimate. He was well aware of how important it was to ensure that he was able to quickly get as many people on his side as possible.

While not the most effective Roman ruler, Emperor Vespasian did have a good understanding of how to win over the people. In an effort to help remove Nero's memory, the Colosseum was built in the location that Nero had owned, where he had kept a garden around a lake. Part of Emperor Vespasian's plan to regain popularity was to dedicate lands associated with Nero's excesses to the people. He wanted to turn those areas into places to celebrate Rome so they would no longer represent the pampered life of a few elites.

Since the plan was to build an enormous theater for sports, the lake, which had been a favorite spot for Nero, had to be drained. This served the dual purpose of clearing the area for a large amphitheater and removing the potential risks that a lake posed in an area where earthquakes remained a threat to the people living in the region. Another measure implemented at the beginning of the Colosseum's construction (specifically to counter the threats posed by earthquakes) was to add concrete foundations that went down six meters, or nearly twenty feet.

Ironically, Nero theoretically allowed everyone access to his lands, but it upset the Roman senators since they didn't think that common people should be allowed to visit locations that they thought should only be used by the elite. Emperor Vespasian was removing a "special place" for the few people who considered themselves above everyone else, and he really couldn't afford to go entirely against them. The structure offered a unique compromise. Nearly anyone would be allowed into the Colosseum, but the more prominent and "important" Romans would be allowed to have areas that were inaccessible to the masses.

Even though Emperor Vespasian was no longer in power when the Colosseum was finished, his descendants kept the same plan, establishing areas where only people who were considered the most important could go. The elite would have places of prominence so they could watch from the best locations. They would also be visible to the masses.

The different seating areas were identified as follows:

- The podium was for the elite members of the Roman Empire.
- The gradation was the seating for important people who had served but had not reached the highest echelons of power.
- The porticus was for the masses, and while it wasn't as comfortable as the other two areas, the people were still able to enjoy the same events. It was far more inclusive than what most other emperors had given them.

The rows closest to the activities belonged to the emperor, his family, and the members of the Senate. The next few rows belonged to those who were a part of the equestrian order (veterans of the Roman cavalry), merchants, bureaucrats, and artisans—people who had managed to earn positions where they would be recognized for their skills. The rest of the seats belonged to the common people, who made up the majority of the Roman Empire. This is actually the way many stadiums are structured today, with the best and most comfortable seats being reserved for people who are considered important (although these people tend to also include relatives to those playing the sport), and the seats higher up are for everyone else. For example, at a basketball game, floor seats would be reserved for important people, and at concerts, the first few rows are often reserved for family, friends, contest winners, and other people who are "important" for some reason.

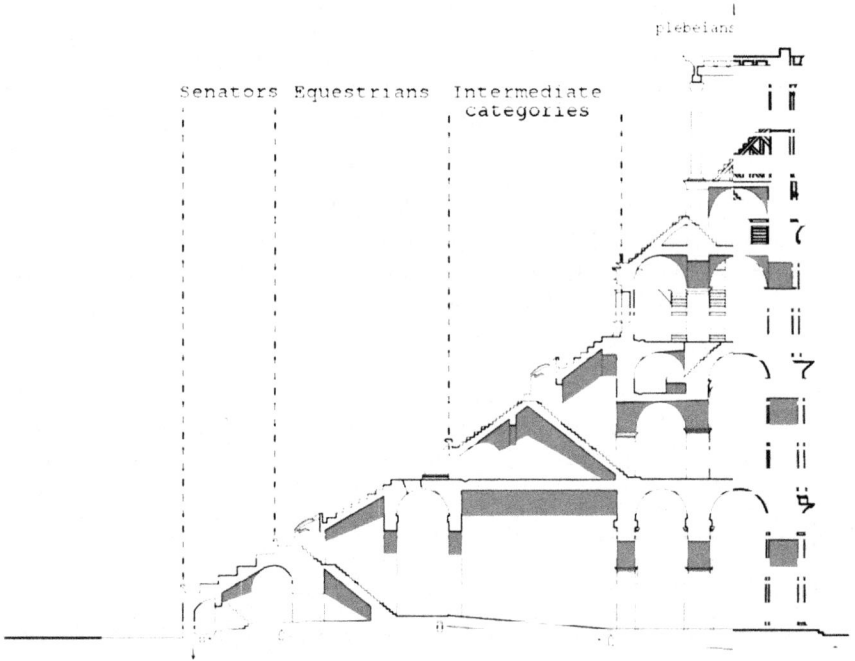

The seating of the Colosseum.[30]

During the design process and construction, the architects provided four entrances exclusively for the important people, who made up roughly 5 percent of the population. For the other 95 percent of people coming to watch the games, there were seventy-six entrances. Separate corridors were made to ensure that the people who were considered important were able to move through the halls without having to mingle with everyone else.

Once people were in their seats, they were largely able to get the same view as everyone else. Obviously, the farther a person was from the action, the less they were able to see, but they weren't entirely excluded from enjoying the games.

Other similar structures of that time were temporary. The Colosseum was unique because it was constructed with a long-lasting material: concrete. The use of this more permanent material has allowed the Colosseum to remain over two thousand years after the people who built it died. It is impressive because the area where it was built was considered a wetland. Even though flooding and poor soil hindered building, the Romans ensured a much more stable structure by digging deep into the dirt, giving it a solid foundation. Concrete was not the only material, though, as it was mixed with travertine stone and bricks.

It included some impressive inner workings as well, things that are not done today. For example, the Romans had a very robust irrigation system that helped them to better tend to farming. They used similar construction methods for the Colosseum, creating a drainage system that allowed them to fill the arena so they could recreate sea battles for people to watch. The builders installed an awning, and the Romans hired sailors who extended and retracted the awning during the rain and heat.

However, perhaps the most impressive part is still visible today: the network of tunnels and chambers under the arena, which was called the hypogeum. An intricate system of gears and levers allowed for people, animals, and props to be lifted into the arena instead of having to walk out onto the field. This made for much more dramatic entrances for battles, plays, and spectacles. The largest participants brought to the arena in this way were elephants, demonstrating that the Romans were able to make devices that were capable of impressive feats.

Because of the turmoil that the Roman Empire was in at the time of Emperor Vespasian's reign, the financial records for this period are unknown. However, there has been speculation that the Romans were able to fund this impressive architectural feat by sacking the Temple of Jerusalem. This ensured that the Roman people didn't feel that their money was being wasted on an awe-inspiring attraction. This would have been an incredibly effective way of showing Roman strength. They could take from the people under their control to celebrate themselves.

As mentioned, Emperor Vespasian started the project around 72 CE, but he did not live long enough to see it completed. His son, Titus, took power following Emperor Vespasian's death, so when the Colosseum was unveiled in 80 CE, he was the one to gain the benefit from it. When it was opened that year, he decreed that there would be one hundred days of games, ensuring that people from far and wide would be able to attend.

This provided a distraction to the problems that were plaguing the empire, and the people thoroughly enjoyed the spectacles.

A coin from Titus's reign celebrating the opening of the Colosseum. [31]

However, the Colosseum wasn't actually completed until 83 CE, by which time Titus had died, and his brother, Domitian, was in power.

Many of the workers on the Colosseum were Jewish slaves brought in after Rome sacked Jerusalem. They not only provided the labor but also a lot of the funding for the impressive structure. The number of estimated slaves used varies, but most agree that it would have required several thousand slaves from start to finish.

When it was finished, the Colosseum was 6 acres inside, with the surrounding entryways creating a circumference of 545 meters. For a long time, it was one of the tallest structures in the world, reaching 48 meters (157.5 feet), which is roughly the height of a 12-story building today.

Chapter 2 – Original Appearance and Early Renovations

Even today, the appearance of the Colosseum is iconic, and it is still easily recognized by people from around the world, despite it being a ruin of its original design.

A view of the Colosseum.[32]

There are many mysteries associated with the structure. The first one goes back to the very core of the Colosseum. The person or people who designed the structure are entirely unknown today. Concrete was used for a lot of the critical components of the Colosseum because its architects understood how strong it was. The Romans had been using the material for some time, but the Colosseum was one of the largest and most extensive uses of concrete in a single structure. The fact that concrete was at the literal foundation of the Colosseum is why it has been able to withstand natural disasters and countless wars.

One of the most noticeable features of the Colosseum is its great height. Four floors surrounded the arena when it was first built. Both the second and third floors were adorned with enormous statues. Although it does look like a circle from some angles, once inside, it is clear that the shape is elliptical to allow for a larger audience. Even today, there are impressive arches that circle three of the four rows. The arches are actually what made the structure so sturdy. Architects used arches because they allowed for substantial weight to be evenly distributed. By using this particular architectural staple, they were able to create buildings that have been able to withstand the test of time. The statues made the building look more regal.

The original Colosseum had brick around the exterior. People plundered different parts of the structure over the years, leaving less than half of the original brick on the structure by the Middle Ages. The interior had marble and other precious resources that were removed over time, so very little of the original opulence has been left. The concrete withstood the thefts because it could not be easily removed, and it is now the most notable material that remains of the impressive structure.

The exterior and the foundation were concrete throughout the arena, but most of the seats were made of stone. The wealthier individuals would bring cushions to sit on. The seats were inclined in a way that is similar to stadiums today, allowing people better visibility, no matter where they were seated.

Not all of the changes made to the Colosseum after its initial construction related to improving the structure. A lot of the later construction work focused on repairs and maintenance, even when it was still fairly young.

Based on more recent understandings of the structure, some of the corridors were painted or covered in colored plaster. It is thought that the colors were black, green, red, and yellow. It is known that there was a devastating fire at the Colosseum in 217 CE, and some archaeologists hypothesize that the original four colors were destroyed in the fire. Instead of spending the time and money to restore the corridors to their original appearance, the Romans opted for a much simpler red and white. The Roman Empire was in decline by this time, so it was likely necessary to be more economical.

The structure was struck by lightning during the 3rd century, causing further fire damage. While repairs were made, it was done at a much slower rate, taking a couple of decades to complete. The repairs were not nearly as thorough or detailed as previous repairs.

The last known time that the Romans worked to repair the structure was around 443 CE. That year, Rome experienced a significant earthquake, resulting in the top tier of seats being almost completely destroyed. By this time, the use for the structure had been altered, as it no longer held gladiator contests, so the Romans did not have nearly as much concern for maintaining the Colosseum. While they did some work, it was not detailed and was much more haphazard than previous restoration and maintenance work. They did not even bother completing the repairs. Less than one hundred years later, the Colosseum saw its last major event, and it soon became repurposed once Rome ceased to rule Europe.

Much of the beauty of the Colosseum that was enjoyed by the Romans is long lost to time. The opulence of what it once was has been lost to the weather, fire, and plundering. It is impossible to know everything that was used or exactly how it looked since most of the important materials have been removed, except for the impressive shell. Even so, the Colosseum remains an incredible piece of history that continues to show that ancient Rome was capable of creating marvelous structures, some of which are possibly even more stable and resilient than any structure being made today.

Chapter 3 – Naming the Architectural Wonder

Although the massive structure has come to be known as the Colosseum, it has had many names since it was first constructed. Originally, it was called the Flavian Amphitheater, although it would have been known as Amphitheatrum Flavium at the time. There is nothing subtle about the name. The title bears the name of the family that commissioned and presented the structure to Rome, the Flavian dynasty, giving them credit for building such an impressive structure. The other part of the name is entirely unimaginative as it simply describes what the structure is—an amphitheater. While histories and history buffs likely know the original name, most people are almost completely unaware of the Flavian dynasty and its role in creating the amazing structure.

At a glance, it is easy to imagine that the name comes from the sheer size of the structure. Perhaps this is one of the easiest ways to remember the name when first learning about it, but that is not where the name derives from.

Ironically, the structure has come to be known by a name that is also attached to Emperor Nero. Since Emperor Vespasian was working to replace the areas associated with his predecessor, one of the things that was located near the place where the Colosseum was to be built was a thirty-meter (nearly one-hundred-foot) statue of the late emperor. The statue was called the Colossus of Nero, and it was considered one of the greatest wonders of the world at that time. The statue was impressive, making it a fairly good complement to the enormous structure. This is an example of how Emperor Vespasian and other rulers of the Flavian dynasty were different from Nero since they made things for everyone to enjoy instead of creating massive to celebrate himself. However, as time progressed and the events of Nero's reign and the tumultuous year of the Four Emperors became something largely lost to time, people failed to realize that the name of the statue was transferred over to the structure, which was meant to be the antithesis of that very statue.

While there were a lot of negative associations with Nero, his statue was still viewed as a wonder and demonstrated the ingenuity of Rome. The people were proud of it. It has been said that Saint Bede the Venerable once wrote, "As long as the Colosseum exists, Rome will exist; when the Colosseum falls, Rome will fall also; but when Rome falls, the world will fall too." He was a monk during the Middle Ages, showing that both the Colosseum and the Colossus were still around or were at least well known around the world (Bede never went to Rome to see either structure).

It seems unlikely that Bede wrote this, but someone from his time period did, so the quote has often been misattributed to him. Some have thought that this writer was talking about the Colosseum, but it is much more likely that he was talking about the statue of Nero. At the time, the structure was probably still known as the Flavian Amphitheater. The writer specifically mentioned the Colyseus, which is generally considered a reference to the statue. As a scholar who was writing around the 7th century, he was more likely to know which of the two structures was at greater risk because the weather and the tectonic plates could do more damage to a single statue than to an entire structure. Also, by that time, Roman power and influence were not what they once had been.

The statue had been repurposed over the years, with people saying that it was Apollo, not Nero, by the time the Colosseum opened. When Emperor Hadrian was in power, it was said that it represented him; the famous wall that he built in modern-day northern England is what this emperor is most remembered for today. Toward the end of the Roman Empire, the people once again decided that it was a representation of Apollo instead of a specific emperor.

The fact that the statue was the focus of so much attention and change indicates that it was an important symbol to Rome. While the purpose of the Colosseum changed over time, its purpose was entertainment, at least while Rome was still an empire. It had a purpose beyond being impressive; the statue was merely a symbol. This is why it is thought that Bede or whoever wrote that passage was referring to the statue, not the structure.

And this author proved to be right. Unlike the Colosseum, the Colossus of Nero did not withstand the test of time. Today, the only remaining part of the once-impressive piece of art is the pedestal on which the statue stood. The statue fell, as did the power of the Roman Empire. However, the Colosseum did not.

By 1000 CE, it seemed as if the Colosseum was no longer being celebrated as an architectural marvel. It seemed that many of the symbols of Roman ingenuity were disappearing. The first time that the term "Colosseum" was used to reference the amphitheater was around 1061 CE when it was documented in the archive of Santa Maria Nova (today known as Santa Francesca Romana, a Catholic church in Rome). In this writing, the structure was referred to as Amphitheatrum Colossei. From there, it began being discussed in other writings, particularly by pilgrims to the region. During this time, the structure came to be known as the Colosseum.

Today, the structure is called the Colosseum, but when spelled out, it is both the Colosseum and the Coliseum. For the most part, the terms are used interchangeably because using either term brings to mind the right structure. However, it has been argued that "Colosseum" is the correct name when talking specifically about the Roman amphitheater, with the "C" being a capital letter.

Chapter 4 –The Arena and Amenities

Today, people often think that the Colosseum was a place for the gladiators and a few theatrics. The structure housed so much more than that. It was a place of games and spectacles that we don't have today. Movies and shows allow us to get a glimpse of that kind of entertainment, though. We don't have any comparable structures today because there is no place to go to witness water battles on that scale in an enclosed arena. You either have to watch them on the actual water or on a screen.

When it was fully completed, between fifty thousand and eighty thousand people could come and watch events and celebrations. Conceived as a way to remind Europe of the might of Rome, the Colosseum was the most complex building of its time and would remain the most complex building for over a millennia. To this day, it is still the largest amphitheater humans have ever completed.

As mentioned in Chapter 2, a lot of considerations went into the design so that the Romans would have the ability to really impress the people who came to the events. The place that remains perhaps the most inspiring is the hypogeum, the area under the Colosseum.

The Arena

Most of us have seen movies or shows that depict what the arena looked like when it was used for spectacles. Actually seeing the structure in person creates an entirely different feeling because it feels so much more real. You can more easily imagine what it was like to attend a game in person back in ancient times. It is somewhat similar to watching a football game versus actually attending one. While you won't be able to watch any games today, you can tour the engineering marvel in a way that was not available to most people who lived in ancient Rome.

Looking at the grounds, the place looks very open. Visitors are able to see the stones that held up the arena and the labyrinthian area under the structure. The arena itself largely isn't there now because it was not made of earth. The mechanisms and other moving parts under the structure would not have worked, nor would they have been able to have the stunning water battle reenactments, if they had been under actual ground. Since the Romans built over a drained artificial lake, the area was already open.

When the Romans began having gladiator fights and other spectacles, they placed wood panels over the underground area. This hid what was happening from the spectators. Once the panels were placed, staff would add layers of sand over them to create a more natural look to the fights. The sand was collected and brought from Monte Mario, a hill in the northwestern part of Rome, which was a fairly short distance from the Colosseum. Still, it was an impressive feat, as they needed enough sand to cover 83 meters by 48 meters (272.3 feet by 157.5 feet). When the panels were placed, they were set up so that animals, people, and props could be brought up through the floor instead of being walked out onto the grounds.

The seating closest to the arena was not on the same level because it could have put the very important spectators at risk. The stands were raised up roughly 3 to 4.5 meters (10 to 15 feet) from the arena, creating a large wall that would be nearly impossible to scale and providing protection from whatever was happening.

Where much of the Colosseum is white or cream colored, the wall around the arena was lined with red or black stones. Considering how much blood was shed on the grounds, it made sense that the wall wasn't a color that could be easily stained. Atop the wall were the caves or seating for the spectators.

The Two Gates: Life and Death

When many events started, people would direct their attention to the gates. Animals were often brought up through the floor. People left through two main gates.

- The Porta Triumphalis was for the gladiators who survived, and the name translates as the "Door of Victory." The gladiators also entered through this gate.

- The Porta Libitinaria was for the people who died in the ring. The name of this arch honored the goddess Libitina, who oversaw tombs.

These two archways made it clear who won and who lost. Gladiators did get to enter through the Porta Triumphalis, but they would not all leave through it. Considering how much time, money, and energy went into training gladiators, it wasn't always guaranteed that they would die.

The second gate was not just for the dead, as death was not always guaranteed. When a participant lost, whether they were injured or dead, they exited through this gate. It led down to the gladiator area underground, where they were able to get immediate medical attention.

Once the dead passed through the Porta Libitinaria, they were taken to the Spoliarium. All of their armor and weapons were removed and placed in the Armamentarium for other gladiators to use.

Amenities

The aqueducts that brought water to the Colosseum allowed for mock water battles, but that was not the sole use of water in the facility. One of the most surprising amenities at the Colosseum was the water fountains, as they were similar to the kinds of water fountains you see in stadiums today. Given that the Colosseum was made to seat tens of thousands of people, hundreds of fountains were added to ensure that people had a way of getting water. To ensure there was water, the ancient Romans ran pipes through the walls, and those pipes stored the water that people would drink.

They also had facilities for removing human waste, as well as restrooms. The restrooms were not quite like what we have today (instead of toilet seats, people had to hover over holes), but people were able to use the bathroom, and the waste was then removed through their sewer system.

Perhaps one of the most innovative aspects of the Colosseum was the velarium, a cover that ensured that the spectators were covered from the elements. It protected them from rain and sun when it was needed. The velarium was retractable, so if it was a beautiful day, the spectators were able to enjoy the open sun. When it was raining or when the summer was at its hottest, they would extend the velarium over much of the stadium, shielding the spectators from the elements. The Romans brought in sailors to control the process of retracting and extending the velarium. The material used to make the cover was a unique type of canvas and netting. While it did not extend over the entire inner arena, it did cover roughly two-thirds of it. The people in the arena were generally exposed, but the spectators were mostly comfortable.

Chapter 5 – The Hypogeum and the Connected Schools

Movies and shows have worked to reenact what the spectators saw in the Colosseum, but there was so much occurring under the boards that even ancient Romans didn't know about. It is much easier to see the underground area today, and it is impressive because the masonry is still largely standing. The engineers made an area that was able to withstand everything happening on the wooden panels above, including elephants that were raised up from the underground regions.

The hypogeum is a complex substructure that runs under the arena, taking up the space that used to be the artificial lake. It was entirely different from the arena that the crowd saw. If a person didn't know where they were going, they could easily get lost. That's why today there are tours to walk people through those areas. What's really impressive is that the hypogeum is two stories underground, demonstrating just how complex the ancient Romans' engineering could be.

A view of the arena with a clear view of the hypogeum. [33]

The large labyrinthian layer of the Colosseum has two main corridors, but looking down on it, the corridors look like a thumbprint. When it was designed, the hypogeum was divided into different areas to handle the activities of a wide range of events. For example, there were places for the gladiators, prisoners, animals, and even storage. It is interesting to think about what it would have been like during an event and how people must have felt as the crowds cheered.

It is also important to note that this area was initially not planned or designed to be what it would eventually become. Neither Emperor Vespasian nor Emperor Titus had thought about the logistics of the activities held in the Colosseum. Emperor Domitian decided to use the location under the Colosseum for preparations, which would largely end the water events, as they would damage the structure.

The Tunnels and Devices

Making the hypogeum took a few years, and it required a considerable amount of work to ensure that the people under the stadium would be safe while things were occurring out in the open. They used stone to create eighty different shafts to transport people and animals to the arena. Some of the shafts were also designed to have moving platforms, known as hegmata. The primary purpose of these was to move larger animals and equipment to the surface.

To ensure that they would be able to bring up the large animals and items to the arena, the builders made thirty-six trapdoors. Occasionally, gladiators would be brought up through the trapdoors, but usually, larger items were transported that way to act as a surprise for the spectators. Many of the people who were employed to work in the hot hypogeum were slaves. They worked the machinery and equipment. They also cleaned and tended to the animals.

The tunnels were made to easily move around under the arena, including being able to get out of the Colosseum. Some of the tunnels led to buildings directly outside of the structure. These structures typically housed the participants of the arena and also acted as storage, where items were saved for later use. The Summum Choragium was an outside building that was used for storage.

There were five tunnels leading under the roads and directly into the hypogeum, but only three of them were for the gladiators. Two of the tunnels were used to bring other items and people into the arena.

The Gladiator Areas

Gladiators did not live under the Colosseum. They had their own special tunnels that led from their schools to the tunnels under the arena. When it was time for their fights, they would leave the hypogeum to face off in front of the crowd. To ensure that fighters would be able to properly prepare and fight, a large part of the underground was dedicated to creating spaces for the different needs of the gladiators, even after death. Most of these spaces were in buildings just outside of the stadium, but they were connected by underground tunnels.

The gladiators had a barracks area and a dedicated place for training under the arena, ensuring that they could sleep and practice leading up to their fights. When it was time for them to enter the arena, they went through the Gate of Life, and those who survived their time in the arena would return through it after they were done. These doors lead to the barracks area and other sections that were used by the athletes of the day.

All four main gladiator schools near the Colosseum focused on different types of training, mostly depending on what the gladiators brought into the ring (weapons and armor). For instance, one school focused on how to fight against a very specific type of opponent. Some of the schools used the same tunnels to get to the Colosseum.

Since death was not inevitable, there were medical experts available to start working on gladiators who survived. People who were victorious in a fight could still be injured. Anyone who survived went there to have their injuries treated because (much like today) a lot of money was invested in these very popular athletes. If a gladiator survived the fight, it was important to get him fixed up and ready for his next fight.

Those who died were also brought through the area, but they were put into a morgue.

The Great School

The Ludus Magnus, or the Great School, was where gladiators trained. In the early days, gladiators were mostly slaves and people of lesser stature, but over time, spectators began to hold the successful gladiators in high esteem. Over time, healthy men (and later women, although female fighters were never as popular) volunteered to become gladiators because they wanted some of the prestige that could be won in the arena.

Regardless of their background, gladiators followed the same rules and were mostly trained in the same school. The conditions were different, of course. Enslaved gladiators were not there of their own free will, so measures, such as chaining them, had to be taken to ensure they did not escape. Women fought as gladiators, but it is uncertain if they were trained at the school as the men.

It isn't possible to use the passage from the school to the Colosseum now because a road and sewage system now run through where the tunnel was. It can be visited during a tour, though, as it is just across the street from the impressive structure.

The Bestiarii School

Known as the Ludus Matutinus, this school was for gladiators who specialized in fighting animals instead of people. This school was established at the same time as the hypogeum and had a tunnel that led from the school to the arena. The name means "of the morning" because that was when fights against animals were generally scheduled.

The school was next to the Ludus Magnus. The school had a place to keep the animals while waiting for fights, and they would be moved under the Colosseum prior to the fight.

The Ludus Dacicus Dacian School

Gladiators in this school were usually from Thracian countries, and their weapons of choice were different from the weapons used by more traditional schools. Their favorite sword was a sica, which had a curved blade that was roughly forty to forty-five centimeters (sixteen to eighteen inches) long.

The Ludus Gallicus School

The least common type of gladiator, those who trained in the Ludas Gallicus, wore more armor than the traditional gladiators. They learned Gallic combat, which consisted of powerful attacks. Then, they had to learn to complement their actions with the teachings of Samnite gladiators, who used a short sword.

Gladiators who followed other similarly heavily armored schools joined this school for training and preparation prior to appearing in the Colosseum.

Passaggio di Commodo

In addition to the tunnels used by the gladiators, there was a fifth tunnel that allowed the emperor to enter the arena. This tunnel went from the palace to the arena, giving the emperor a way to avoid being seen coming and going if he wished.

Chapter 6 – Early Uses

Emperor Titus opened the structure to the public around 80 CE with a grand event that lasted one hundred days. The original structure was not fully complete. That would happen about two years later under Emperor Domitian, although by the time of Titus, the structure was completely functional; there was just still work to be done on the upper stories of the structure.

The freestanding structure was like a beacon to people who came to Rome because it was so easily visible from nearly any angle. Most amphitheaters were largely built into hillsides to reduce how much had to be built. By using sturdy arches and columns, the Romans were able to construct something that was solid enough to literally stand on its own. Between the games and the opulence of the structure, word of the Colosseum spread, and it became a significant draw for people well outside of the Roman Empire.

The Colosseum was said to be a gift to the Roman people, and when it opened to one hundred days of games, it was a spectacle that was unlike anything that had come before it.

Emperor Commodus: Failing to Understand the Point of the Colosseum

Following the games, the Flavian Amphitheater became a destination for a wide range of activities. The gladiator matches remained the most famous, but the Romans were able to do a lot more with the large arena. However, it has been noted that Emperor Commodus actually participated in gladiator fights at the Colosseum.

When Commodus began his reign, he was a co-emperor with Marcus Aurelius, his father, starting around 177 CE. At the time, the young emperor was fifteen years old, something that would prove to be incredibly problematic. Marcus Aurelius failed to acknowledge that his son showed signs of being a poor choice to rule. As one historian, Aelius Lampridius, would eventually write about this early co-emperor situation, "Even from his earliest years he was base and dishonorable, and cruel and lewd, defiled of mouth, moreover, and debauched."

Marcus Aurelius was a beloved emperor, having expanded the empire and understood how to keep the people on his side. He was related to members of the Flavian dynasty, and his family had a prominent place in the empire. As he grew, he learned how to govern. His rise to power is unknown today because he was not the chosen successor to Emperor Hadrian. He was meant to be a joint emperor around his seventeenth birthday, but something happened that meant he did not actually become emperor until he was forty years old. However, he won over a lot of people over those years. He was a great strategist, which was why he was able to help expand the empire, and he was also considered very intelligent. Marcus Aurelius is still known for his philosophy and intellectual pursuits.

Unfortunately, Marcus Aurelius's son did not take after him, and their shared reign did not last long. It is unknown if it would have helped Commodus to learn how to be a better ruler since he was eighteen when his father died, but he certainly was not up to filling his predecessor's shoes. Like Nero and Caligula, Commodus preferred to indulge in all of the benefits of being an emperor without paying enough attention to the people under him. With a large harem and no interest in working, he spent much of his time delegating the important work to other people.

What seemed to interest Commodus the most was gladiator fights. Sometimes, he would attend them, but the emperor was said to have participated in over one hundred events. Not that most of those were particularly fair. The odds were heavily stacked in his favor. It is said that he once killed one hundred bears (which could be an exaggeration) by killing the bears with spears from his seat in the stands. It is also said that he had put men who had lost their feet in the arena. They were forced to dress as snakes and throw sponges at him. Commodus clubbed all of them to death. The only opponents that he treated well were actual gladiators who posed a real threat to him. He would occasionally hurt them by cutting off an ear or part of their nose, but he did not do anything that would result in death. It is almost certain that the only reason he was able to draw blood was because the gladiators understood that the emperor needed to be allowed to win the fight.

By the time he died, Commodus had bragged about having beaten twelve thousand opponents in the ring while fighting with his left hand. This might have been a sign of some kind of mental disorder, but it was certainly a sign that he was very sheltered from reality. Considering how intelligent and capable his father was, it seems that Commodus's hedonistic approach to life was more a result of him not being taught better when he was young and people being willing to enable his horrible tendencies. Whatever the case, he seemed to have come to the conclusion that he was Hercules reincarnated, and he tried to convince his people of this fact.

Unfortunately for him, Commodus seemed to become more like Nero during his time as emperor, even going as far as to remove the head of Nero's statue (the one from which the Colosseum was named). He had a new statue head created that resembled him. He further changed the statue to make it look like Hercules by adding a club to the statue's hand and a lion at the statue's feet. Both of these were images closely associated with Hercules. This was not the only statue that Commodus created that was meant to compare him to the legendary fighter. As additional evidence of his delusions, he renamed all of the months of the year after himself, with one of those months being Hercules. Other months reflected other names and titles that he gave himself.

His rule was more tyrannical, so people did not tend to confront him in person. In 182 CE, his sister tried to get others to rise against him and assassinate the emperor. The people who conspired with her were killed. She was sent into exile for a short period of time, and then she, too, was killed. There was a second attempt on his life in 187 CE. It was only in 192 CE that one of the attempts was actually successful. It is believed that one of Commodus's women (a mistress or someone part of his harem) helped two of his officials to poison him. The poison did not finish him off, though, so they hired Narcissus, a wrestler, to ensure that the emperor died. The professional wrestler succeeded in strangling Commodus to death. Commodus was thirty-one years old.

While most people know of the corruption and excess of Caligula and Nero, Commodus is far less well known. He seemed to be just as horrible and incompetent as they were. He was finally brought to the public's attention in the movie *Gladiator*, which was released in 2000. The movie was far from accurate, as he did not kill his father, and he did not die after killing a gladiator. Still, it was good to see the historical villain brought to life (and back to people's attention) by the capable hands of Joaquin Phoenix. While the movie got a lot wrong, Phoenix masterfully created a loathsome and horrible figure who more accurately reflected how most of Rome felt about the man who ruled for far too long.

The Mock Water Battles

Probably the most impressive events that occurred in the amphitheater were the mock water battles called naumachia. There are indications that the first one of these occurred in 46 BCE, so it was not a new thing when the Colosseum was finally finished. However, it was by no means a normal spectacle because of how much work was required to hold such an extravagant event. It is thought that only four or five were held throughout the entire Roman Empire because these events were so time intensive and required a level of planning that went far beyond any other type of event. It is thought that at least two of these events occurred at the Colosseum in the early days (before the hypogeum was completed).

These events were heavily orchestrated, and some of them included water monsters. We don't even have anything similar today. At best, we have water scenes on screen, but most of those are created with a computer. There was also a lot that could go wrong. Since the emperor would be in attendance, security was necessary.

The first recorded naumachia was in honor of Julius Caesar, and it occurred in 46 BCE. It was meant to celebrate the ending of four wars. The naumachia wasn't the only event, but it was certainly the most awe-inspiring. There were horse races that were held away from the water battles, musical entertainment, and other nonviolent entertainment. However, there were also some other violent spectacles, including land combat (such as infantrymen and cavalry). This first recorded mock water battle occurred in an artificial basin created near the Tiber River. There were four thousand oarsmen and two thousand men who were to do the fighting as a part of the battle.

Everyone knew there would be an impressive water battle, so the event attracted thousands of people. It is unclear just how much of what they witnessed was planned and choreographed and how much was the men just improvising and attacking each other. With a large number of attendees and not enough control over a huge crowd, some of the people who came to witness the spectacle were trampled and killed. Ovid would write of the event, "With such a throng, who could not fail to find what caught his fancy?" This indicates that the entertainment went much further than merely spectating, with the event having plenty of debauchery. And this went beyond just drinking, as was highlighted by the number of surrounding brothels and the number of sex workers at the event.

Even though a lot of consideration and care went into making the Colosseum, there was still an element of danger, particularly when it came to filling it with water for the mock battles. Cassius Dio, a Roman historian, would write about the preparation for such a battle at the Colosseum around 235 CE. According to his writings, the mock battle occurred at a time when there was also heavy rain. This account relays that both participants in the battle and members of the audience died during the deluge. If this account is correct, it would explain why the Romans altered the structure, adding the hypogeum to be used for safer events or at least safer events for the spectators.

Chapter 7 – Death in the Colosseum

We largely associate the Colosseum with fighting, whether individuals or mock battles. This was obviously one of the biggest draws to the arena, but fighters were not the only people sent into the Colosseum to die. Rome ruled a large part of Europe, North Africa, and part of the Middle East at its height. The reputation Rome has today was earned through centuries of treating certain populations of their growing empire in ways that would be considered war crimes today.

This chapter looks at the people who were singled out for death in the Colosseum, whether or not that death was inevitable. The amphitheater was open for a little under four hundred years. In that time, historians have estimated that 400,000 people died in the arena. That means that in a single year, one thousand people died to entertain the audience. The gladiators were not the only ones who entered the Colosseum, although they were almost certainly seen as the most valuable people. A lot of those deaths were people whose deaths would be seen as beneficial to the empire.

The Gladiators

It shouldn't come as a surprise that gladiators were the biggest draw. When these athletes were set to fight against other gladiators, the fighters were paired up in a way that is similar to how athletes are assessed for fights today. For example, we have heavyweight boxing matches now.

Gladiators were set to face each other based on their size, skill, school, and record.

In the early days, gladiators were slaves or prisoners. Then, soldiers joined the arena, and eventually, people would voluntarily become fighters. The shift in participants was because of how much respect a gladiator could receive if he was successful in the arena. This raised those in the lower classes if they were successful, especially slaves, as they could be freed. With the chance to gain fame, people were more likely to put their lives on the line.

Regardless of who a gladiator was, they were expected to die without showing any fear of what was to come. They were supposed to entertain the spectators by being honorable, even as they died.

Prisoners and Execution

Public executions were common in Rome, just like they were around the world until the 20th century. However, it wasn't quite like today. Prisoners could be executed in many different ways, and it was often horrific for the people put into the arena for the expressed purpose of dying.

Perhaps the most well-known prisoners to be put into the ring were Christians. There are actually no records of Christians being killed in the Colosseum as martyrs. It's possible that these kinds of killings occurred elsewhere in the empire, but it's not certain that this type of entertainment was brought into the heart of Rome. Early Christians were killed because they were pacifists and refused to worship the Roman gods. They seemed fearless in following their convictions, and by doing so, they helped to spread their religion much farther and faster than nearly any other group. This happened in part because the Romans held bravery in high esteem. It's possible that no Christians were actually killed in the Colosseum, as that would bring a growing religion into the capital and would have shown the spectators just how far the Christians were willing to go for their beliefs.

There are unconfirmed stories of Christians being killed in the amphitheater, with the most famous being St. Ignatius of Antioch. He was said to have been the first Christian put in the Colosseum. He allegedly faced lions. Those reports have him saying, "I am as the grain of the field and must be ground by the teeth of the lions, that I may become fit for His table." Following his execution, over one hundred Christians were shot by archers. It's also possible that this occurred somewhere other than the Colosseum because Christians were killed all across the empire. It is reported that Christians were executed in front of Nero's statue, with the poor people being placed in a brazen bull. These were large bulls that were made of bronze and were hollow inside. People would be placed into the bulls, and then a fire would be set under it. The person inside of it would be burned alive.

Most executions were carried out around noon, allowing people to take a break from their regular activities to watch people be executed. These people had committed major crimes in the empire. Young children were strongly encouraged to watch. This was considered a way of discouraging young people from committing the same crimes.

The heinous crimes that were considered worthy of being shown publicly started as a fairly short list:

- People who deserted from the military

- Rebels against the empire

- Fugitives

It didn't take long for that list of crimes to grow exponentially. Things like crop destruction, theft of goods or cattle, arson, deceiving a customer, being profane in a temple, going back on a promise, perjury, and rape were just a few of the crimes that were added to the list.

The manner of execution also varied based on the citizenship status of the person to be executed. If someone was a Roman citizen, they were decapitated. Since the condemned would not have a long, drawn-out death, it was considered an honorable way to go. This is fairly ironic as the people being executed might have committed some very horrific crimes, so the thought of letting them die honorably was less of a deterrent. For those who weren't Roman citizens, the manner of death was often related to the person's social status and the crime that they committed. People were burned, slain with a sword, crucified, and tortured. Some of the most brutal methods of execution were to have the criminal reenact a myth or historical scene in which the character they portrayed was bound to die. Perhaps the cruelest was throwing the people to a wide range of animals who were just as doomed as the criminal. Naturally, the animals almost always won in those cases, but the animals would eventually be killed during gladiator fights or animal hunts.

Animals Were a Part of the Deadly Entertainment

People were not the only ones to die to entertain the masses. It's been estimated that over one million animals were killed as a part of the spectacles in the Colosseum. Besides the gladiators who were trained to kill them as a part of the regular fights, there were events called venatio, which were animal hunts. The Romans brought animals from all across their sprawling empire just to have them killed in the arena. This was seen as a way of proving just how dominant the empire was since they could bring exotic animals from pretty much anywhere in the known world. Since it was expensive to do this and there was no real financial benefit to the empire, it showed off Rome's wealth too.

Many types of animals were sent into the arena to die, and not all of them were ferocious. Besides elephants, bears, lions, and tigers, the Romans sent rabbits, crocodiles, goats, boars, dogs, deer, and hippopotamuses into the ring. Although there is no solid evidence, it has been reported that so many animals were killed in the arena that a few species went extinct as a result.

Notably missing from the animals who died in the Colosseum were wolves. Romans held wolves in high regard because they saw the animal as religiously significant. This meant that one of the most ferocious animals in the empire, an animal that could fight well as a pack, was not included as entertainment.

Chapter 8 – Medieval Uses of the Iconic Structure

As the Roman Empire crumbled, repairs and renovations on the Colosseum became less frequent. By the Middle Ages, nature and time had ravaged the structure. Humans would further reduce the once-magnificent structure into a literal shell of itself.

Natural Disasters

The first natural disaster to occur at the Colosseum was a fire started by a lightning strike, which caused significant damage in 217 CE. It managed to burn many of the wooden levels on the inside of the structure, and it took over one hundred years to fully repair all of the damage. Final repairs were coupled with renovations, which was why it wasn't done until 320 CE. It is thought that this caused significant structural damage as well, so the interior of the Colosseum wasn't quite the same after the fire was extinguished.

The next major natural disaster that is thought to have affected the amphitheater was the earthquake of 443 CE. This happened toward the end of the Western Roman Empire (historians usually put the fall of Rome around 470 to 500 CE). With the empire in decay, the records were not nearly so well kept, so it is not sure just how much damage the Colosseum suffered because of the earthquake.

There were other fires and earthquakes, but they weren't as significant or costly. The Colosseum ceased to be used for entertainment after Rome fell, which was when people became the primary means of destroying the historic location. They would begin to plunder it for its valuable materials.

Housing

The rise of Christianity across Europe changed the focus of the power structure. People who were higher up in the religious establishment began to take control over the important structures of the empire, and the Colosseum was a building that offered a lot of potential for use. It came into the hands of friars who lived nearby from 800 to 1349 CE. The place already had a sewage system and other amenities that made it comfortable, and with the tunnels under the arena, it was easy to repurpose the Colosseum into a rental space. The area where animals and gladiators used to wait until they were brought out was changed into living quarters. Walls were built to divide the space into units. The center became a communal area.

The arrangement ended when an earthquake made the residents realize just how dangerous it was to live in this magnificent ruin. With no one having the dedicated time or money to maintain the structure, it was clear to the people who lived in it that the Colosseum wasn't a safe place to live.

The prominent Frangipani family took control of parts of the iconic landmark around 1200 CE. Not much is known about what they did with it, but they did claim the entire structure for a while. It seems likely that they were the ones benefiting from people living in the Colosseum.

Intentional Destruction and Farther Attempts at Use

It isn't clear what happened to the Colosseum over the years once it was clear that the building wasn't a place that had much practical use. However, Rome was the center of the Catholic Church, and Christians wanted to leave their mark around the city and in nearby locations, particularly the Vatican. The Catholic Church firmly believed that the Colosseum was a place where Christians were sacrificed for entertainment. They used the claim that many Christians were martyred in the stadium to claim it for themselves.

The 1349 CE earthquake saw some additional destruction to the structure; it lost some of its concrete and stone, which were critical parts for some of the arches. Large rock and stone chunks lay around the Colosseum, but they did not remain there forever. Christians took these chunks and used them in the construction of several cathedrals, including St. John Lateran and St. Peter. Pieces of the Colosseum were also used in the construction of the Palazzo Venezia and along the Tiber River.

As they built their own structures and less impressive works of architecture, the people who lived around Rome began mining precious materials from the structure. Essentially, they used the Colosseum as a quarry, taking any material that was still usable. By this time, the wood was rotten and not usable, but nearly everything else could be removed, including the marble and more decorative rocks and bricks.

The Catholic Church would try again to use the structure, but this time, the pope was the one who wanted to make the Colosseum something that would be financially beneficial to the area. Pope Sixtus decided that it would be a good place to make wool, so it was transitioned into a wool factory around 1500 CE. After his death, the factory was quickly shut down.

Unfortunately, people would continue to strip parts of the Colosseum away, leaving deep scars from where hinges and bronze clamps had been removed from the walls and doors.

The plundering of the structure was finally declared over by Pope Benedict XIV. He said that it was wrong to do this in the place where so many Christians were martyred. He was the first pope to push for renovations to the structure. People finally began to want to preserve the building that was once the pride of the Roman Empire. It isn't certain when the Catholic Church began to protect the Colosseum (sometime during the 16th and 17th centuries), but it finally started to recognize the importance of preserving one of the greatest engineering feats in human history.

Chapter 9 – The Colosseum in Modern Times

There is no picture of what the Colosseum used to look like. What we recognize today is how it has looked for several hundred years, which is unfortunate because even the ruins are impressive. However, there were events and situations that would continue to threaten the landmark, including two world wars.

During the 19th century, some of the efforts to preserve the structure had evolved from trying to remember the Christians who were supposedly martyred in the Colosseum into an archaeological marvel. People who were interested in understanding more about the structure and the ancient Roman civilization began excavations to understand what their mindset was. Even then, people were aware that the main draw was the gladiator battles, not killing Christians or criminals.

When Italy was reunited in 1870, the Colosseum became a symbol of Italian heritage, not a structure tied to Christianity. It was one of many historical sites that received attention and funding to preserve Italian history. The biggest concern was that the structure was not stable, so they began to fortify some of the weakest parts by adding buttresses. Ironically, the newer buildings around it were torn down to protect the Colosseum and make it easier to conduct necessary repairs.

It doesn't seem that World War I resulted in any problems for the Colosseum, but it was definitely harmed during World War II, mostly because of the dictator Benito Mussolini. He had many of the buildings around the structure demolished, which meant evicting a lot of people around it. This was enforced around the city as a part of a push to highlight ancient artifacts, and it cost thousands of people their homes. This would have a lasting effect on the city since it literally changed the landscape; the historic structures had already been incorporated into daily life. These changes made it so that the Colosseum and many other ancient artifacts were isolated. While this made it easier for tourists, it took away from their historical significance as part of the fabric of the city's life; they were supposed to be more than just shrines to a bygone era.

The dictator and his regime made a lot of changes, leaving their stamp on the capital city. This occurred before World War II began. Once the fighting started, the efforts to change the city to look the way Mussolini wanted ended. He was killed by his people. When the Allies finally took Rome, their tanks moved past the Colosseum. While it did not play a big role in the war, it did have an interesting place in the history of Italy during that time. The Italians quickly surrendered to the Allies, so retaking Italy and Rome was not a significant fight, unlike in Germany and Japan. Still, the ancient structure saw the arrival of a major force, and pictures were taken of the event.

Allied troops outside of the Colosseum on leave in Italy in June 1944. [34]

It is estimated that only a third of the original structure remained by the time restoration began in earnest during the 20th century. A serious project to start bringing it back to its former glory began during the 1990s. Costing an estimated forty billion lire, the project lasted from 1993 until 2000. Work was done to prop up the weaker parts of the structure, ensuring that no more of the foundation was damaged. While the major project ended at the turn of the century, restoration work continues to this day. Italians strive to preserve this piece of their history.

Chapter 10 – Its Role in Rome and the World Today

In 2007, the Colosseum was named one of the New Seven Wonders of the World. The original seven wonders were constructed in ancient times, but most of them have not survived to the modern day. The Seven Wonders of the Ancient World were the following:

- The Great Pyramid, the largest of the pyramids of Giza, is still standing despite it being over four thousand years old.

- Hanging Gardens of Babylon was thought to have been built as far back as 600 BCE, but nothing of it remains today.

- The Statue of Zeus was said to have been as tall as twelve meters (forty feet), but nothing of it remains today. It was destroyed in an earthquake before the Roman Empire rose to power.

- Temple of Artemis in Ephesus (modern-day Turkey) was destroyed by Herostratus, who reveled in the idea of obliterating the famous temple.

- The Mausoleum of Halicarnassus was built for Maussollos of the Persian Empire. It did not withstand the millennia of earthquakes; only small pieces of the foundation still remain.

- The Colossus of Rhodes was a huge statue of Helios, the personification of the sun. It only stood for about fifty-six years, as earthquakes destroyed everything above the knees (people continued to visit it for nearly another millennia to marvel at what little remained).

- The Pharos of Alexandria, or the Lighthouse of Alexandria, was located near Alexandria, Egypt, from roughly 285 BCE until 1323 CE. It was destroyed by numerous earthquakes by 1500 CE.

With only one remaining ancient wonder and few historians having even a hint of what some of these wonders looked like, it was decided to identify other ancient marvels that have withstood the test of time. This time, the people would look around the world, not just around Europe, North Africa, and the Middle East. The new list started to be compiled in 2000. It had been more than two thousand years since a list had been made, so the Swiss Foundation decided to determine new ancient structures that actually were wonders. These structures were not only impossibly large and detailed, but they were also ingenious creations that could largely withstand the tests of time.

The new list includes the following wonders.

- The Colosseum is nearly two thousand years old and has managed to withstand earthquakes, time, and humans. While it isn't the gorgeous structure that it once was, it is still a marvel that seems to have been built long before it should have been possible.

- The Great Wall of China may not be complete today, but long stretches of it still remain (it is thought to have been over 8,850 kilometers or 5,500 miles). It stretches out longer than the eye can see when standing in the middle.

- Chichén Itzá was a city of the Maya, and much of the ruins of the city remain (even though the people are long gone).

- Petra is an ancient city that was built into the walls of a cavern. Located in Jordan, the city is removed from civilization today, but it was once a popular trade center for the region. It is thought to have been abandoned after several major earthquakes between 360 and 600 CE and was only found again in 1912.

- Machu Picchu is an Incan city that was rediscovered in 1911. There are many theories of what it was meant to be, but there are no real records, as it was abandoned. Located on top of the Andes Mountains, it would have been incredibly isolated from the rest of the Inca population, but it is impressive, even by today's standards. There are tours where people can walk up the Andres over a few days to walk around what remains of the location.

- *Christ the Redeemer,* which is perhaps comparable to the Colossus of Rhodes, is an enormous statue that stretches its arms over Rio de Janeiro, Brazil. It is the youngest wonder on this list; it was built following the end of World War I.

- The Taj Mahal, located in Agra, India, was built to remember Mumtaz Mahal, the wife of Emperor Shah Jahan in the 17th century. It is made of white marble and includes impressive gardens and a reflection pool.

These wonders are awe-inspiring, and almost all of them are sought out by tourists who want to feel the weight of history and the marvel of human ingenuity. The Colosseum is one of the oldest wonders, and it is also one of the most visited because of how steeped in history it is, as well as how innovative its internal workings are.

Conclusion

The Colosseum is famous around the world, and it is recognizable in most places just from a picture of it. Despite being nearly two thousand years old, it remains the largest amphitheater in the world. It offered a place for anyone who wanted to witness the grand events and feel a communal spirit. Food, water, and entry were free, demonstrating the power and wealth of the empire for several hundred years.

Fires and earthquakes continued to damage the majestic structure. Time and people proved to be far more detrimental, though, and it would be over 1,800 years before serious effort and money would be spent to try to restore the impressive building to a more stable state.

Billions of lire have been spent to ensure that no more of the structure is lost, and the building is more stable than it has been in hundreds of years. It is the biggest tourist destination in Rome, and it continues to draw millions of people a year from all over the world. However, the entertainment today is in imagining what it once was like, how people lived, and to marvel at just how advanced the Romans were.

If you enjoyed this book, a review on Amazon would be greatly appreciated because it would mean a lot to hear from you.

To leave a review:
1. Open your camera app.
2. Point your mobile device at the QR code.
3. The review page will appear in your web browser.

Thanks for your support!

Here's another book by Captivating History that you might like

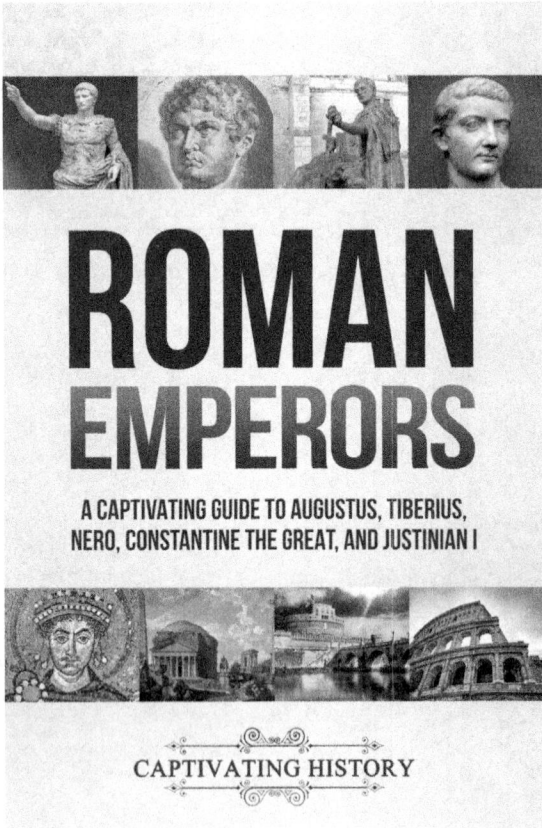

ROMAN EMPERORS

A CAPTIVATING GUIDE TO AUGUSTUS, TIBERIUS, NERO, CONSTANTINE THE GREAT, AND JUSTINIAN I

CAPTIVATING HISTORY

Free Bonus from Captivating History (Available for a Limited time)

Hi History Lovers!

Now you have a chance to join our exclusive history list so you can get your first history ebook for free as well as discounts and a potential to get more history books for free!

Simply visit the link below to join.

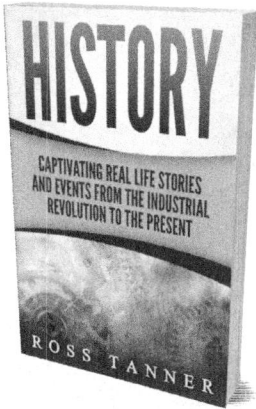

Or, Scan the QR code!

captivatinghistory.com/ebook

Also, make sure to follow us on Facebook, X, and YouTube by searching for Captivating History.

Resources

Part 1

The Cambridge Companion to Ancient Rome, Edited by Paul Erdkamp, Cambridge University Press, 2013.

Christopher Mackay, *Ancient Rome. A Military and Political History,* Cambridge University Press, 2004.

Norman Davies, *Europe: A History,* Pimlico, 1997.

Part 2

The Roman Games: A Sourcebook. Alison Futrell. 2006.

Arena: The Story of the Colosseum. John Pearson. 2013.

The Gladiator: The Secret History of Rome's Warrior. Alan Baker. 2002.

Gladiatrix: The True Story of History's Unknown Woman Warrior. Amy Zoll. 2002.

Cruelty and Civilization: The Roman Games. Roland Auguet. 1994.

Gladiators: Violence and Spectacle in Ancient Rome. Roger Dunkle. 2008.

Part 3

The Fires of Vesuvius: Pompeii Lost and Found 1st Edition, Mary Beard, 2008. ISBN-13: 978-0674045866, ISBN-10: 0674045866

The World of Pompeii, Pedar Foss, John Joseph Dobbins, 2008, Routledge, ISBN 9780415475778.

SPQR: A History of Ancient Rome, Mary Beard, 2016.

The Storm Before the Storm: The Beginning of the End of the Roman Republic, Mike Duncan, 2017.

Roman Pompeii: Space and Society, Ray Laurence, 1994.

Pliny the Younger. *Letters,* translated by William Melmoth; revised by F. C. T. Bosanquet. Vol. IX, Part 4. The Harvard Classics. New York: P.F. Collier & Son, 1909–14; Bartleby.com, 2001.

Nigel Bagnall, *The Punic Wars: Rome, Carthage and the Struggle for the Mediterranean*, London: Pimlico. ISBN 978-0-7126-6608-4, 1999.

Walbank, Polybius; transl. by Ian Scott-Kilvert, *The Rise of the Roman Empire*, Harmondsworth: Penguin. ISBN 978-0-14-044362-2, 1981.

"August 24th, 79: An Hour-By-Hour Account of Vesuvius' Eruption on Its 1,937th Anniversary", Sarah Bond, Forbes, retrieved on 25th February, 2021.

Pompeii – The Living City, Alex Butterworth, 2005, St Martin's Press; 1st edition. ISBN 978-0-312-35585-2

The Beginnings of Rome—Italy and Rome from the Bronze Age to the Punic Wars (c. 1000-264 BC), T. J. Cornell, 1995, New York: Routledge. ISBN 978-0-415-01596-7

A Critical History of Early Rome, Gary Forsythe, 2005, Berkeley: University of California Press. ISBN 0-520-24991-7

Magna Graecia: Greek Art from South Italy and Sicily, Michael J. Bennett, Aaron J. Paul, Mario Iozzo, & Bruce M. White, 2002, Cleveland, OH, Cleveland Museum of Art

Greek and Roman Religions, Rebecca I. Denova, 2018, John Wiley and Sons, Inc. ISBN 9781119392552

Streets, Spaces, and Places: Three Pompeiian Movement Axes Analysed, appendix by Karin Fridell Anter, Uppsala Universitet, 2011, ISBN 978-91.554-8103-2.

Part 4

24 Facts About The Colosseum, The Colosseum, May 10, 2024, thecolosseum.org

7 Blood-Soaked Facts about the Colosseum, DarkRome, May 15, 2024, City Wonders Limit, darkrome.com

Afterlife: 18th Century to 20th Century, Piranesi in Rome, May 15, 2024, Omeka, omeka.wellesley.edu

Christian martyrs in the Colosseum, Maria Milani, 2017, Ancient Roman History, mariamilani.com

Colosseum arena, Rome, Italy, The Editors of Encyclopedia Britannica, March 29, 2024, Britannica.com

Colosseum Definition, Mark Cartwright, May 29, 2018, World History Encyclopedia, worldhistory.org

Colosseum, Civitatis, May 10, 2024, civitatis Rome.com

Colosseum, History.com Editors, July 11, 2022, History.com

Colosseum, rome.info, May 10, 2024

Colosseum, The Editors of Encyclopedia Britannica, March 29, 2024,

Britannica, britannica.com

Culture in the Ancient Roman Republic, N.S. Gill, September 3, 2019, ThoughtCo, thoughtco.com

Fascist Archeology in Mussolini's Rome, Christopher Siwicki, May 11, 2020, Art&Object, artandobject.com

From Flavian Amphitheater to Colosseum, N.S. Gill, August 5, 2019, ThoughtCo, thoughtco.com

Gladiator Schools in Rome, Linda Alchin, 2017, tribunesandtriumphs.org

History of the Colosseum, The Colosseum, May 10, 2024, thecolosseum.org

History, Facts and Information about Hypogeum, Linda Alchin, 2017, Hypogeum, tribeandtriumphs.org

How Did The Colosseum Get Its Name?, kissformitaly, Sep 29, 2013, kissfarmitaly.com

How the Colosseum Was Built, Farell Evans, July 15,2022, History.com, history.com

Hypogeum of Colosseum, colosseumrometickets, 2018, colosseumrometickets.com

Ludus Magnus Gladiator School in Ancient Rome, Colosseum Rome, 2024, visit-colosseum-rome.com

New Seven Wonders of the World, Amy Tikkanen, "New Seven Wonders of the World," Encyclopedia Britannica, Feb 14, 2018, www.britannica.com

Roman Executions in the Colosseum: The Stories of Laureolus and Androcles, Mauro Poma, May 28, 2017, Ancient Origins, ancinents-origins.net

Romans Once Filled the Colosseum with Water and Staged an Epic Mock Sea Battle, Tao Tao Holmes, January 27, 2016, Atlas Obscura, atlasobscura.com

Secrets of the Colosseum, Tom Muller, January 2011, Smithsonian Magazine, smithsonianmagazine.com

Seven Wonders of the Ancient World, National Geographic, May 15, 2024, education.nationalgeographic.org

The Colosseum, May 13, 2024, thecolosseum.org

The Colosseum, National Geographic Society, October 19, 2023, NationalGraphic.com

The Colosseum: An Engineering Marvel of the Roman Empire, Kashyap Vyas, March 1, 2018, Interesting Engineering, interestingengineering.com

The Colosseum's History, Natasha Sheldon, May 12, 2022, History and Archaeology Online, historyandarchaeology.com

Why is the Colosseum broken?, Rome Tours, May 15, 2024, Sightseeing Tours, romecitytour.it

Image Sources

1   NormanEinstein, CC BY-SA 3.0 <http://creativecommons.org/licenses/by-sa/3.0/>,
    via Wikimedia Commons
    https://commons.wikimedia.org/wiki/File:Etruscan_civilization_map.png

2   Etnoy (Jonathan Fors), CC BY-SA 3.0 <https://creativecommons.org/licenses/by-
    sa/3.0>, via Wikimedia Commons
    https://commons.wikimedia.org/wiki/File:20090414-Civit%C3%A0-di-Bagnoregio.jpg

3   Louvre Museum, CC BY-SA 3.0 <http://creativecommons.org/licenses/by-sa/3.0/>,
    via Wikimedia Commons https://commons.wikimedia.org/wiki/File:Paris_-
    Louvre-_Sarcophage.jpg

4   Carole Raddato from FRANKFURT, Germany, CC BY-SA 2.0
    <https://creativecommons.org/licenses/by-sa/2.0>, via Wikimedia Commons
    https://commons.wikimedia.org/wiki/File:House_of_the_Faun,_the_second_peristyl
    e_occupying_more_than_a_third_of_the_insula,_Pompeii_(14857443457).jpg

5   sabrina roberjot, CC BY-SA 3.0 <http://creativecommons.org/licenses/by-sa/3.0/>,
    via Wikimedia Commons
    https://commons.wikimedia.org/wiki/File:StatueFaunePomp%C3%A9i,JPG

6   Magrippa at the English Wikipedia, CC BY-SA 3.0
    <http://creativecommons.org/licenses/by-sa/3.0/>, via Wikimedia Commons
    https://commons.wikimedia.org/wiki/File:Alexandermosaic.jpg

7   Hibernian, CC BY-SA 3.0 <https://creativecommons.org/licenses/by-sa/3.0>, via
    Wikimedia Commons https://commons.wikimedia.org/wiki/File:HAVE_-
    _House_in_Pompeii.jpg

8   https://commons.wikimedia.org/wiki/File:The_Three_Graces,_from_Pompeii.jpg

9   Naples National Archaeological Museum, CC BY 2.5
    <https://creativecommons.org/licenses/by/2.5>, via Wikimedia Commons

https://commons.wikimedia.org/wiki/File:Doryphoros_MAN_Napoli_Inv6011-2.jpg

10 https://commons.wikimedia.org/wiki/File:Wedding_Zeus_Hera_MAN_Napoli_Inv9559.jpg

11 https://commons.wikimedia.org/wiki/File:Achille,_Patrocle,_Bris%C3%A9is_-_Maison_du_po%C3%A8te_tragique_-_Pomp%C3%A9i.jpg

12 https://commons.wikimedia.org/wiki/File:Theatre_mask_mosaic_MAN_Napoli_Inv9994.jpg

13 Lord Pheasant at en.wikipediaLord Pheasant, CC BY-SA 3.0 <https://creativecommons.org/licenses/by-sa/3.0>, via Wikimedia Commons https://commons.wikimedia.org/wiki/File:Pompeii_-_Temple_of_Apollo_1400px.png

14 https://commons.wikimedia.org/wiki/File:Roman_fresco_Villa_dei_Misteri_Pompeii_001.jpg

15 https://commons.wikimedia.org/wiki/File:Roman_fresco_Villa_dei_Misteri_Pompeii_009.jpg

16 AlMare Attribution-ShareAlike 2.5 Generic (CC BY-SA 2.5). https://creativecommons.org/licenses/by-sa/2.5/deed.en via Wikimedia Commons, https://upload.wikimedia.org/wikipedia/commons/b/bc/Pompeji_Casa_Dei_Vettii_Hercules_Child_Detail.jpg

17 Juliana Bastos Marques, CC BY-SA 4.0 <https://creativecommons.org/licenses/by-sa/4.0>, via Wikimedia Commons https://commons.wikimedia.org/wiki/File:Temple_of_Isis_-_Pompeii.jpg

18 Miguel Hermoso Cuesta, CC BY-SA 4.0 <https://creativecommons.org/licenses/by-sa/4.0>, via Wikimedia Commons https://commons.wikimedia.org/wiki/File:Jard%C3%ADn_Villa_Poppaea_04.JPG

19 No machine-readable author provided. Buckeye~commonswiki assumed (based on copyright claims)., CC BY-SA 3.0 <http://creativecommons.org/licenses/by-sa/3.0/>, via Wikimedia Commons https://commons.wikimedia.org/wiki/File:Pompeji_-_Arena.jpg

20 https://commons.wikimedia.org/wiki/File:Pittura_di_pompei_con_zuffa_tra_pompeiani_e_nocerini.jpg

21 Daderot, CC0, via Wikimedia Commons https://commons.wikimedia.org/wiki/File:Lucius_Caecilius_Iucundus,_plaster_cast_of_Roman_bronze_and_marble_original,_House_of_Caecilius_Iucundus_(V-i-26),_Pompeii,_c._79_AD,_National_Archaeological_Museum,_Naples_-_Spurlock_Museum,_UIUC_-_DSC05672_(cropped).jpg

22 https://commons.wikimedia.org/wiki/File:Oplontis_Caldarium_room8.jpg

23 https://commons.wikimedia.org/wiki/File:Poppaea_Olimpia.jpg

24 Smuconlaw., CC BY-SA 4.0 <https://creativecommons.org/licenses/by-sa/4.0>, via Wikimedia Commons

https://commons.wikimedia.org/wiki/File:Statue_of_Eumachia,_Life_and_Death_in
_Pompeii_and_Herculaneum,_British_Museum,_London,_UK_-_20130706.jpg

25 https://commons.wikimedia.org/wiki/File:Pompeii_-
_Fullonica_of_Veranius_Hypsaeus_1_-_MAN.jpg

26 Museum of Fine Arts of Lyon, CC BY 2.5
<https://creativecommons.org/licenses/by/2.5>, via Wikimedia Commons
https://commons.wikimedia.org/wiki/File:Statuette_Vulcanus_MBA_
Lyon_A1981.jpg

27 https://commons.wikimedia.org/wiki/File:Karl_Brullov_-
_The_Last_Day_of_Pompeii_-_Google_Art_Project.jpg

28 https://commons.wikimedia.org/wiki/File:Destruction_of_Pompeii_and_
Herculaneum.jpg

29 Lancevortex, CC BY-SA 3.0 <http://creativecommons.org/licenses/by-sa/3.0/>, via
Wikimedia Commons
https://commons.wikimedia.org/wiki/File:Pompeii_Garden_of_the_Fugitives_02.jpg

30 https://commons.wikimedia.org/wiki/File:Colosseum-profile-english.png

31 Rc 13, CC BY-SA 3.0 <https://creativecommons.org/licenses/by-sa/3.0>, via
Wikimedia Commons;
https://commons.wikimedia.org/wiki/File:Colosseum_Ses_Titus_80AD.JPG

32 FeaturedPics, CC BY-SA 4.0 <https://creativecommons.org/licenses/by-sa/4.0>, via
Wikimedia Commons; https://commons.wikimedia.org/wiki/File:Colosseo_2020.jpg

33 Charlottev96, CC BY-SA 4.0 <https://creativecommons.org/licenses/by-sa/4.0>, via
Wikimedia Commons; https://commons.wikimedia.org/wiki/File:ColosseumInt.jpg

34 https://commons.wikimedia.org/wiki/File:The_British_Army_on_Leave_
in_Italy,_June_1944_TR1959.jpg

Printed in Dunstable, United Kingdom